WORD ATTACK JOY

Joy L. Keith
M. A. University of Colorado
Reading Teacher

Reference Illustrations:
Frank H. Keith

READING JOY, INC.

P.O. Box 404
Naperville, Illinois 60540

5 6 7 8 9 — STR — 80 79 78

Special thanks to Nancy Pohovey for her assistance in augmenting the word reference lists for this second edition.

TABLE OF CONTENTS

WORD REFERENCE LISTS:

WORD ATTACK SKILLS LIST

Word attack skills are those "sounding" and "word analysis" skills which one uses to decode (or unlock) and read unfamiliar printed words. Three general types of word attack skills can be identified:

I. CONSONANT SOUNDING

Individual Consonants
    Beginning Sounds
    Ending Sounds
Consonant Blends
    Two-letter Blends
    Three-letter Blends
    Final Blends
Consonant Digraphs
Variant Consonant Sounds
Silent Consonant Letters

II. VOWEL SOUNDING

Short Vowels
Long Vowels
"R" Controlled Vowels
Vowel Diphthong
Vowel Digraphs
Miscellaneous Vowel Sounds
Pronunciation Rules ($\breve{v}c$ $c\bar{v}$ $\bar{v}\not{v}$ $\bar{v}c\not{e}$)

III. STRUCTURAL ANALYSIS

Rhyming
Compound Words
Contractions
Plurals
Possessives
Verbs
Roots and Affixes
    Roots
    Prefixes
    Suffixes
Syllabication (vc/cv $\bar{v}$/cv $\breve{v}$c/c   /_le   /p/r/s)
Adjectives
Homonyms
Synonyms
Antonyms
Heteronyms
Accent

1

Consonants - Speech sounds which are modified by the lips, teeth, tongue, and/or palate. Consonants are basically "closed-mouth" sounds as opposed to vowels which are basically "open-mouth" sounds.

b c d f g h j k l m n p r s t v w y z

Consonant Blends - A combined or "blended" sound of two or three consonant letters which appear consecutively. Each of the consonants involved retains its own sound.

"L" Blends: bl   cl   fl   gl   pl   sl

"R" Blends: br   cr   dr   fr   gr   pr   tr

"S" Blends: sc   sk   sl   sm   sn   sp   st   sw

"W" Blends: dw   tw   sw

"3-letter" Blends: scr   spr   squ   str   spl   shr   thr

Final Blends   (appearing at the ends of words)

ct   ft   ld   lf   lk   lm   lt   lp   mp   nc

nch   nd   nk   nt   pt   rb   rd   rg   rk   rl

rm   rn   rp   rs   (etc.)

Consonant Digraphs - Two consecutive consonants which produce a single sound (not a blended sound). The single sound produced does not sound like the individual consonants involved.

ch (chick)   sh (ship)   wh (whale)

ph (phone)   th (this/thumb)*   ck (duck)

ng (hang)   gh (laugh)   qu (queen)

Notes: ph and gh have the sound of "f"

th can be voiced (vocal cords vibrate) this
can be unvoiced (vocal cords do not vibrate)
                   thumb

gh is silent when it follows i (light)

ch sometimes sounds like sh (chef, chiffon)

<u>Variant Consonant Sounds</u> - Several of the consonant letters use more than a single sound. (Exceptions to the "rules" exist).

<u>c</u>   hard "c" sounds like "k" (cat, come, cut) when followed by <u>a</u>, <u>o</u>, or <u>u</u>.
soft "c" sounds like "s" (cent, city, cycle) when followed by <u>e</u>, <u>i</u>, or <u>y</u>.

<u>g</u>   hard "g" sounds like "g" (game, good, guy) when followed by <u>a</u>, <u>o</u>, or <u>u</u>.
soft "g" sounds like "j" (gem, ginger, gym) when followed by <u>e</u>, <u>i</u>, or <u>y</u>.

<u>s</u>   "s" sounds like "s" (some, seven)
"s" sounds like "z" (run<u>s</u>, hi<u>s</u>, bear<u>s</u>, wa<u>s</u>)
"s" sounds like "sh" (<u>s</u>ugar) and "zh" (trea<u>s</u>ure) when followed by <u>u</u>.

<u>q</u>   "q" sounds like "kw" (quick, queen, quite)
"q" sounds like "k" (liquor, picturesque)

<u>d</u>   "d" sounds like "d" (dog, dance, dime)
"d" sounds like "j" (gra<u>du</u>al, indivi<u>du</u>al) when followed by <u>u</u>.

<u>x</u>   "x" sounds like "ks" (box, mix) at the ends of syllables
"x" sounds like "gz" (<u>ex</u>it, <u>ex</u>amine) when <u>ex</u> appears
"x" sounds like "z" (xylophone, xerox)

<u>t</u>   "t" sounds like "t" (top, tail)
"t" sounds like "sh" (vaca<u>ti</u>on, mo<u>ti</u>on) when followed by <u>ion</u>.
"t" sounds like "ch" (vir<u>tu</u>e, mu<u>tu</u>al)

<u>Silent Consonant Letters</u> - Some consonant letters are silent (do not make a sound) in certain combinations of two or three letters.

<u>Double letters</u>: pul̸l   fluf̸f   bal̸loon   sud̸den

<u>silent k</u>	<u>kn</u> combination:	̸knot	̸knit
<u>silent g</u>	<u>gn</u> combination:	̸gnaw	̸gnash
<u>silent w</u>	<u>wr</u> combination:	̸write	̸wrong
<u>silent b</u>	<u>mb</u> combination:	lam̸b	com̸b
<u>silent t</u>	<u>tch</u> combination:	ma̸tch	i̸tch
<u>silent c</u>	<u>ck</u> combination:	du̸ck	tri̸ck
<u>silent gh</u>	<u>igh</u> combination:	lig̸h̸t	sig̸h̸

<u>Vowels</u> - Vowels are speech sounds which are produced by a relatively free passage of air from the lungs through the lips without intervening stops or obstructions. The mouth is in a somewhat "open" position during pronunciation.

>   <u>Vowels</u>: a e i o u
>
>   <u>"y" and "w" sometimes function as vowels</u>:
>
>   1) "y" is a vowel when:
>
>   >   it follows one of the vowels (d<u>ay</u>, k<u>ey</u>, t<u>oy</u>)
>   >   it is the only vowel in the wor<u>d</u> (by, fly)
>   >   it is the only vowel in the syllable (fun/ny)
>
>   2) "w" is a vowel when:
>
>   >   it follows one of the vowels (n<u>ew</u>, s<u>aw</u>, h<u>ow</u>)

<u>Short Vowels</u> - A word normally uses the short vowel sound when there is just one vowel in the word or in the syllable and that vowel is followed by a consonant. (hĕlp, ĭn, lĕm/on)

ă - apple	ĕ - elephant	ĭ - Indian
ŏ - octopus	ŭ - umbrella	

<u>Long Vowels</u> - The sound of the long vowel is the same as its alphabet name. A word normally uses the long vowel sound when there is a final silent e in the syllable (bīke), or when it is the only vowel in the word or syllable with no consonants following (hē), or with many two-vowel combinations known as digraphs (bōat).

ā - cake	ē - tree	ī - pie
ō - boat	ū - cube	

<u>"R" Controlled Vowels</u> - (Murmur Dipthongs) When a vowel is followed by the consonant letter "r", the "r" controls the sound of the preceding vowel, giving it an "_r" sound.

ar - car   er - her   ir - bird   or - fork   ur - turtle

Note: er, ir, ur have identical sounds.

<u>Vowel Diphthong</u> - A combined vowel sound appearing in one syllable (having one sound) with a unique sound.

oy - boy   oi - oil   ow - cow   ou - out

4

<u>Vowel Digraphs</u> - Two vowels appearing consecutively having a single long vowel sound. (usually the first vowel is long and the second is silent/*exceptions)

e̅e̸ - sweet	e̅i̸ - ceiling	*ei - vein (a̅)
o̅e̸ - toe	ī̸e̸ - pie	e̅a̸ - easy
*ea̅ - great	a̅i̸ - rain	o̅a̸ - boat
e̅y̸ - key	a̅y̸ - play	o̅w̸ - grow

<u>Miscellaneous Vowel Sounds</u>

o̅o̅ - moon	y̅ - my (one-syllable words y = ī)
ŏŏ - book	y̆ - funny (two syllable words y = e̅)

e̅a - re̅ad	aw - saw
ĕa - bread	au - auto
ea̅ - grea̅t	
	ew - new
al - ball	ue - blue

<u>Pronunciation Rules</u>: (Apply to single syllable words and individual syllables within polysyllabic words).

	RULE	EXPLANATION	EXAMPLES	EXCEPTIONS
SHORT	V̆C	Use the short vowel sound when there is only one vowel followed by a consonant letter(s).	pĭg shĭps crămp	old find sign
LONG	CV̅	Use the long vowel sound when there is only one vowel in the syllable and it ends the syllable.	me̅ go̅ hī	to ma
	V̅V̸	When two vowels come together, the first is usually long and the second is usually silent.	boat me̅e̸t tra̅i̸n	build steak learn
	V̅CE̸	When "e" ends a word in the "vce" pattern, "e" is usually silent and the vowel is long.	bīke̸ mu̅le̸ ho̅pe̸	love have give

v - vowel   c - consonant

5

A GUIDE TO STRUCTURAL ANALYSIS

<u>Rhyming</u> - Words which correspond in final "vowel + consonant" or "vowel sound." (note: there are usually multiple spellings for the same rhyming sound: eg. āne-ain, ĕd-ĕad, ue-ew, etc.).

b<u>ake</u>, c<u>ake</u>, r<u>ake</u>	rhyme	(vowel + consonant)
h<u>e</u>, sh<u>e</u>, thr<u>ee</u>	rhyme	(vowel sound)

h<u>o</u>t, h<u>i</u>t, h<u>a</u>t	do not rhyme because the vowel sound differs
b<u>ad</u>, b<u>ag</u>, b<u>at</u>	do not rhyme because the consonant differs

<u>Compound Words</u> - A compound word is composed of two or more words, each of which must retain its own meaning.

Compound Words:

birdhouse	-	a house for birds
inside	-	the side which is in
sunburn	-	a burn from the sun

Not Compounds:

about	-	is <u>not</u> a fight
again	-	is <u>not</u> a gain

<u>Contractions</u> - A contraction is a shortened form of two words formed by omitting some of the letters and/or sounds in the second word. An apostrophe (') holds the position of the omitted letters and/or sounds.

can nøt	can't	we áre	we're
he i∮	he's	she wíll	she'll
they wøúld	they'd	I háve	I've

Note: It's is a contraction (it is)

<u>Plurals</u> - A plural is a grammatical form which designates more than one of the object named.

Form plurals by:

1)	adding -s	boat - boats
2)	changing "y" to "i" + es	baby - babies
3)	add -es after s, sh, ch, x, z	flash - flashes
4)	changing "f" to "ve" + s (or just add -s)	leaf - leaves puff - puffs
5)	noting irregulars	foot - feet shrimp - shrimp

<u>Possessives</u> - Possessives are formed by adding 's to most proper names, nouns, and irregular plurals to indicate ownership.

boy's	children's	boss's	('s)
girls'	wolves'	families'	(' alone after plurals ending in s)

Note: Exception: <u>its</u> is the possessive - eliminate the apostrophe.

<u>Verb Forms</u> - Verb forms indicate the tense (time of action):

Present tense (root alone or root + s) <u>walk</u> or <u>walks</u>

Present Participle Tense (root + ing) <u>walking</u>

Past Tense (root + ed) walked

Forming verb tenses: (spelling hints) v-vowel
c-consonant

aim-aiming-aimed   - 1) Verb ends in a $\overline{V}\!\!\!/VC$ pattern, add -ing/-ed

lock-locking-locked   - 2) Verb ends in a $\breve{V}CC$ pattern, add -ing/-ed

bake-baking-baked   - 3) Verb ends in a $\overline{V}C\!\!\!/E$ pattern, drop "e" and add -ing/-ed

chop-chopping-chopped - 4) Verb ends in a $\breve{V}C$ pattern, double the final consonant and add -ing/-ed

cry-cried   - 5) "y" is the only vowel, change "y" to "i" + ed

<u>Roots and Affixes</u> - A root word is a base morpheme (a meaningful word or part of a word which cannot be further divided) to which affixes may be added to alter the meaning. Affixes are commonly prefixes and suffixes added to root words to vary, modify or change the base word meaning.

<u>Prefix</u>	<u>Root</u>	<u>Suffix</u>		
<u>un</u>-	happy		happy	<u>not</u> happy
	price	-<u>less</u>	price	<u>without</u> price
<u>bi</u>-	cycl	-<u>ist</u>	cycle	<u>one who</u> <u>two</u> wheels

<u>Syllabication</u> - Syllabication is the process of dividing words into syllables or speech parts. A <u>syllable</u> consists of a <u>single vowel sound</u> (Recall: many single vowel sounds are spelled with two vowel letters: e $\overline{a}$, ow, $\overline{a}$y, etc.).

bl   shr   m   nts - are not syllables
                          (no vowel sound)
I   me   ship - are syllables (vowel sound)

<u>A word has as many syllables as it has vowel sounds.</u>

m $\overline{a}$d¢ (1 vowel sound/1 syllable)
p $\overline{a}$ ᷉nting (2 vowel sounds/2 syllables)

Syllabication Rules: (note: many exceptions exist)

v - vowel   c - consonant

VC/CV	<u>vowel-consonant-consonant-vowel</u> divide between the two consonant letters	mar/ket pen/cil bas/ket
$\overline{V}$/CV	<u>long vowel-consonant-vowel</u> divide after the long vowel	$\overline{o}$/pen p $\overline{i}$/rate d $\overline{e}$/mand
$\breve{V}$C/V	<u>short vowel-consonant-vowel</u> divide after the consonant which follows the short vowel	c $\breve{a}$b/in s $\breve{e}$v/en tr $\breve{a}$v/el
/_le	<u>word ending in "le"</u> the last syllable is made up of a consonant + <u>le</u>.	ap/ple jun/gle pud/dle
P/R/S	<u>Prefix-Root-Suffix</u> prefixes, roots, and suffixes all form separate syllables. (Note: there are many polysyllabic roots.)	de/part/ment im/port/er dis/a/gree/ment
Exceptions: do not divide "r" controlled vowels (for/age) consonant digraphs are not divided (au/thor) (recall that consonant digraphs have a single sound - see Page 2)		

<u>Adjective Forms</u> - Adjectives are used to describe or indicate a degree of comparison between things.

>Positive (a single subject......tall)
>
>Comparative (two subjects......tall<u>er</u>)
>
>Superlative (three or more......tall<u>est</u>)

<u>Homonyms</u> - Homonyms are words which have the same sound (name), but have different meanings and spellings.

spelling:	I - eye	to - two	sale - sail
meaning:	first person- body part	toward- number	marketing - ship movement

<u>Synonyms</u> - Synonyms have a similar meaning.

>cool - chilly   job - work   fact - truth

<u>Antonyms</u> - Antonyms have an opposite meaning.

>big - small   dark - light   winter - summer

<u>Heteronyms</u> - Heteronyms have the same spelling, but a different pronunciation and meaning.

rēcord	(to tape something)	wĭnd	(air)
rĕcord	(phonograph)	wīnd	(a clock)
prĕsent	(a gift)	tear	(cry)
present	(to announce)	tear	(rip)

Note: <u>Onym</u> means "name"

Accent: Words of two or more syllables are generally pronounced with more stress on one of the syllables. An accent mark (✓) is placed just after the syllable which receives the major stress.

Accent rules: (generally hold true)

1) In two-syllable words, accent the first syllable:

>pu´pil   ti´ger

2) In two syllable words where the second syllable contains two vowels (but only one vowel sound), accent the second syllable:

>un·safe´   re·play´

9

3) The root word is accented in affixed forms:

    re·turn´ed   art´ist

4) Accent the syllable preceding <u>ious</u>, <u>ic</u>, <u>ity</u>, <u>ion</u>, <u>ical</u>, <u>ian</u>, <u>ial</u>, <u>tion</u>, or <u>sion</u>.

    sec´tion   com´i·cal

5) Accent the third-to-last syllable in a three or more syllable word ending in silent "e."

    grad´u·ate

6) Polysyllabic words usually have a major´and minor´accent (alternating syllables).

    dis´ap·point´ment

GROUP WORD ATTACK-SYNTHESIS TEST

Purpose: This group test has been designed to be used in two ways:

1) As an initial screening device to aid the teacher in identifying those children who may need additional instruction in word attack skills. In this case, it is highly recommended that such children be given the diagnostic Individual Oral Word Attack Test so that an appropriate instructional plan can be designed based on specific areas of skill weaknesses.

2) As a supplement to the Individual Oral Word Attack Test. This test provides information about a child's ability to use the isolated Consonant and Vowel sounding principles in decoding total words. Some children who possess skills in isolation cannot effectively decode words--they do not apply the skills they possess.

Note: Although this test does sample test all of the basic Consonant and Vowel sounds and pronunciation rules, it does not test the Structural Analysis Skills. (See the test for these skills on pages 16-20.)

Administration: This test is designed to be used with children who are reading at the 2-2 level or above; therefore, it may be used at any age level.

Produce copies of the test for each child (making sure that the copies are clearly printed. You may wish to make a thermal master of test and run ditto copies). Next, distribute the test forms and review the procedure for answering by circling the two possible endings which make words when combined with the circled letter or letters. If the children need additional practice, work through the second item on the test. The children are to complete the rest of the test items on their own. Set a time limit of 30 minutes.

Scoring: There are a total of 128 possible points on this test. Any child who scores below 110 points (or makes 18 or more incorrect responses) should be given the Individual Oral Word Attack Test. There is a correction key following the student form.

Student Form: Pages 12 and 13

Answer Key: Pages 14 and 15

GROUP WORD ATTACK-SYNTHESIS TEST

Name_____Grade_____Date_____Score_____

Circle two word endings which will form a word using the beginning letter or letters circled. The first one is completed for you.

(t) (op) ive (en) as	(b) ice at one age	(c) eef ube eab an	(d) ime ape ip ack	(f) et ig eam ake
(g) eet ame ant um	(h) ab ine en ail	(j) end ob ad oke	(k) ey ag id oss	(l) op ike ail ot
(m) ed ile ab et	(n) ipe ut im ail	(p) oke og en ob	(r) it ipe ast ub	(s) et en oap ict
(t) ant ept an oe	(v) ade an eek ine	(w) ave int ud et	(y) ide ell es aint	(z) asp eed ip ing
(bl) ill ank aze id	(cl) ote am end ay	(fl) ent oat ame ug	(gl) ass ad ink ell	(pl) each ax ant ug
(sl) ake eep unt am	(br) ave it en ush	(cr) one in ack isp	(dr) ain aze ove un	(fr) oke ipe esh ee

(gr) and ape ell uck	**(pr)** eck og ess ize	**(tr)** uff ick ibe and	**(sc)** alp est ale ix	**(sk)** ock ime ate in
(sm) oke ick ell amp	**(sn)** ess ap ail eat	**(sp)** one ash eed ill	**(st)** ing amp ike end	**(sw)** ip oan eet im
(scr) ing am eam ank	**(spr)** ot ay ing ub	**(squ)** ish am eak ay	**(str)** ike ame og eet	**(spl)** ug ing it ash
(shr) ub en ink one	**(thr)** um ill ee ap	**(ch)** ent un ain amp	**(th)** ull at ung ink	**(wh)** eat ud ich ump
(sh) ang eet unk ame	**(qu)** ake um ix een	**(kn)** ung ock it amp	**(wr)** ite ap unch et	**(fr)** ark own y all
(n) awl ir ew oise	**(bl)** oom ow out oup	**(thr)** ew oot ow ald	**(m)** ouse alt ird arm	**(h)** urt ard owp oon
(b) ark urn oop ort	**(c)** orch oin ool ound	**(h)** ood aup urf erd	**(f)** erd oot oil awk	**(r)** oy aw orn erch

GROUP WORD ATTACK-SYNTHESIS TEST

Name_____ Grade_____ Date_____ Score_____

Circle two word endings which will form a word using the beginning letter or letters circled. The first one is completed for you.

(t) (op) (ive) (en) as	b ice (at) (one) age	c eef (ube) eab (an)	d (ime) ape (ip) ack	f et (ig) eam (ake)
g eet (ame) ant (um)	h ab ine (en) (ail)	j end (ob) ad (oke)	k (ey) ag (id) oss	l op (ike) ail (ot)
m ed (ile) ab (et)	n ipe (ut) im (ail)	p (oke) og (en) ob	r it (ipe) ast (ub)	s (et) en (oap) ict
t ant ept (an) (oe)	v ade (an) eek (ine)	w (ave) int ud (et)	y ide (ell) (es) aint	z asp eed (ip) (ing)
bl ill (ank) (aze) id	cl ote (am) end (ay)	fl ent (oat) (ame) ug	gl (ass) (ad) ink ell	pl each ax (ant) (ug)
sl ake (eep) unt (am)	br (ave) it en (ush)	cr one in (ack) (isp)	dr (ain) aze (ove) un	fr oke ipe (esh) (ee)

14

gr — (and), (ape), ell, uck	**pr** — eck, og, (ess), (ize)	**tr** — uff, (ick), (ibe), and	**sc** — (alp), est, (ale), ix	**sk** — ock, ime, (ate), (in)
sm — (oke), ick, (ell), amp	**sn** — ess, (ap), (ail), eat	**sp** — one, ash, (eed), (ill)	**st** — (ing), (amp), ike, end	**sw** — ip, oan, (eet), (im)
scr — ing, (am), (eam), ank	**spr** — ot, (ay), (ing), ub	**squ** — (ish), am, (eak), ay	**str** — (ike), ame, og, (eet)	**spl** — ug, ing, (it), (ash)
shr — (ub), en, (ink), one	**thr** — um, (ill), ee, ap	**ch** — ent, un, (ain), (amp)	**th** — ull, (at), ung, (ink)	**wh** — (eat), ud, (ich), ump
sh — ang, (eet), unk, (ame)	**qu** — (ake), um, ix, (een)	**kn** — ung, (ock), (it), amp	**wr** — (ite), ap, unch, et	**fr** — ark, (own), (y), all
n — awl, ir, (ew), (oise)	**bl** — (oom), (ow), out, oup	**thr** — (ew), oot, (ow), ald	**m** — (ouse), (alt), ird, arm	**h** — (urt), (ard), owp, oon
b — (ark), (urn), oop, ort	**c** — orch, (oin), (ool), ound	**h** — (ood), aup, urf, (erd)	**f** — erd, (oot), (oll), awk	**r** — (oy), (aw), orn, erch

15

GROUP STRUCTURAL ANALYSIS TEST

(For children reading on the 3-1 to 6th grade level)

Purpose: This group test has been designed to be used as a
screening device to:

    1) Locate children who possess inadequate
       structural analysis skills.

    2) Aid in the identification of specific
       structural analysis skill deficiencies
       so that a program of instruction can
       be initiated.

Note: This test does not cover the consonant and vowel
sounding skills. Therefore, be sure to also
administer the Group Word Attack Synthesis Test (Pgs. 11-15).

Administration: You may produce a thermal ditto master of the
students' test copy on the following two pages and
run copies for your class. Distribute the tests and
have the class work through each item as follows:

    1) You introduce test A and read the
       instructions aloud.

    2) Allow the class 3 minutes to do the items.

Repeat steps 1 & 2 for each of the following tests:
B, C, D, E, F, G and H.

Scoring: Passing scores for each test (A, B, C, D, E, F, G and H)
are indicated on the Teacher's Answer Key which follows
the Student Form.

Student Form: Pages 17 and 18

Answer Key: Pages 19 and 20

GROUP STRUCTURAL ANALYSIS TEST
(for readers on the 3-1 - 6 levels)

Name_____ Grade_____ Date_____

A PRONUNCIATION

Mark every vowel in the words below:

(e.g. long $\bar{u}$ short $\breve{u}$ silent u̸   special sound (u))

1. crew	4. beef	7. baker	10. roast	13. thief	16. paint
2. salt	5. nurse	8. rest	11. cube	14. drove	17. bread
3. shout	6. third	9. dark	12. sixth	15. she	18. toil

B SYLLABICATION

Divide every word below into syllables with / marks:

(e.g. peo/ple)

1. pattern	4. limit	7. comic	10. metal
2. cider	5. hotel	8. simple	11. waffle
3. able	6. blanket	9. private	12. center

C COMPOUND WORDS

Circle the first word and underline the second word in each compound word below: (e.g. (bird)house)

1. baseball	3. downtown	5. moonlight	7. snowflake
2. cardboard	4. fireplace	6. notebook	8. teaspoon

D CONTRACTIONS

Write the word which each contraction represents: (e.g. 'm am)

1. 've_____	3. n't_____	5. 'll_____
2. 's _____	4. 're_____	6. 'd _____

E ROOTS AND AFFIXES

Circle the root word in each word below: (e.g. (girl)s)

1. lightest	6. slower
2. department	7. unhappiness
3. percentage	8. doing
4. invisible	9. walks
5. reported	10. patches

F. HOMONYMS

Write the letter which gives each homonym meaning on the line.

_____ 1.	new	A.	because of
_____ 2.	flower	B.	ground grain
_____ 3.	male	C.	a blossom
_____ 4.	for	D.	number
_____ 5.	mail	E.	to print letters
_____ 6.	flour	F.	a man
_____ 7.	right	G.	not old
_____ 8.	knew	H.	understood
_____ 9.	four	I.	letters
_____ 10.	write	J.	correct

G. SYNONYMS

Write the letter for each synonym pair (same meaning) on the line:

_____ 1.	town	A.	begin
_____ 2.	problem	B.	small
_____ 3.	little	C.	like
_____ 4.	stop	D.	end
_____ 5.	enjoy	E.	city
_____ 6.	big	F.	hate
_____ 7.	close	G.	puzzle
_____ 8.	start	H.	large
_____ 9.	dislike	I.	leader
_____ 10.	chief	J.	shut

H. ANTONYMS

Write the letter to make an antonym pair (opposite meaning) on the line:

_____ 1.	sunrise	A.	man
_____ 2.	boy	B.	off
_____ 3.	up	C.	night
_____ 4.	near	D.	never
_____ 5.	on	E.	there
_____ 6.	here	F.	pull
_____ 7.	morning	G.	far
_____ 8.	always	H.	down
_____ 9.	push	I.	sunset
_____ 10.	woman	J.	girl

18

GROUP STRUCTURAL ANALYSIS TEST
(For readers on the 3-1 - 6 levels)

Name_____ Grade_____ Date_____

(A) PRONUNCIATION (15)

Mark every vowel in the words below:

(e.g. long ū   short ŭ   silent u̸   special sound (u))

1. cr(ew)	4. bēe̸f	7. bāker	10. rōa̸st	13. thi̸ef	16. pāi̸nt
2. sa̸lt	5. nûrse̸	8. rĕst	11. cūbe̸	14. drōve̸	17. brĕa̸d
3. sh(ou)t	6. thîrd	9. da̋rk	12. sĭxth	15. shē	18. t(oi)l

(B) SYLLABICATION (10)

Divide every word below into syllables with / marks:

(e.g. peo/ple)

1. pat/tern	4. lim/it	7. com/ic	10. met/al
2. ci/der	5. ho/tel	8. sim/ple	11. waf/fle
3. a/ble	6. blan/ket	9. pri/vate	12. cen/ter

(C) COMPOUND WORDS (7)

Circle the first word and underline the second word in each compound word below: (e.g. (bird)house)

1. (base)ball	3. (down)town	5. (moon)light	7. (snow)flake
2. (card)board	4. (fire)place	6. (note)book	8. (tea)spoon

(D) CONTRACTIONS (5)

Write the word which each contraction represents: (e.g. 'm am)

1. 've _have_	3. n't _not_	5. 'll _will_
2. 's _is_	4. 're _are_	6. 'd _would_

(E) ROOTS AND AFFIXES (8)

Circle the root word in each word below: (e.g. (girl)s)

1. (light)est	6. (slow)er
2. de(part)ment	7. un(happi)ness
3. per(cent)age	8. (do)ing
4. in(vis)ible	9. (walk)s
5. re(port)ed	10. (patch)es

(F) HOMONYMS (8)

Write the letter which gives each homonym meaning on the line.

G	1. new	A.	because of
C	2. flower	B.	ground grain
F	3. male	C.	a blossom
A	4. for	D.	number
I	5. mail	E.	to print letters
B	6. flour	F.	a man
J	7. right	G.	not old
H	8. knew	H.	understood
D	9. four	I.	letters
E	10. write	J.	correct

(G) SYNONYMS (8)

Write the letter for each synonym pair (same meaning) on the line:

E	1. town	A.	begin
G	2. problem	B.	small
B	3. little	C.	like
D	4. stop	D.	end
C	5. enjoy	E.	city
H	6. big	F.	hate
J	7. close	G.	puzzle
A	8. start	H.	large
F	9. dislike	I.	leader
I	10. chief	J.	shut

(H) ANTONYMS (8)

Write the letter to make an antonym pair (opposite meaning) on the line:

I	1. sunrise	A.	man
J	2. boy	B.	off
H	3. up	C.	night
G	4. near	D.	never
B	5. on	E.	there
E	6. here	F.	pull
C	7. morning	G.	far
D	8. always	H.	down
F	9. push	I.	sunset
A	10. woman	J.	girl

20

INDIVIDUAL ORAL WORD ATTACK TEST - Administration Guide

Purpose: To determine strength and weakness in the three areas of Word Attack: 1) Consonant Sounding, 2) Vowel Sounding, and 3) Structural Analysis.

This is an <u>oral test</u> and is preferable to a written test because when a child has to decode an unknown word, he must <u>vocally produce sounds</u>--he does not <u>write letters;</u> <u>two different skills</u> are involved.

Administration: Give the child the <u>Test Copy</u>. The teacher uses the <u>Answer Key</u> as her reference for correct sounding and structural analysis answers. For children in first or second grade, use tests A, B, D(1-4), F, G, and N. Children in third grade and above may take every test.

(A) <u>Consonants</u>   (the child produces the <u>sound</u> the letter makes/ 17, 18 and 19 - give the two sounds for s, c, and g)

(B) and (C) <u>Consonant Blends</u>   (the child produces the blended sound)

(D) Consonant Digraphs (the child produces the sound)

(E) <u>Silent Consonant Letters</u>   (the child identifies the silent letter(s) in each combination of letters)

(F) <u>Short Vowels</u>   (the child gives the short vowel sound)

(G) <u>Long Vowels</u>   (the child gives the sound of the long vowels)

(H) <u>"R" Controlled Vowels</u>   (the child gives the sound)

(I) <u>Miscellaneous Vowel Sounds</u>   (the child gives the sound)

(J) <u>Pronunciation Rules</u>   (the child identifies the rule and tells if the vowel (v) would be long, short or silent)

(K) <u>Applying Pronunciation Rules</u>   (the child pronounces the nonsense words--check for long and short vowel sounding)

(L) <u>Syllabication Rules</u>   (the child identifies the rule and tells where the patterns divide into syllables)

21

(M) Applying Syllabication Rules (the child tells where each nonsense word would divide into syllables)

(N) Compound Words (the child names the two words in each compound word)

(O) Contractions (the child gives the word which each contraction represents)

(P) Root & Base Words (the child identifies the root word in each word given)

(Q) Homonyms (the child gives the meaning difference for each set of homonyms)

(R) Synonyms (the child gives a synonym for each word - sample answers are given; accept any correct response)

(S) Antonyms (the child gives an antonym for each word - sample answers are given; accept any correst response)

Scoring: Use any errors made on tests A, B, C, D, E, F, G, H, I, J, K, L, and O as a probable indication of a need for instruction.

For tests K, M, N, P, Q, R, and S, use 80% correct as a general "rule of thumb" for a passing score.

Student Form: Pages 23 and 24

Answer Key: Pages 25 and 26

INDIVIDUAL ORAL WORD ATTACK TEST

A

1. m
2. d
3. l
4. r
5. z
6. k
7. h
8. j
9. w
10. b
11. f
12. n
13. y
14. t
15. p
16. v

17. s
18. c
19. g

B

1. pr
2. fl
3. br
4. sc
5. fr
6. sp
7. gl
8. dr
9. sn
10. bl
11. tw
12. cl
13. sl
14. gr
15. sm
16. cr
17. st
18. sw
19. tr
20. pl
21. sk

C

1. str
2. spl
3. thr
4. squ
5. scr
6. shr
7. spr

D

1. th
2. ch
3. wh
4. sh
5. qu
6. ck
7. ph
8. ng

E

1. mb
2. kn
3. wr
4. igh
5. tch
6. gn

F

1. e
2. u
3. a
4. o
5. i

G

1. i
2. a
3. u
4. o
5. e

H

1. ur
2. or
3. ir
4. ar
5. er

I

1. oy
2. $\overline{ow}$
3. $\overline{ea}$
4. oi
5. ou
6. $\overline{y}$
7. o͝o
8. al
9. ew
10. au
11. y̆
12. aw
13. ow
14. ĕa
15. $\overline{oo}$

Ⓙ

1. vc
2. cv
3. vv
4. vce

Ⓚ

1. moke
2. pu
3. fis
4. neeb
5. sot
6. em
7. ri
8. goam
9. lipe
10. suff

Ⓛ

1. vccv
2. v̄cv
3. v̆cv
4. _le

Ⓜ

1. ōmed
2. rĭsup
3. taple
4. fissek
5. minjut
6. vigdle
7. sugtin
8. prisdeens

Ⓝ

1. birdhouse
2. workshop
3. anywhere
4. wintertime
5. highway
6. plaything
7. someone

Ⓞ

1. n't
2. 're
3. 've
4. 's
5. 'll
6. 'd

Ⓟ

1. boys
2. liked
3. colder
4. longest
5. discolor
6. thankful
7. unclean
8. hopeless
9. movement
10. reheatable
11. mistakes
12. reaction
13. dangerously
14. punches
15. walking
16. monkeys
17. dripped

Ⓠ

1. to too two
2. here hear
3. sun son
4. buy by bye
5. write right
6. sale sail

Ⓡ

1. cold
2. large
3. work
4. city
5. like
6. pretty
7. true
8. woman

Ⓢ

1. under
2. left
3. empty
4. father
5. slow
6. laugh
7. morning
8. start

INDIVIDUAL ORAL WORD ATTACK TEST

The sounds the child produces should sound just like the sound in the sample words provided for your reference only.

(A) CONSONANT SOUNDS

1. <u>m</u> an
2. <u>d</u> og
3. <u>l</u> ook
4. <u>r</u> un
5. <u>z</u> oo
6. <u>k</u> ey
7. <u>h</u> elp
8. <u>j</u> ump
9. <u>w</u> in
10. <u>b</u> all
11. <u>f</u> at
12. <u>n</u> et
13. <u>y</u> es
14. <u>t</u> op
15. <u>p</u> in
16. <u>v</u> et

ask for 2 sounds

17. <u>s</u>/ <u>s</u>et / hi<u>s</u>
18. <u>c</u>/ <u>c</u>ap / <u>c</u>ell / <u>g</u>o
19. <u>g</u>/ <u>g</u>ym

(B) CONSONANT BLENDS (2-letter)

1. <u>pr</u> oud
2. <u>fl</u> ag
3. <u>br</u> own
4. <u>sc</u> at
5. <u>fr</u> ee
6. <u>sp</u> ice
7. <u>gl</u> eam
8. <u>dr</u> op
9. <u>sn</u> ow
10. <u>bl</u> ack
11. <u>tw</u> in
12. <u>cl</u> ean
13. <u>sl</u> eep
14. <u>gr</u> ape
15. <u>sm</u> all
16. <u>cr</u> eam
17. <u>st</u> and
18. <u>sw</u> eep
19. <u>tr</u> ade
20. <u>pl</u> ate
21. <u>sk</u> ate

(C) CONSONANT BLENDS (3-letter)

1. <u>str</u> ipe
2. <u>spl</u> ash
3. <u>thr</u> ee
4. <u>squ</u> eak
5. <u>scr</u> ap
6. <u>shr</u> ink
7. <u>spr</u> ay

(D) CONSONANT DIGRAPHS

1. <u>th</u>/<u>th</u>in / the
2. <u>ch</u> ick
3. <u>wh</u> ip
4. <u>sh</u> ell
5. <u>qu</u> een
6. <u>ck</u>/du<u>ck</u>
7. <u>ph</u> one
8. <u>ng</u>/ha<u>ng</u>

(E) SILENT CONSONANT LETTERS

1. mb/lam<s>b</s>
2. kn/<s>k</s>not
3. wr/<s>w</s>rap
4. igh/sig<s>h</s>
5. tch/i<s>t</s>ch
6. gn/<s>g</s>naw

(F) SHORT VOWELS

1. <u>e</u> nd
2. <u>u</u> nder
3. <u>a</u> pple
4. <u>o</u> x
5. <u>i</u> t

(G) LONG VOWELS

1. <u>i</u> sle
2. <u>a</u> pe
3. <u>u</u> se
4. <u>o</u> at
5. <u>e</u> agle

(H) "R" CONTROLLED VOWELS

1. <u>ur</u> ge
2. <u>or</u> der
3. <u>ir</u> k
4. <u>ar</u> t
5. <u>er</u>/her

(I) MISCELLANEOUS VOWEL SOUNDS

1. b <u>oy</u>
2. sn<u>ow</u>
3. <u>eat</u>
4. <u>oi</u>l
5. <u>out</u>
6. b<u>y</u> ($\bar{i}$)
7. b <u>oo</u> k
8. <u>a</u>lso
9. n <u>ew</u>
10. <u>au</u> to
11. <s>y</s>/pony ($\bar{e}$)
12. s <u>aw</u>
13. c <u>ow</u>
14. br <u>ea</u> d
15. m <u>oo</u> n

Legend (top left):
- ˘ short
- ‾ long
- / silent

J — PRONUNCIATION RULES

1. v̆c
2. cv̄
3. v̄y̸
4. v̄c¢

K — APPLYING PRONUNCIATION RULES (nonsense words)

1. mōk¢
2. pū
3. fĭs
4. ne̸b
5. sŏt
6. ĕm
7. rī
8. go̸m
9. līp¢
10. sŭff

L — SYLLABICATION RULES

1. vc/cv
2. v̄/cv
3. v̆c/v
4. /_le

M — APPLYING SYLLABICATION RULES

1. ō/med
2. rĭs/up
3. ta/ple
4. fis/sek
5. min/jut
6. vig/dle
7. sug/tin
8. pris/deens

N — COMPOUND WORDS

1. bird house
2. work shop
3. any where
4. winter time
5. high way
6. play thing
7. some one

O — CONTRACTIONS

1. n't   not
2. 're   were
3. 've   have
4. 's   is
5. 'll   will
6. 'd   would

P — ROOT & BASE WORDS

1. boy s
2. like d
3. cold er
4. long est
5. dis color
6. thank ful
7. un clean
8. hope less
9. move ment
10. re heat able
11. mis take s
12. re act ion
13. danger ously
14. punch es
15. walk ing
16. monkey s
17. drip ped

Q — HOMONYMS

1. to   too   two
   toward/also/number
2. here   hear
   place/listen
3. sun   son
   star/boy
4. buy   by   bye
   purchase/near/farewell
5. write   right
   print/correct
6. sale   sail
   marketing/ship movement

Note:
the child can
use each form
in a sentence
Example:
(I walk to schoo[l]

R — SYNONYMS

1. cold   cool
2. large   big
3. work   job
4. city   town
5. like   love
   (similar)
6. pretty   beautiful
7. true   fact
8. woman   lady

S — ANTONYMS

1. under   over
2. left   right
3. empty   full
4. father   mother
5. slow   fast
6. laugh   cry
7. morning   night
8. start   stop

READING GAMES

On the following pages you will find many "Sparkling Ideas for Teaching Word Attack"--all of these games have been used with great success in both remedial reading and classroom instruction. In fact, I have written this booklet for all the boys and girls in my remedial reading classes who have said, "Gee, this is so much fun. I sure am glad I have games class instead of reading group!" So come along...cut and paste...and who knows what may happen...those bored, ditto-drowned kids in your class may really learn something and even say "Gee, this is so much fun!"

All of the ideas on the following pages are intended to tickle your creative bone...try the ideas as given or use them as a basis for designing your own original materials.

Supplies you will need (sufficient supply for 20 games):

20	sheets	12x18" oaktag paper or index board
5	sheets	22x28" poster board (white)
10	sheets	22x28" poster board (assorted colors)
5	pkgs.	3x5" plain index cards (assorted colors)
100		wooden (spring-type) clothespins
20	strands	36" rug yarn scraps (assorted colors)
1	set	water base magic markers (12 assorted colors)
10	yards	clear, adhesive Contact Paper (optional to protect materials)—always use water-base magic markers under contact paper (permanent markers bleed).

yarn needle
rubber cement
Elmer's Glue
ruler
pair scissors
black magic marker (permanent black)
red magic marker (permanent red)

Optional: white-out typist's paint (Stationery Stores)
fluorescent crayons

You will also need many small pictures, and good sources for these are:

Ginn Publishing Co.	Word Enrichment Workbooks (levels 1, 2, 3, 4, 5)
Harper & Row	The Reading Road to Spelling Book 1-A
Harcourt Brace Jovanovich	First Grade Workbooks
Scott Foresman	The Talking Alphabet
Lyons & Carnahan	The New Phonics We Use Workbooks

HELPFUL HINTS FOR GAME-MAKING

Notch the right-hand corner of all playing cards as a method to keep cards sorted, right-side-up.

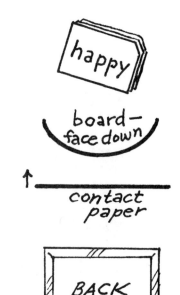

Apply contact paper by placing it sticky-side-up on a table or on the floor. Come down on top of the contact as illustrated to avoid wrinkles. Be sure to bend the game surface and center in the middle of the contact paper.

Always overlap contact paper one or two inches to the back side of the board to avoid peeling edges. It is actually best to cover both the front and back surfaces of game materials.

Use permanent magic markers on playing cards which will not be covered with contact paper. Use water-base magic markers on cards which will be covered with contact paper. Remember: permanent magic markers will "bleed" under contact paper, so always use water-base magic markers.

Use bright colors—colorful game boards, colorful playing cards and colorful illustrations really make games look exciting and interesting. Be sure to try using the new fluorescent crayons—they make striking game boards.

To store cards, produce oaktag envelopes using a 12x18" sheet of oaktag. Cut off a 2x12" strip. Fold and staple the envelope together as illustrated. Clip the flap corners. Glue the envelope to the back of the game board, insert the cards and tuck the flap under the strip.

To make spinners that really spin, use a hole punch to make a round hole in the spinner arrow. Be careful not to make a round hole in the playing board. Place a brass fastener through the spinner and plunge the fastener into the spinner game board. Then elevate the brass fastener ¼" as illustrated.

When printing and lettering boards and cards, be sure to print the lower-case "a" as it appears in reading materials.

To store a "multitude of games" make a shelving
unit out of bricks and boards (or tri-wall cardboard). Label the front of each shelf with a skill
title and place games on the shelf by skill. Now
you and the children can find materials quickly.

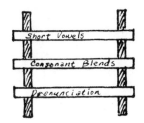

Another storage method: Drill a hole in each of two
opposite walls about five feet above the floor and
18" from the rear wall. Insert a 1" diameter screw
eye (1) in each hole. Attach a 20 gauge wire to one
hook and then place 20-50 clamps (2) through the wire.
Secure the wire to the second screw eye. Attach games
to the clamps for an instant display-storage unit.

(1)

(2)

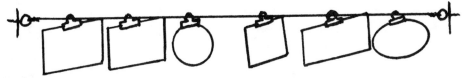

Always use acrylic rug yarn when making yarn games or
mobiles. Worsted woolen yarn tends to stretch, break
and untie itself when knotted.

acrylic

worsted

Always use a double thickness of 4-ply poster board
for the top section of all mobiles. Using lots of
Elmer's Glue between the layers will strengthen the
cardboard and prevent bending.

When labeling clothespins, it is a good idea to wrap
the top of each clothespin using cloth or plastic
scotch tape (colored tape). It is easy to write on
the tape using a permanent fine-point magic marker.

Color directly on tongue depressors using permanent
magic markers. Try fluorescent magic markers to color
the tongue depressors prior to lettering -- they add
"color appeal." If you wish, seal with a light coat
of spray varnish.

Use zip lock sandwich bags for storing playing cards
on the back side of game boards.
Open the bag by slitting through
the contact with a razor blade
or exacto knife. Insert the
playing cards and zip the bag
closed.

If contact paper is too expensive for your budget,
make a protective holder (not as good as contact,
yet quite serviceable). Using scotch plastic tape
(1" width), tape a 18x24" piece of clear polyester
or acetate film to a piece of 19x24½ poster board
leaving one side open. Game boards may be inserted
and changed as the need arises. You can write on
this surface using a Listo or china marker and wipe
clean using a soft cloth.

Materials: 4-ply poster board (white and colors)
            rug yarn (assorted colors)
            water-base magic markers (assorted colors)
            jumbo paper clips (to attach mobile to ceiling)

Directions: Plan to make mobiles large enough to read easily from
            the back of the classroom. The overall size when
            assembled should range from 18-24" x 24-36". Lettering
            can range from 1½-5" in height. By color-coding the
            sub-categories (e.g. each of the consonant digraph
            circles represents a different sound, so use a
            different colored poster board for each), you can help
            the children visually organize the skills to be learned.

            Begin by cutting all needed pieces and assemble
            them on a table or on the floor as they will appear
            in the completed mobile. Make sure to use a double
            thickness of 4-ply poster board for the top (title)
            section of your mobiles. Use plenty of Elmer's Glue
            between the thicknesses—this will prevent your mobile
            from drooping. Check the sizes of objects and make
            sure that they will not bump into one another and
            partially cover objects hanging nearby. Now continue
            by using colored water-base magic markers to letter and
            illustrate each of the pieces front and back. Now
            reassemble the mobile on a table or on the floor, placing
            objects as illustrated. Using a paper punch, punch
            holes ½"from the edges where yarn is to be attached.
            Now string the mobile by tying the yarn—I frequently
            use a color identical to the poster board used. Finally,
            attach a paper clip to the top piece of yarn and hang
            from the ceiling or lighting fixture.

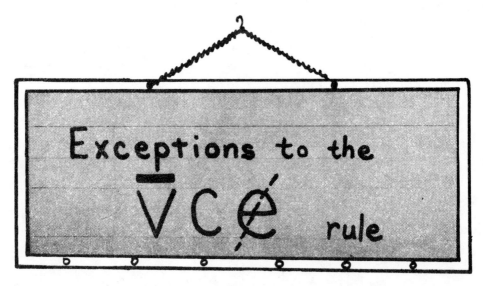

Title card
must be a
double or
triple thick-
ness of 4-ply
poster board.

LETTER SOUNDS

b boy
h hat
n nine

c cat
j jar
p pig
v vest
y yarn

d dog
k king
r rabbit

f fish
l lamp
s sun
w web
z zipper

g girl
m mop
t top

31

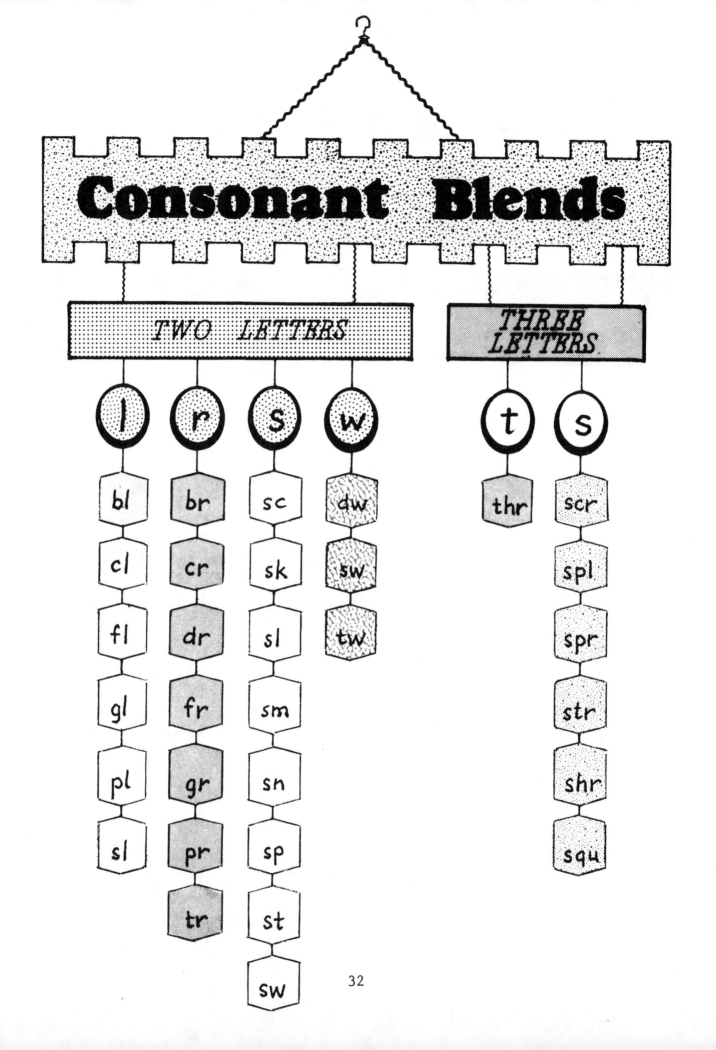

Consonant Blends

TWO LETTERS

l
- bl
- cl
- fl
- gl
- pl
- sl

r
- br
- cr
- dr
- fr
- gr
- pr
- tr

s
- sc
- sk
- sl
- sm
- sn
- sp
- st
- sw

w
- dw
- sw
- tw

THREE LETTERS

t
- thr

s
- scr
- spl
- spr
- str
- shr
- squ

32

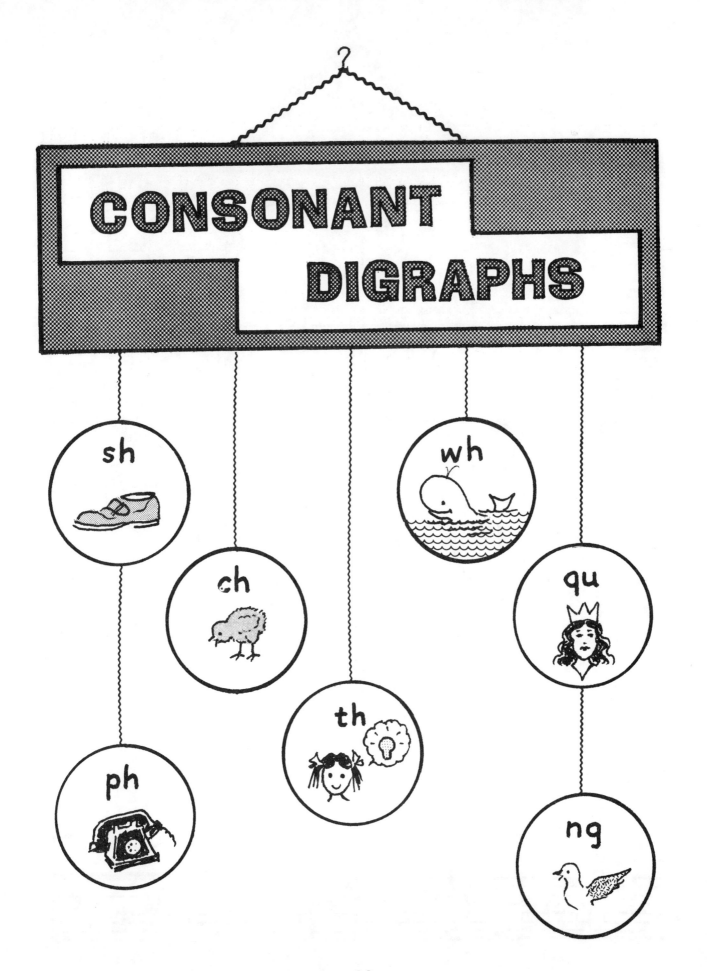

CONSONANT DIGRAPHS

sh

ch

th

wh

qu

ng

ph

short vowel

MOBILE

a e i o u

y = ī
fly

y = ē
puppy

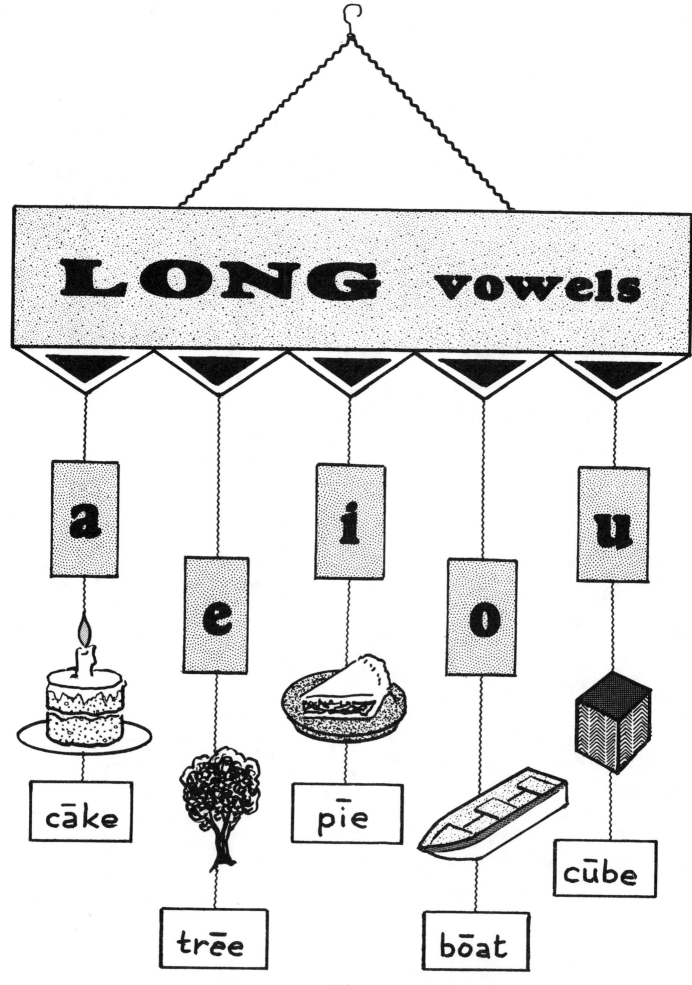

LONG vowels

a — cāke

e — trēe

i — pīe

o — bōat

u — cūbe

36

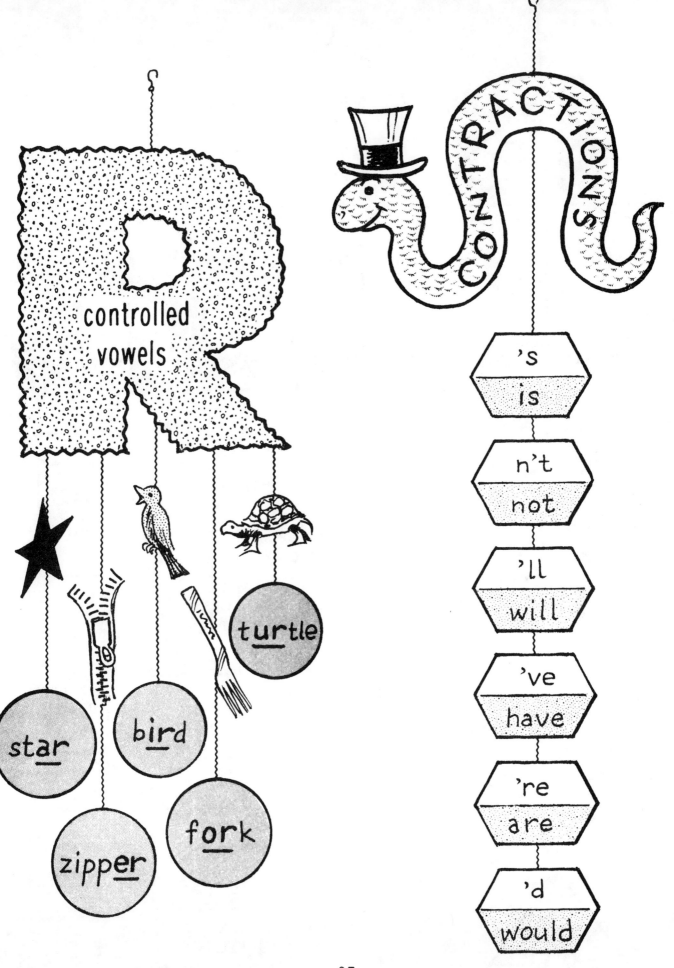

R controlled vowels

star

zipper

bird

fork

turtle

CONTRACTIONS

's is

n't not

'll will

've have

're are

'd would

37

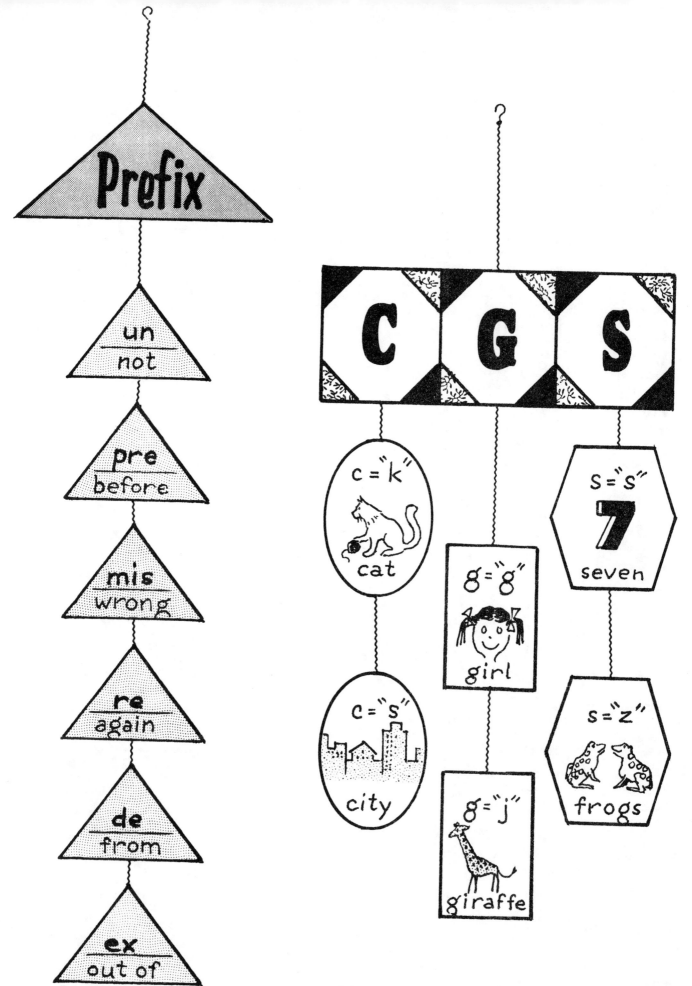

Prefix

un / not

pre / before

mis / wrong

re / again

de / from

ex / out of

C G S

c = "k" — cat

c = "s" — city

g = "g" — girl

g = "j" — giraffe

s = "s" — 7 seven

s = "z" — frogs

38

Suffix

able — capable

ful — full of

ment — doing

er — one who

less — without

ly — like

oi

ow

$\overline{oo}$

oy

ou

$\breve{oo}$

39

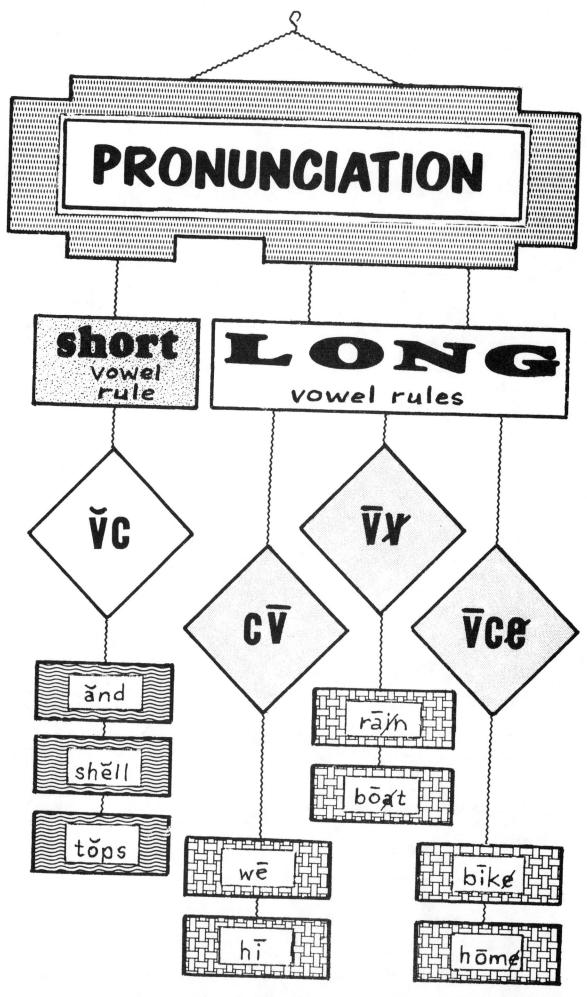

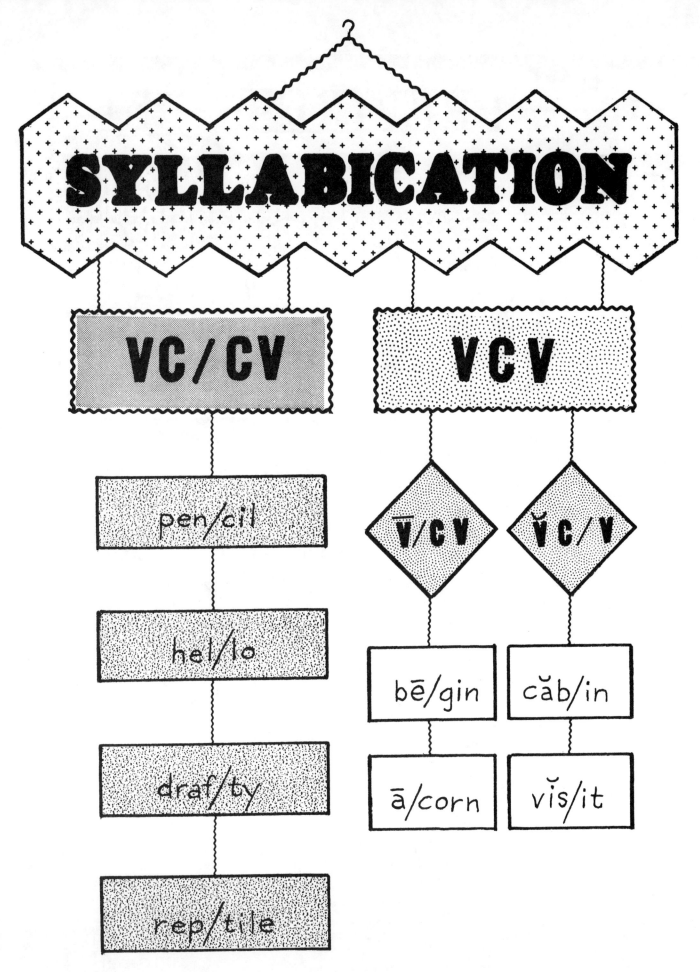

SYLLABICATION

VC/CV

VCV

pen/cil

hel/lo

draf/ty

rep/tile

$\overline{V}$/CV

$\breve{V}$C/V

bē/gin

căb/in

ā/corn

vĭs/it

41

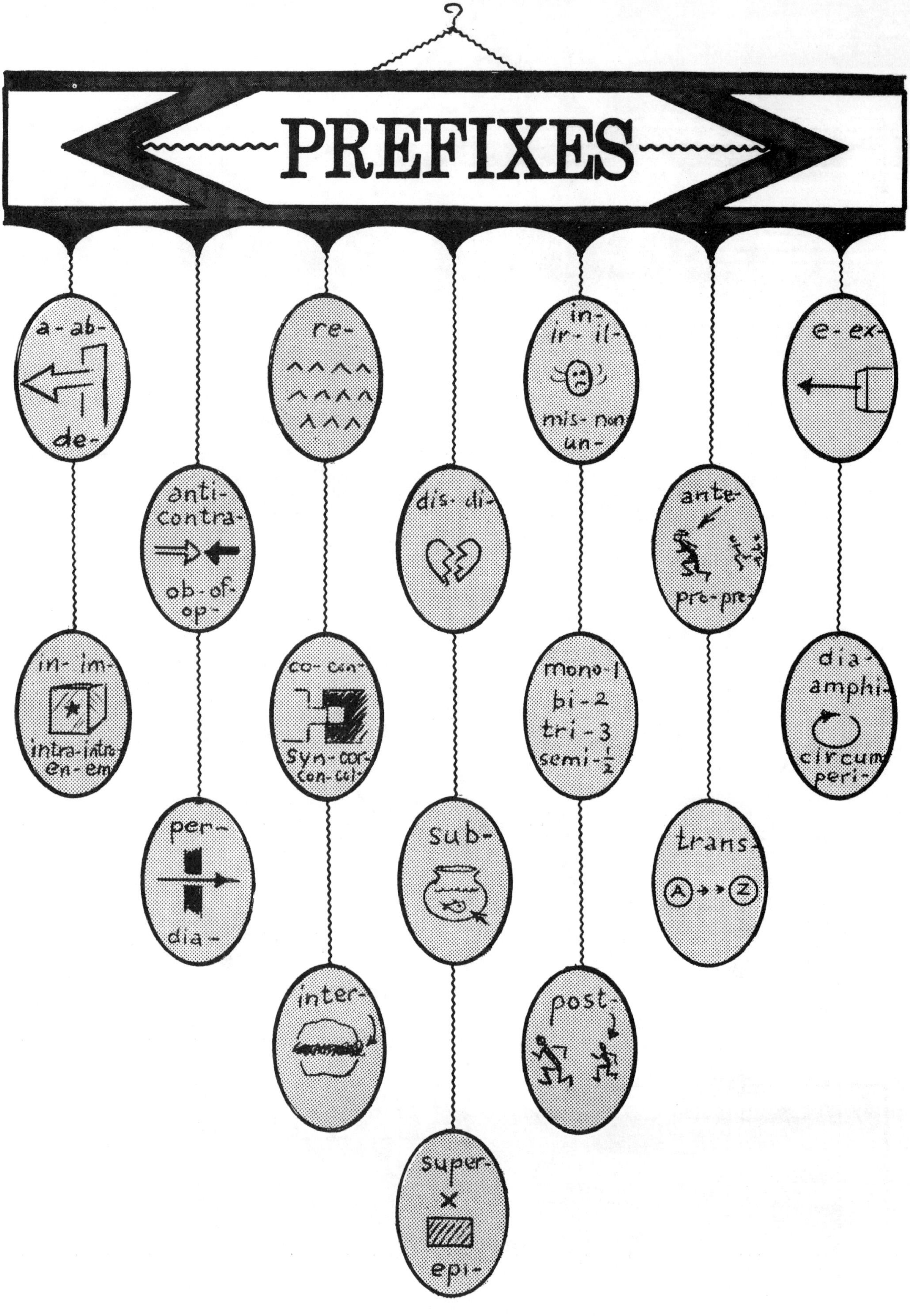

PREFIXES

a- ab-
de-

re-

in- ir- il-
mis- non-
un-

e- ex-

anti-
contra-
ob- of-
op-

dis- di-

ante-
pre- pro-

in- im-
intra- intro-
en- em-

co- con-
syn- cor-
con- col-

mono- 1
bi- 2
tri- 3
semi- $\frac{1}{2}$

dia-
amphi-
circum-
peri-

per-
dia-

sub-

trans-
Ⓐ ➔ ➔ Ⓩ

inter-

post-

super-
×
epi-

SUFFIXES

-ward

-ful -some
-ous -ious
-cous

-et -let
-icle -ule
-cule

-ence -ance
-sion -tion
-tude

-ance -ence
-ment

-al -eal -ial
-ic -ive -ly

-able -ible
-ile

-less

-ar -er
-an
-or -ist

-acy -dom
-ness -hood
-ant -ism
-ity -ty

-fy -ify
-en -ize

43

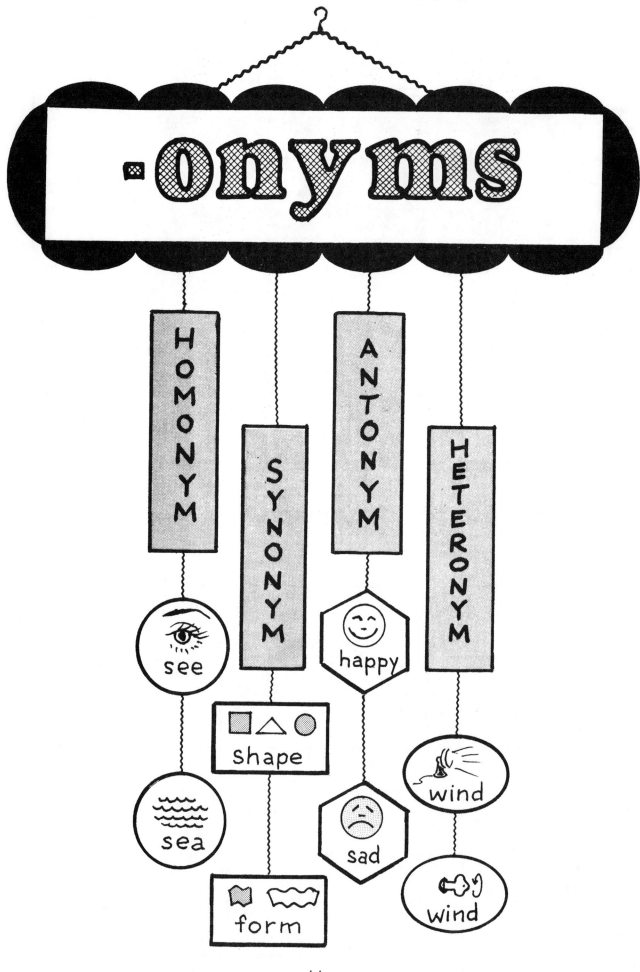

-onyms

HOMONYM

SYNONYM

ANTONYM

HETERONYM

see

sea

shape

form

happy

sad

wind

wind

THE SYNTHESIZE ENTERPRISE

Materials: white oaktag paper 12x18"
3x5" plain index cards (various colors)
4-ply poster board (assorted colors)
water-base magic markers (assorted colors)
permanent black and red magic markers (for
cards which need not be covered with contact
paper)
clear contact paper for covering game boards

Directions: Specific directions are included for each game.
Generally, the object is to match word parts to
form words. In all games any beginning part may
be combined with any medial and/or ending part
to form words. Most games have key sounds illustrated for the child's reference to help him recall
and eventually memorize the specific sound or
skill being studied. Produce large, colorful game
boards and always remember to color-code specific
categories of cards (e.g. all beginning sound cards--
blue; all medial sound cards--yellow; and all ending
sound cards--pink). This will not only aid in
keeping the cards sorted, but also adds delight-
ful color to the game.

Rules for winning can vary: The child who uses up
all of his cards first, the one who completes his
word-building card first (and correctly), the one
who accumulates the largest number of words, or
the one who accumulates the greatest number of
points (as in Word Factory and Point Partners).

Self-Correction: Master lists of possible combinations can be
designed or possible endings for each beginning
sound can be printed on the back of each beginning
sound card.

Skill: Short Vowel Word Synthesis

Word Whale - Board size - 22x28"
                40 1x1½" pink cards (beginning sound)
                40 1x1½" green cards (ending sound)

See: Consonant Sound List (beginning sounds)
       List of Rhyming Endings (VC - short vowel
       endings) (use the lists at the back of this
       book to produce the beginning and ending
       sound cards).

Play: Stacks of beginning and ending sound cards are
       placed face-up on the board as illustrated.
       Children take turns making words by combining
       beginning sound and ending sounds to make words.
       As cards are removed, new sounds will appear.

Self-Correction: On the reverse side of each ending
       word part card, print all the words which can
       be made using that ending.

Adapt: To use the board for long vowel words, place
        long-vowel key pictures over the short vowel
        pictures and provide green cards with long vowel
        sounds (e.g.ate, oap, etc.).

Skill: Word Synthesis

Word Line - 20-40 2x4" white cards
                   / is green
                   beginning sound is printed in red
                   ending sound is **printed in black**

Play: Cards **are** distributed to players and words **are** built
        in both directions from any starting card.

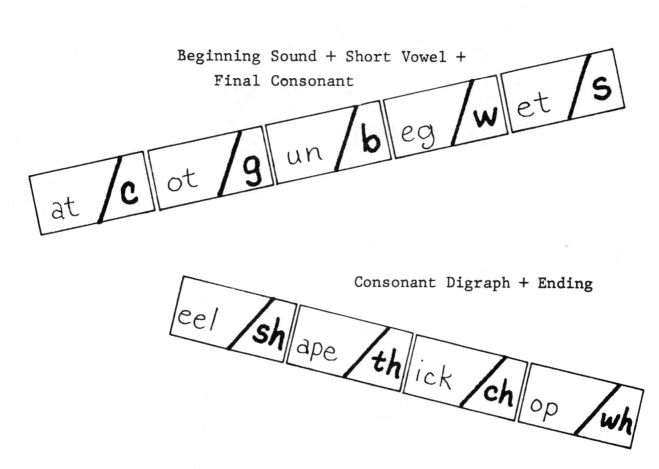

Beginning Sound + Short Vowel +
Final Consonant

at /c ot /g un /b eg /w et /s

Consonant Digraph + Ending

eel /sh ape /th ick /ch op /wh

b - bl - br + Word Ending

ush /br ake /b ike /bl ock /b ee /br

Skill: Word Synthesis

<u>Word Building Cards</u> - Board size 12 x 18" oaktag
Letter cards 1" square
Affix cards 1½ x 3½"

Play: Children play alone or on teams. The object is to
build as many words as possible.

48

Skill: Word Synthesis (using any desired sounds)

Word Factory - Board size - 22 x 18" (bright green)
               1½ x 3" yellow beginning
     sound cards (need 50-75)
               1½ x 3" pink ending sound
     cards (need 50-75)

Play: Place stacks of beginning and ending sound cards
       face up as illustrated. Taking turns, the children
       make words by combining yellow and pink cards and
       scoring the total associated points (e.g. spool
       3-sp + 6-ool = 9 points). The winner at the end
       of the game (when all cards have been used) is the
       one with the greatest number of points.

Adapt: See the following page for additional skill
        practice ideas.

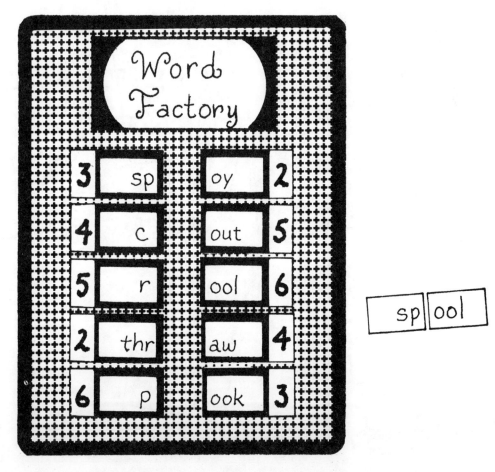

49

WORD FACTORY

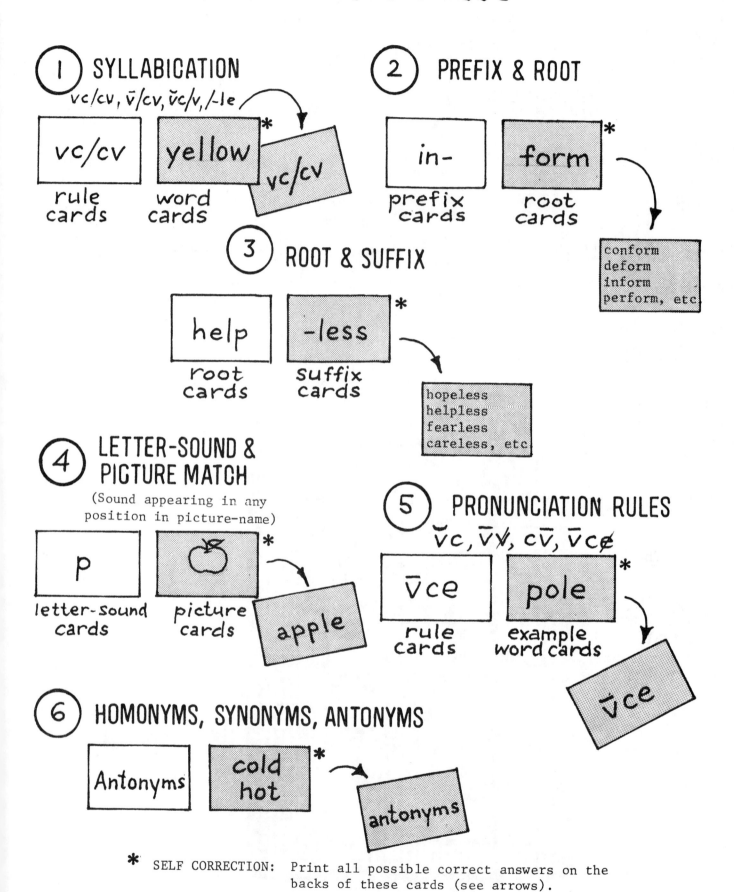

① SYLLABICATION
vc/cv, v̄/cv, v̆c/v, -le

vc/cv	yellow
rule cards	word cards

vc/cv *

② PREFIX & ROOT

in-	form
prefix cards	root cards

*

conform
deform
inform
perform, etc

③ ROOT & SUFFIX

help	-less
root cards	suffix cards

*

hopeless
helpless
fearless
careless, etc

④ LETTER-SOUND & PICTURE MATCH
(Sound appearing in any position in picture-name)

p	🍎
letter-sound cards	picture cards

* apple

⑤ PRONUNCIATION RULES
v̆c, v̄v̸, cv̄, v̄cȩ

v̄ce	pole
rule cards	example word cards

* v̄ce

⑥ HOMONYMS, SYNONYMS, ANTONYMS

Antonyms	cold hot

* antonyms

* SELF CORRECTION: Print all possible correct answers on the backs of these cards (see arrows).

Horse-Turtle-Shark-Beaver-Bird

The WORLD'S ONLY

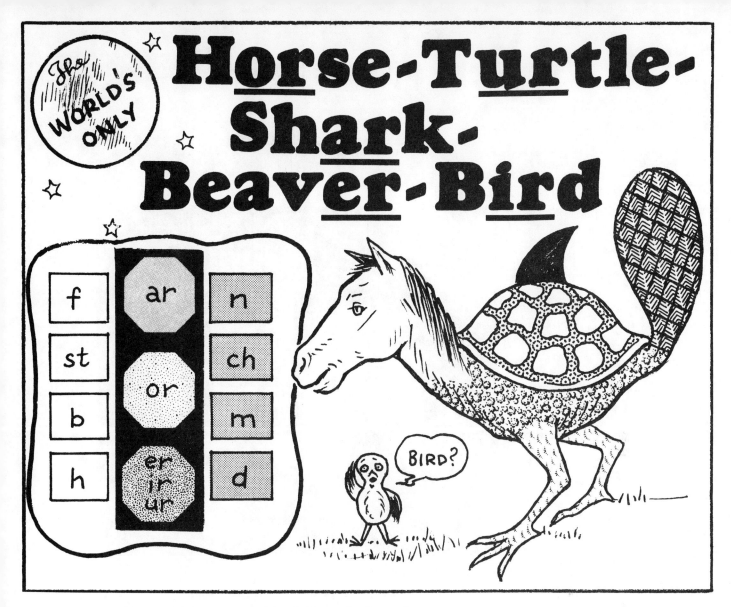

BIRD?

Skill: "R" Controlled Vowel Sounds

The World's Only Horse-Turtle-Shark-Beaver-Bird

Board size 20 x 28"
Cards: 60   2x3" yellow beginning sound
        60   2x3" blue ending sound
        20   3" diameter pink "ar"
        20   3" diameter green "or"
        30   3" diameter orange "er-ir-ur"

Play: In turn, each player produces "R" controlled vowel
       sound words by combining cards as illustrated. By
       placing stacks of cards on the board, new cards will
       appear as children remove those cards they are using
       to form words. By printing a 1, 2, or 3 on the back
       of each card, the children can add up the points for
       individual cards used and receive a "word score."
       At the end of the game, the child with the greatest
       number of "word points" earned wins.

Self-Correction: Duplicate the list of "R" Controlled Vowel
       Sound words provided in the reference section so
       children can check their responses.

Skill: Short ĕ word synthesis

<u>ĕlephant</u> - Board size 12 x 14"
        40 1¼ x 1¼" pink cards (beginning sounds)
        40 1¼ x 2½" yellow cards (short ĕ ending sounds)

Play: Stacks of pink and yellow cards are placed on the elephant's
       blanket. Children make words by combining beginning sounds
       and ending sounds.

Self-Correction: A master list of possibilities can be made
       available to help children check their responses.

52

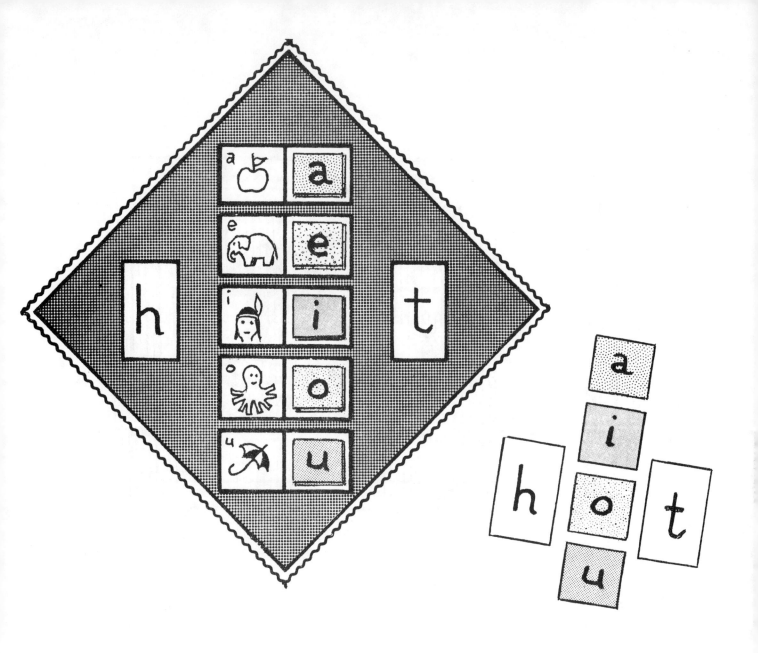

Skill: Short Vowel - substitution and word synthesis

Short Vowel Change - Board size 22x22" (dark color)
                    40 2½x4" beginning and ending
                              cards on white oaktag
                    20 3x3" cards for each short vowel
                              (make the cards for different
                              vowels different colors).

Play: Stacks of cards are placed face-up on the board as illustrated. In turn, the child pronounces each short vowel
word using the given beginning and ending consonant sounds
(e.g. "hat, het, hit, hot, hut") and if the combination
produces a real word, the child picks up the vowel card
used (e.g. for h and t he would pick up a i o u). The
next child plays using the next set of beginning and
ending cards. The winner is the child with the greatest
number of vowel cards.

53

Skill: Short Vowel Word Synthesis

Short Vowel Worm - Board size 18 x 28"
                30-50 1½x3" yellow cards (beginnings)
                30-50 1½x3" green cards (endings)

Play: (Note: the short vowel worm's boots give letter and
       picture clues to the five short vowel sounds). Place
       stacks of beginning and ending sound cards on the
       umbrella. Children play by combining any beginning
       and ending sound to produce real words. At the end
       of the game, the child who has made the greatest number
       of words wins.

Self-Correction: The backs of the ending sound cards should
       list all the possible words. (See arrow)

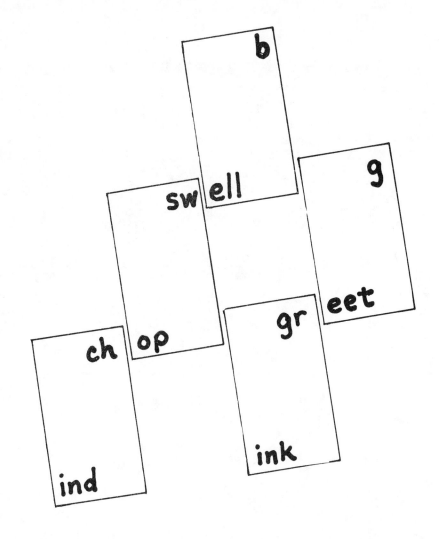

Skill: Word Synthesis   (Game Board shown on Page 56)

Point Partners - Board size 22 x 28" (dark color)
                Card size 1 3/4 x 2½" (need 75-100 cards)

Play: The cards are dealt out to three or four players. One
       card is placed face-up on each of the ten spaces as
       shown to begin play. In turn each player builds a
       "partner" by combining one of his cards with one on the
       board to make a word or complete a pair (e.g. Homonyms)
       A sample play would be to take the "g/eet" card
       illustrated and place it on the board next to the
       "gr/ink" card to produce the word "greet". Such a play
       would give the child a score of 5 points because he
       placed his card on a 5-point space. Another play would
       be to place the "ch" on the 4-space next to the "op"
       to form "chop." In this case, 4 points would be scored.
       Play continues until all spaces on the board are filled.

Self-Correction: Write all the possible word combinations on
       the back of each card (see arrow) according to ending
       sounds page 56.

55

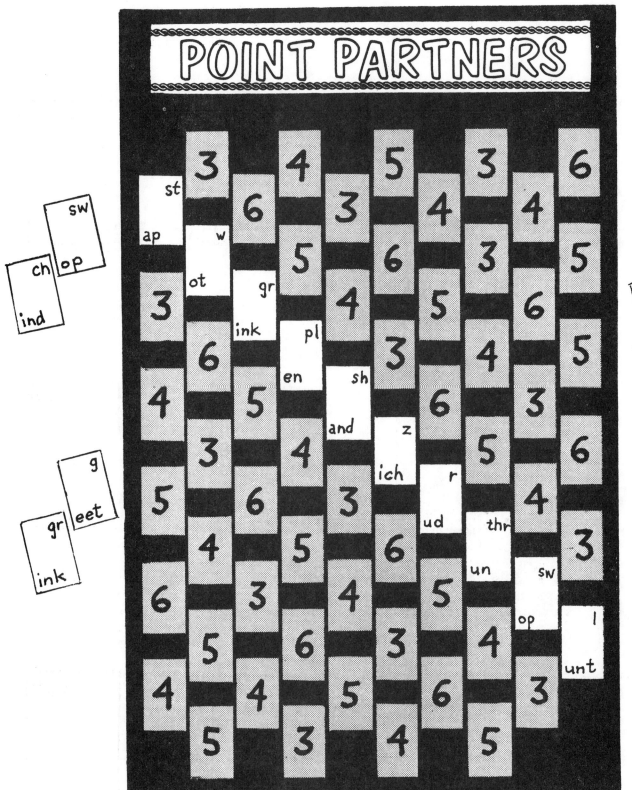

POINT PARTNERS

Point Partners - Sample cards for additional word attack skills:

Always print the top word in red, the bottom
word in black. This helps the child to more
clearly visualize combinations.

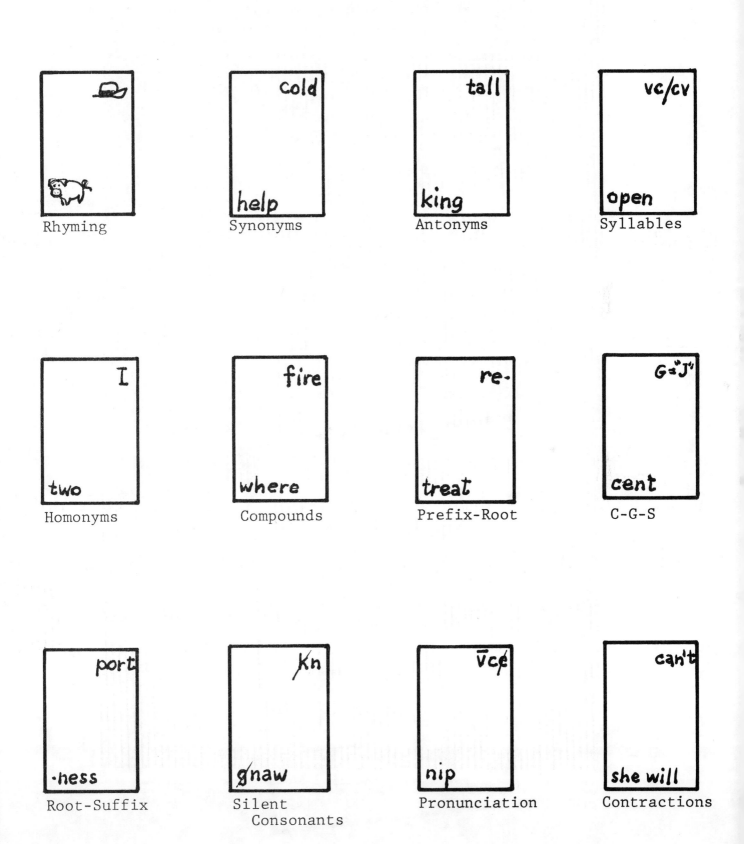

Rhyming	Synonyms	Antonyms	Syllables
Homonyms	Compounds	Prefix-Root	C-G-S
Root-Suffix	Silent Consonants	Pronunciation	Contractions

PEEK-A-BOO GAMES

Materials: Order the "PEEK-A-BOO POCKET KITS" described on the following page. These kits contain all the materials needed for the production of the games on the following pages.

Magic markers (both water-base and permanent)

Directions: Complete directions are included with each kit. Although possible skill applications vary, the twenty-five or more skill suggestions include those illustrated on the following pages.

The kits come with:

        A heat-sealed Vinyl plastic "Peek-A-Boo Pocket"
        Six open-ended game cards
        Twelve pre-printed skill cards
        Wooden playing sticks
        Instructions and suggested skills list

You can utilize the materials in your kit to teach your choice of skills by simply filling in the card spaces with skill items and the wooden playing sticks with answers. Each game takes approximately 15 minutes to complete.

Self-Correction is explained on the following page.

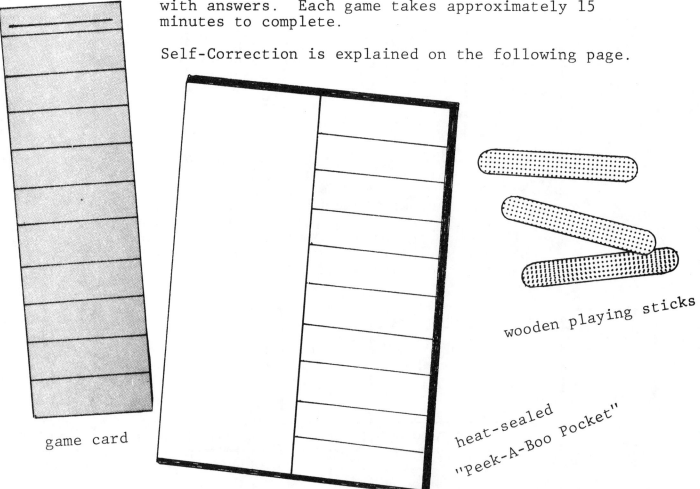

game card

wooden playing sticks

heat-sealed
"Peek-A-Boo Pocket"

Self-correction

Reverse side of game

Peek-A-Boo Pocket games self-correct. After the child inserts all answer playing sticks, he turns the plastic pocket to the reverse side and corresponds numbers to check his work.

PEEK-A-BOO POCKET KITS:

Each kit contains one heat-sealed vinyl plastic "Peek-A-Boo Pocket" and the materials needed to make eighteen games of your choice (playing cards, playing sticks, and instructions for more than twenty-five skill applications).

"Peek-A-Boo Pocket Kit"

Single-sided pocket for answers to be placed on the right side only.
18 games per kit.

"Double Peek-A-Boo Pocket Kit"

Double-sided pocket for answers to be placed on the right and left sides.
18 games per kit.

*Postpaid

PEEK-A-BOO POCKETS

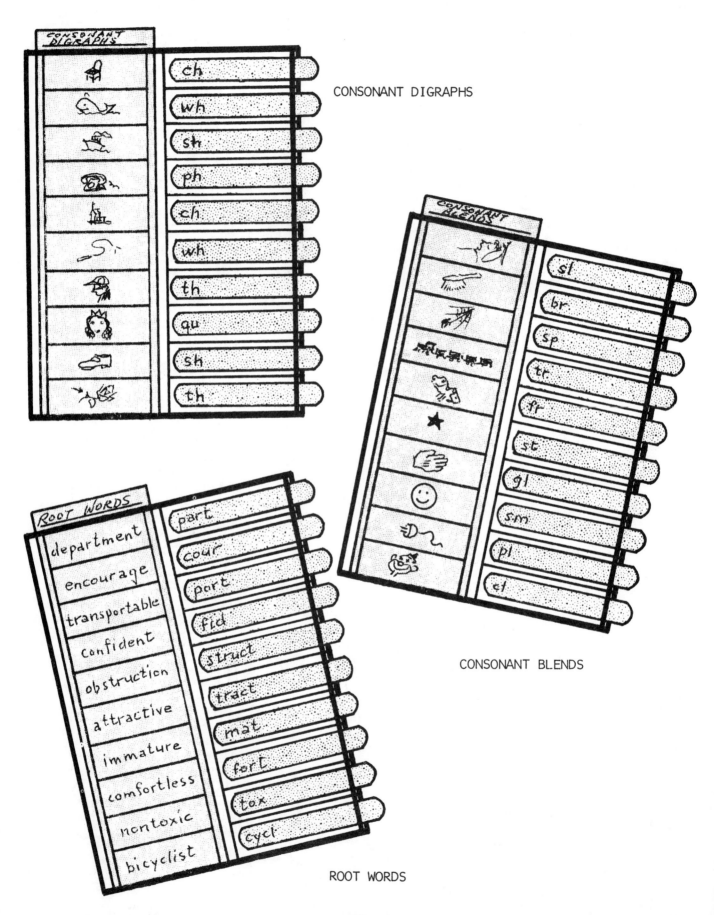

CONSONANT DIGRAPHS

CONSONANT BLENDS

ROOT WORDS

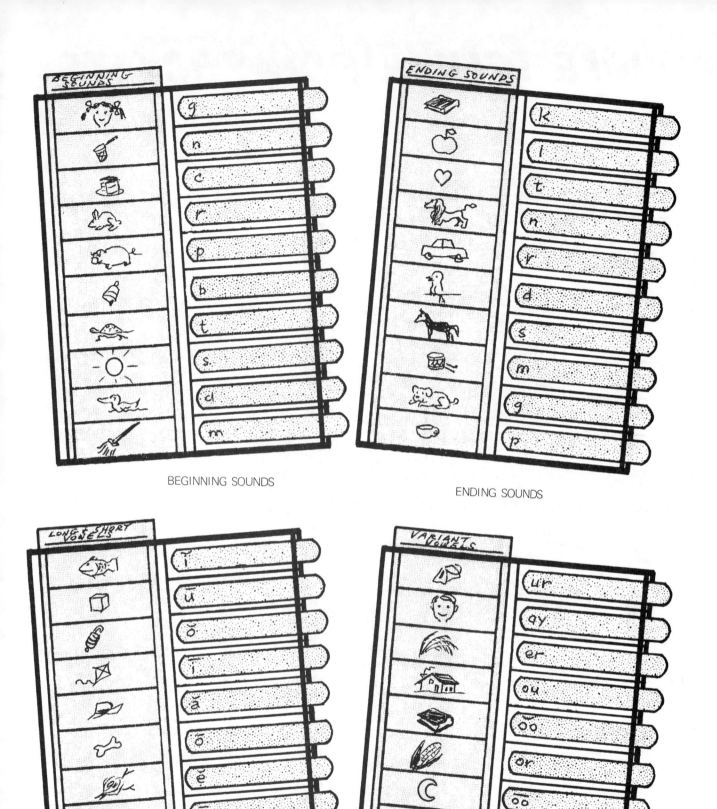

BEGINNING SOUNDS

ENDING SOUNDS

LONG AND SHORT VOWELS

VARIANT VOWELS

61

DOUBLE PEEK-A-BOO POCKETS

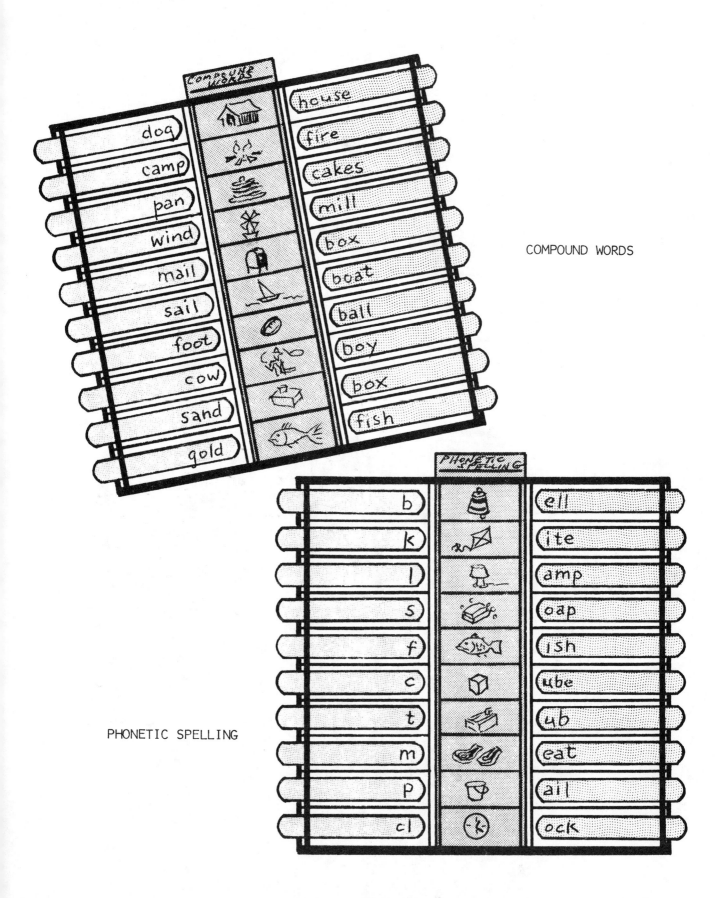

COMPOUND WORDS

PHONETIC SPELLING

62

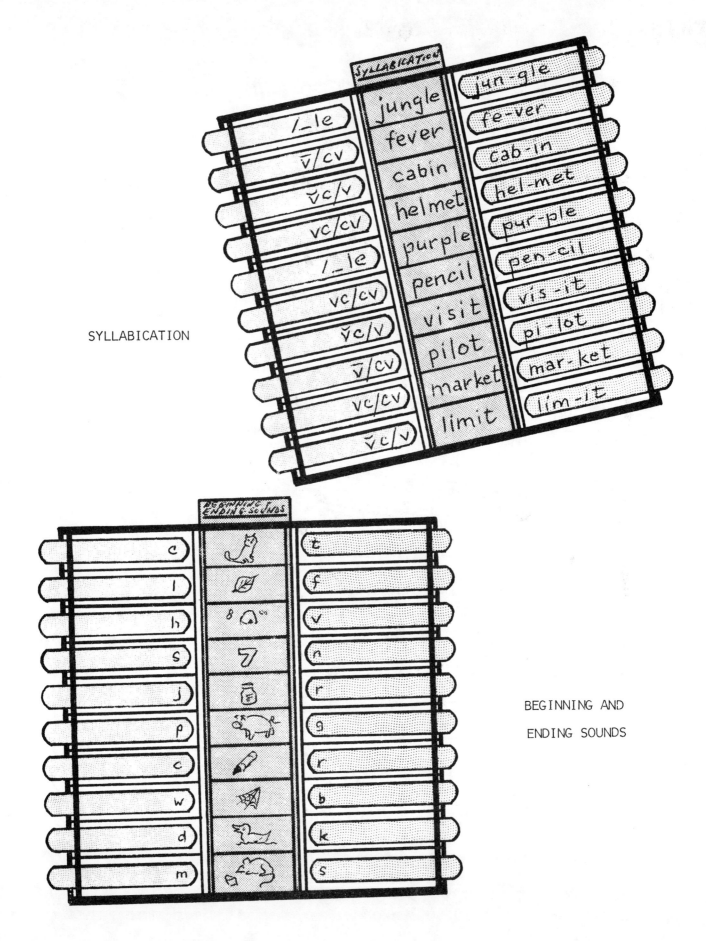

SYLLABICATION

BEGINNING AND

ENDING SOUNDS

63

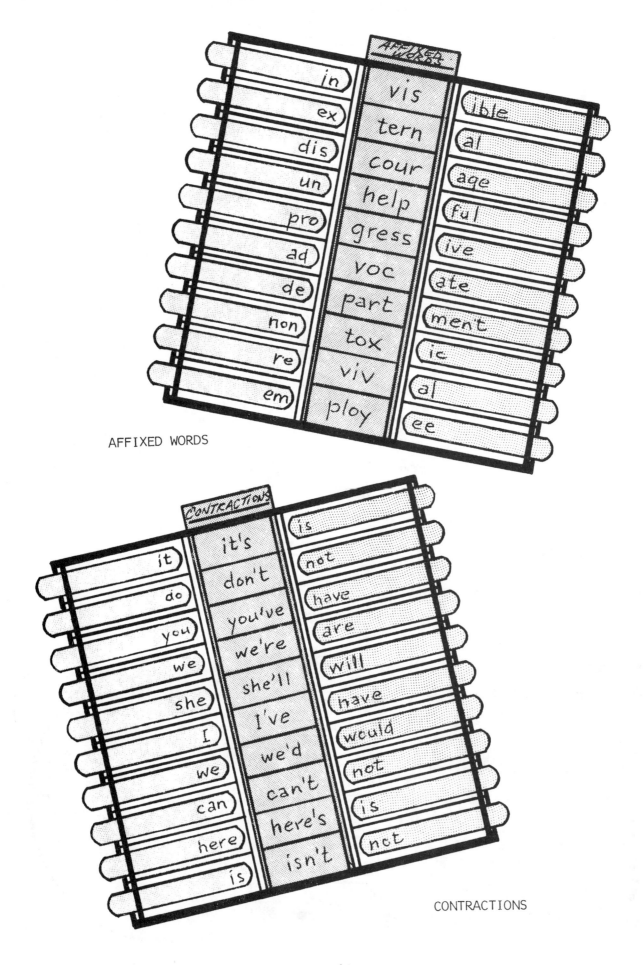

AFFIXED WORDS

CONTRACTIONS

Materials: 12" diameter oaktag, index or poster board circle
                11" diameter oaktag, index or poster board circle
                water-base magic markers
                clear contact paper
                ruler & glue

Directions: Each shape-up game will require one 12" diameter
                circle and one 11" diameter circle. Rule off both
                circles into eight or sixteen sections as illustrated.
                You may wish to use a pencil compass to lightly in-
                dicate a smaller circular area in the center of the
                11" circle. Using magic marker, scallop or zig zag
                an irregular design along the area indicated by the
                penciled circle. Print the desired skill information
                on the inside "pie-shaped" areas and their correspond-
                ing answers on the outside "pie-shaped" areas of the
                11" circle.

                Next, cut along one of the lines to reach the inner
                circular area and cut along the scalloped or zig zag
                outline. Glue this "center section" to the larger
                12" circle and then cover the playing circle with
                clear contact paper. Next, cover the playing cards
                with contact and cut them apart.

Play: Children play by placing answer cards next to the
                appropriate items on the playing board.

Self-Correction: When any answer is placed, self-correction is
                evident: if the answer card fits the design, then
                the answer is correct.

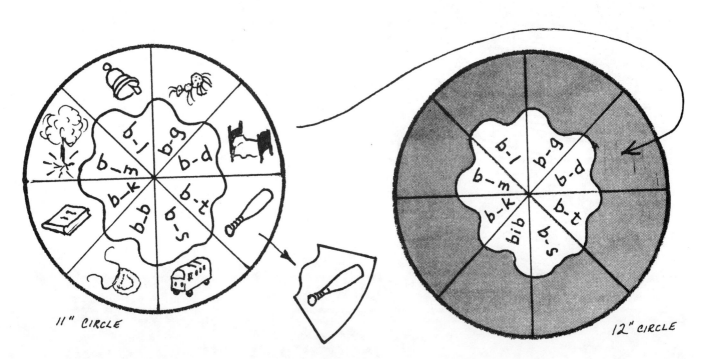

11" CIRCLE   12" CIRCLE

65

SHAPE-UPS

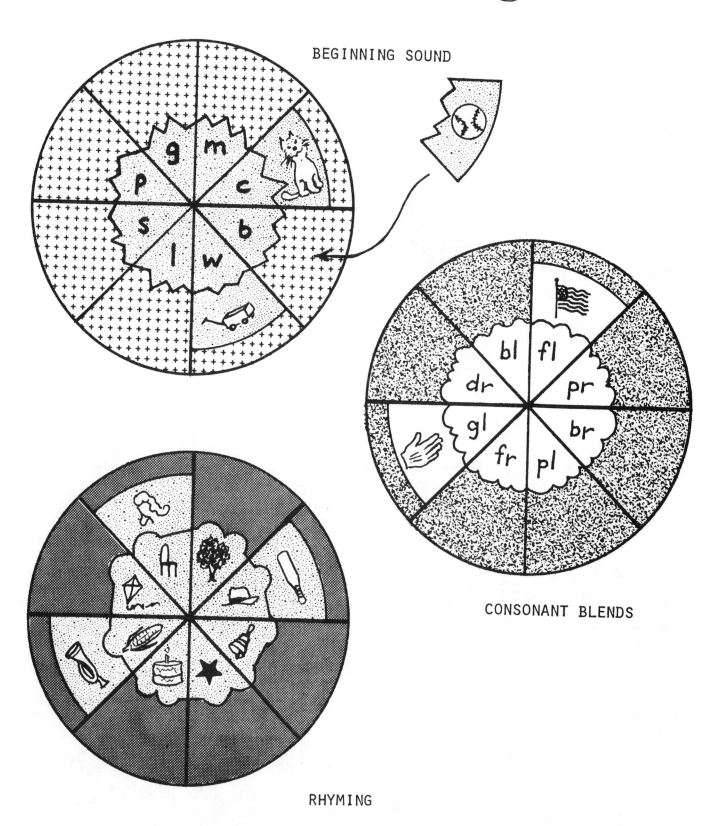

BEGINNING SOUND

CONSONANT BLENDS

RHYMING

66

COMPOUND WORDS

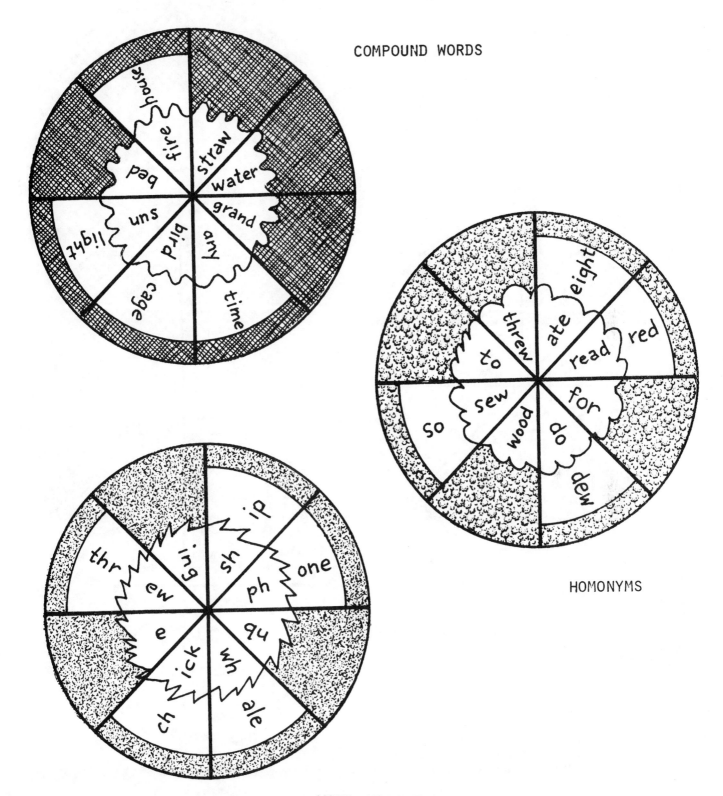

HOMONYMS

WORD SYNTHESIS

PLURALS

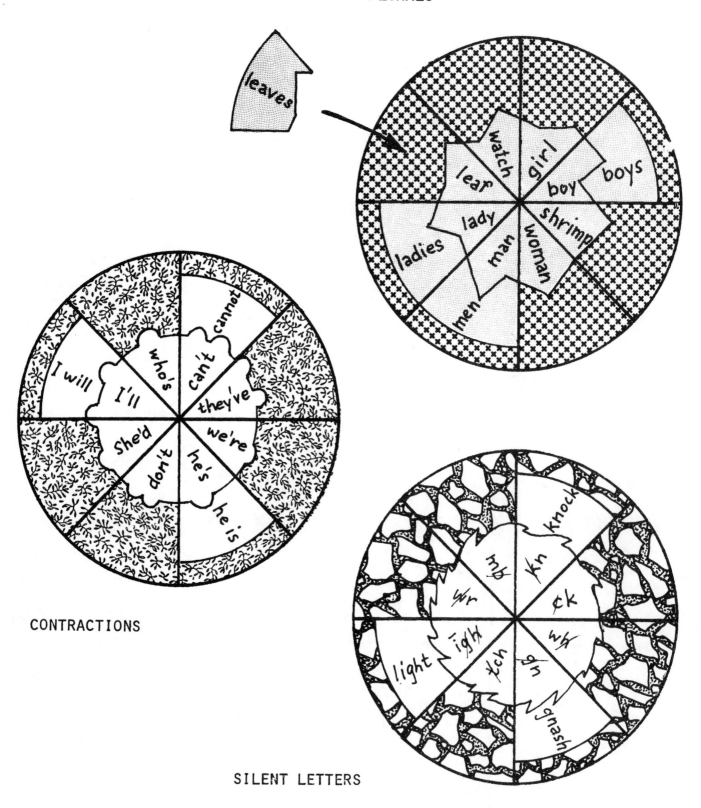

leaves

watch
girl
boy
boys
leaf
shrimp
lady
woman
ladies
man
men

CONTRACTIONS

I will
I'll
who's
can't
cannot
they've
She'd
we're
don't
he's
he is

SILENT LETTERS

knock
mb
kn
wr
ck
light
igh
wh
tch
gn
gnash

68

VARIANT VOWELS

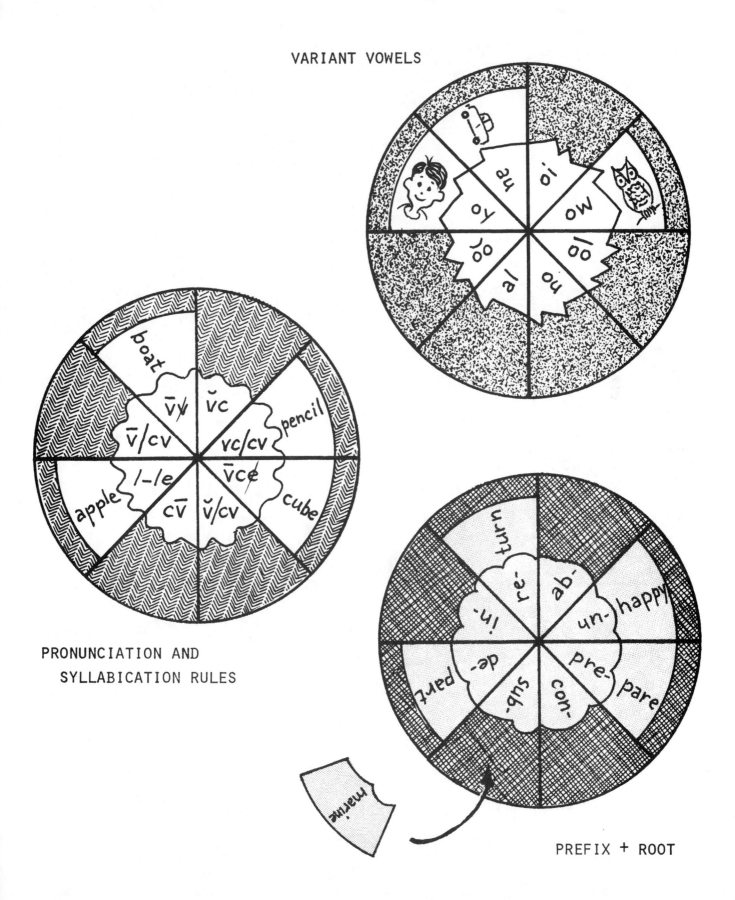

PRONUNCIATION AND
SYLLABICATION RULES

PREFIX + ROOT

69

Materials: White oaktag paper
water-base magic markers
small pictures (where needed)
clear contact paper

Directions: Dominoes - Rule off a 12x18" piece of oaktag into 2x4" rectangles. Outline the edges with red, green or blue magic markers. Divide each 2x4" rectangle into 2x2" squares using a black magic marker. On each 2x2" square print a word or glue a picture as needed. The center of each domino is indicated by the black lines. Be sure to print letters or words and glue pictures with their tops facing toward the black line. Print the first item eg. "bl" where you see #1 and glue a picture of "blocks" where you see the second #1. Continue until all number pairs are filled. Cover both sides of the sheet with clear contact paper and cut apart the dominoes (2x4" rectangles with black center lines). To play, the dominoes are dealt out to two, three, or four players. One is placed face-up in the center of the table and players pronounce sounds, picture names, and/or words as they place their corresponding cards next to cards on the table. The only thing to be careful of is to not place non-corresponding cards adjacent to each other.

1 card

27	1	9	10	18	19
1	2	10	11	19	20
2	3	11	12	20	21
3	4	12	13	21	22
4	5	13	14	22	23
5	6	14	15	23	24
6	7	15	16	24	25
7	8	16	17	25	26
8	9	17	18	26	27

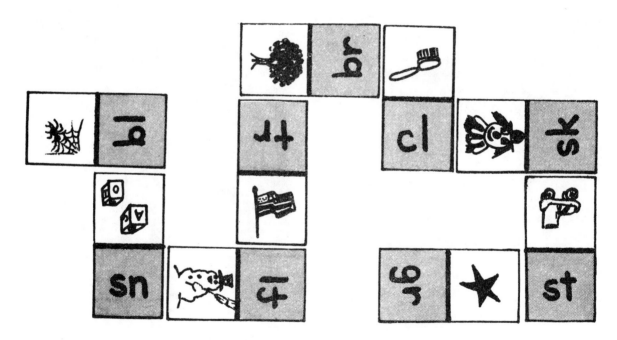

Consonant Blend Dominoes

70

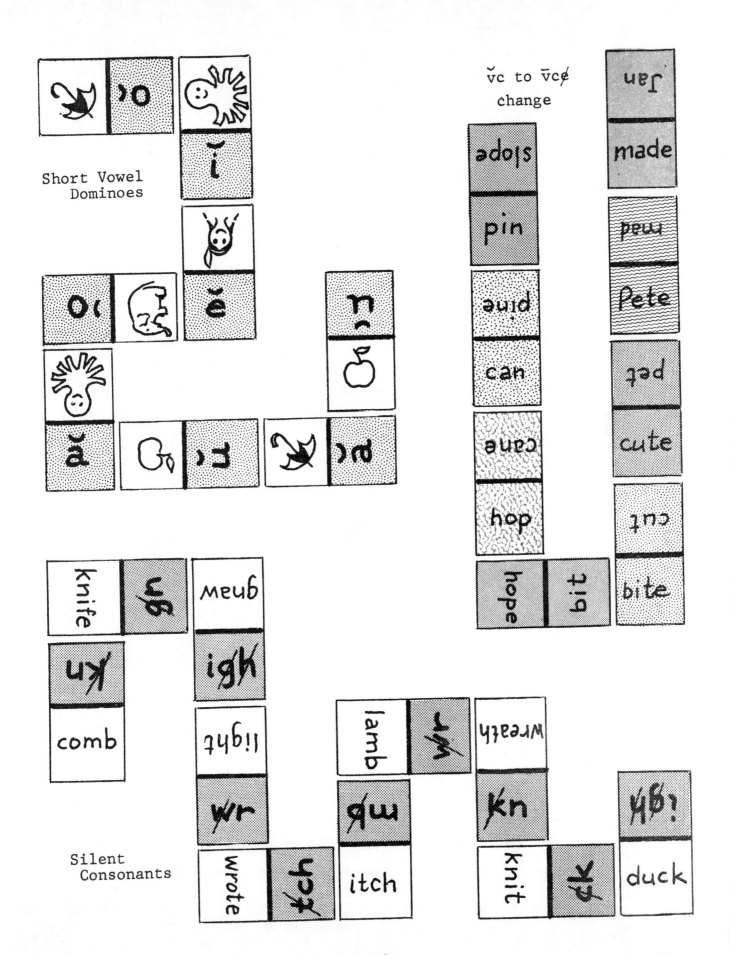

Short Vowel
Dominoes

Silent
Consonants

v̆c to v̄cé
change

71

Antonym Dominoes

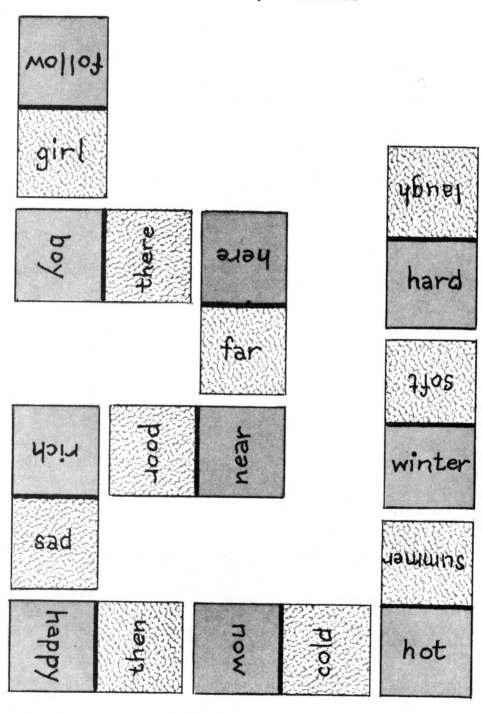

Synonym Dominoes

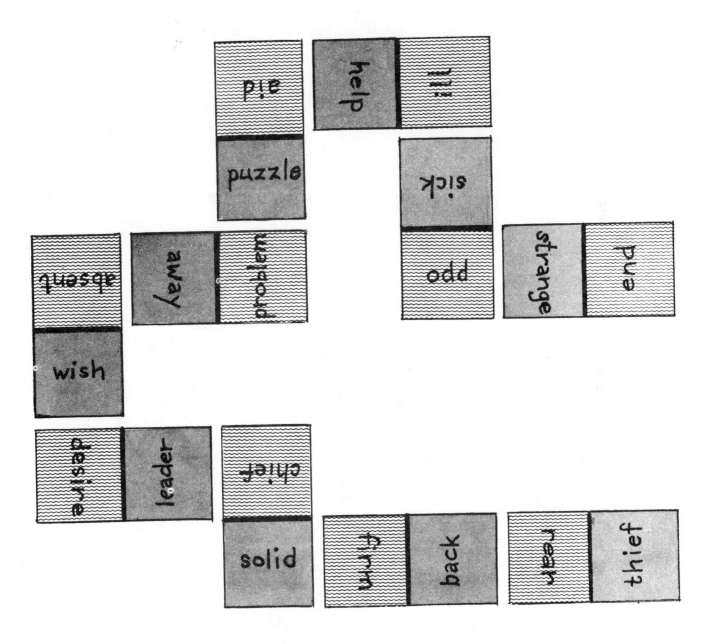

Trionomoes - Cut equilateral triangles 4x4x4" -
you will need at least 20 white oaktag triangles
which will have words exemplifying the sounds or
principles being studied and at least 20 colored
poster board triangles which illustrate the skill
to be practiced. In the Short Vowel Trionomoes
Game illustrated below, there are four colored
poster board triangles for each of the five short
vowel sounds. I used a different color of poster
board for each different vowel sound (eg. all
short a triangles are pink). So that this partic-
ular game can be played in two ways, I wrote words
on one side and glued pictures on the opposite
side. Children play by dealing out all the tri-
nomoes except one which is placed in the center
of the table or on the floor. The idea is to
match words or pictures to sounds (see illustration)
and pronounce the word or picture name when placed
in position.

Self-Correction: The game can be made self-correcting by indicating
the correct sound match on the reverse side of each
small picture on the white triangle.

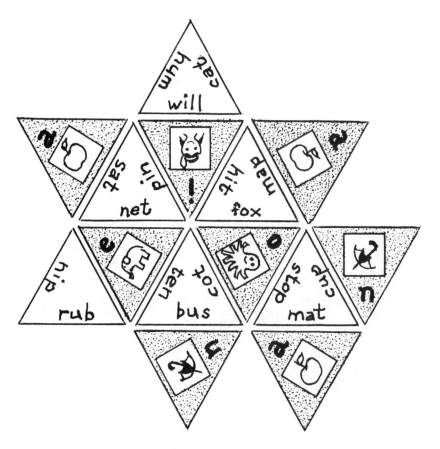

Short Vowel Trionomoes

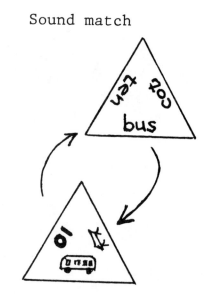

Sound match

Reverse side

Additional Skill Cards for "Trionomoes":

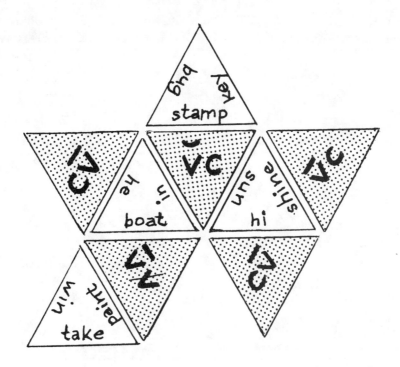

Pronunciation Rules

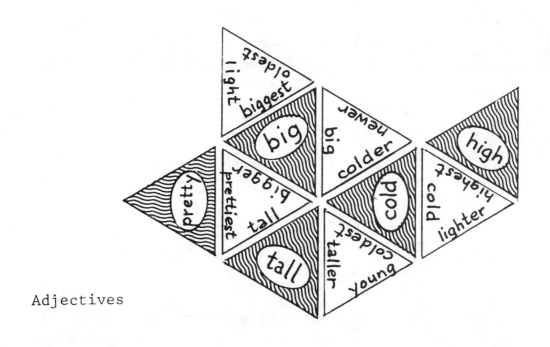

Adjectives

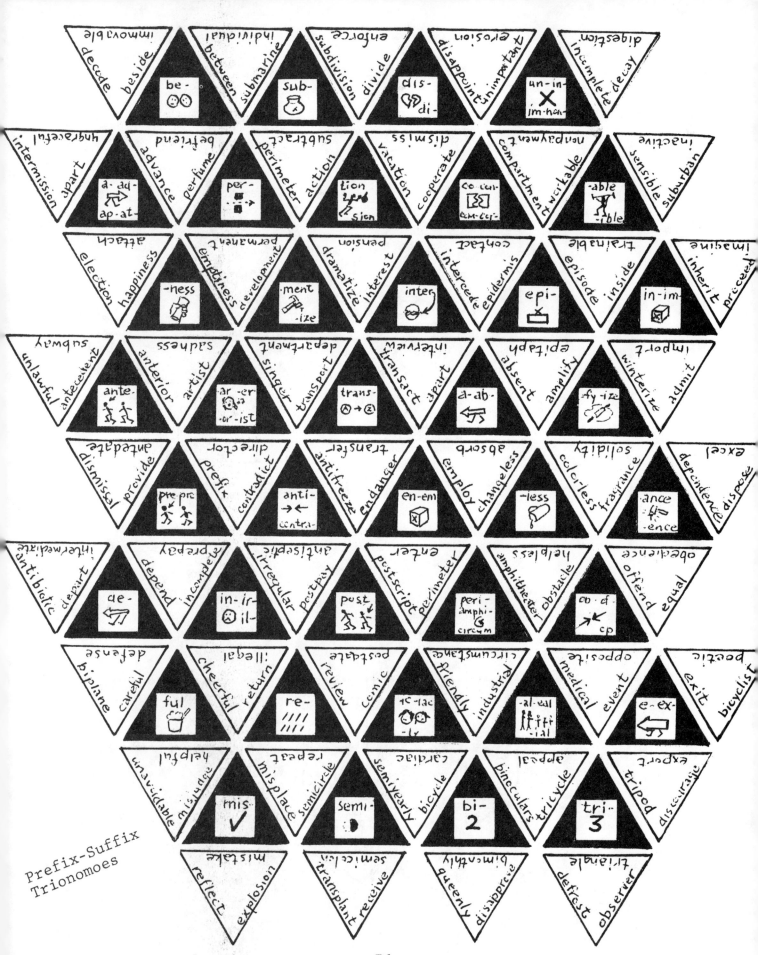

Prefix-Suffix
Trionomoes

Quadronomoes: 12 - 4" square yellow poster board squares
                 12 - 4" square pink poster board squares

Directions: Divide each square into four triangles by drawing
               black lines between opposite corners. When printing
               letters or writing word parts, be positive to print
               beginning sounds or words extending out to the
               right-hand side of the square's center. Print
               ending sounds or words moving in toward the square's
               center as illustrated:

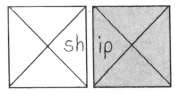

               Cover completed cards with contact paper if desired.
               Now they are ready to be dealt to players. Begin
               with one card face-up in the center of the table.
               Players pronounce the words as they place their
               cards next to those already on the table. Note:
               any cards which touch must make correct responses
               in all directions (on all sides). The winner is
               the first child to place all his cards correctly.

Self-Correction: The back of each word ending card can be coded
                  with possible answers (beginning sounds). (see arrows)

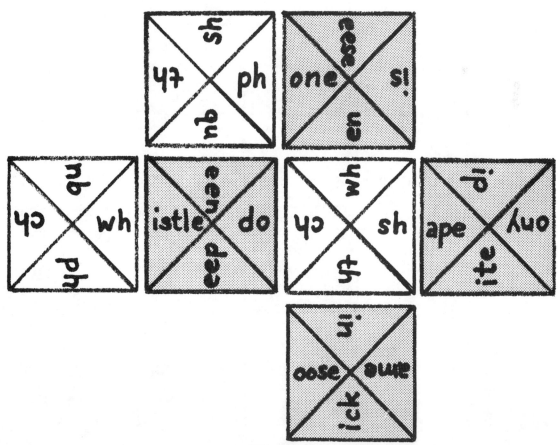

77

Additional Skills for "Quadronomoes"

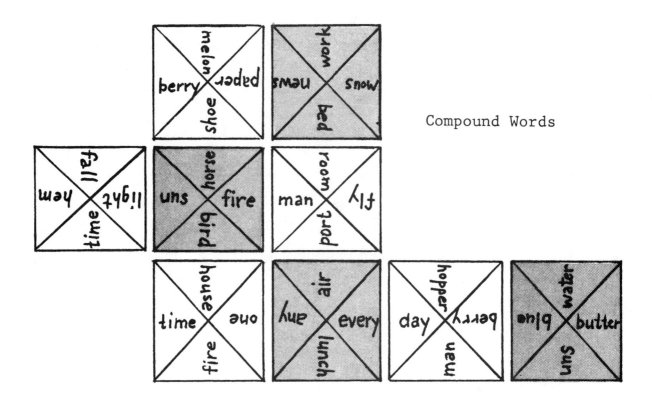

Compound Words

Rhyming
(word & picture)

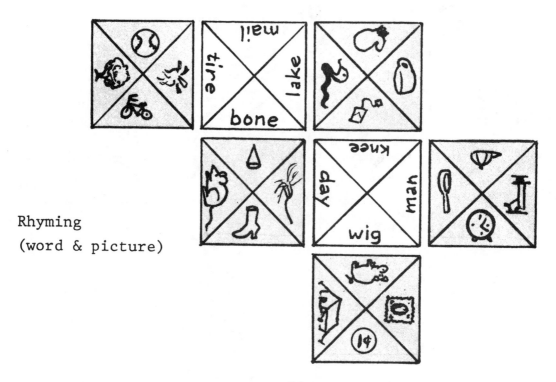

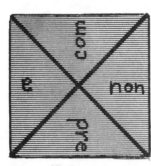

Prefix & Root Quadronomoes

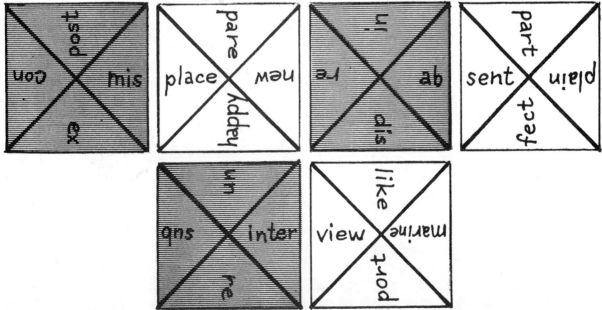

79

Materials: 4-ply poster board (white and assorted colors)
3x5" plain index cards (assorted colors)
12x18" white oaktag
clear contact paper
water-base magic markers
black and red permanent magic markers
brass fasteners (for "spinner-type" games)
colored buttons, golf tees or other place-markers.

Directions: Specific directions for each game are given. In
general, play involves pronouncing consonant and
vowel sounds in isolation or reading words which
provide practice in a specific word attack skill.
Many of the games involve moving along a trail by
reading words or giving letter sounds. One game,
"Toss and Score" involves the use of a playing
cube keeping a record of points earned. Plan to
cover all base boards with clear contact paper for
protection. Many of the boards are "basic boards"
and different sets of cards may be produced which
emphasize different skills utilizing the same board.
To make some of the games self-correcting, pictures
illustrating the word to be pronounced can be glued
to the reverse side of the cards (in this case, place
the word cards face-up on the boards--covering the
picture side).

Directions: Produce the game board as illustrated, but do not attach
the spinner until after the board is covered with contact
paper. Play involves spinning the spinner and moving the
number of spaces indicated by pronouncing sounds. The
first child who reaches the Hound's tail wins.

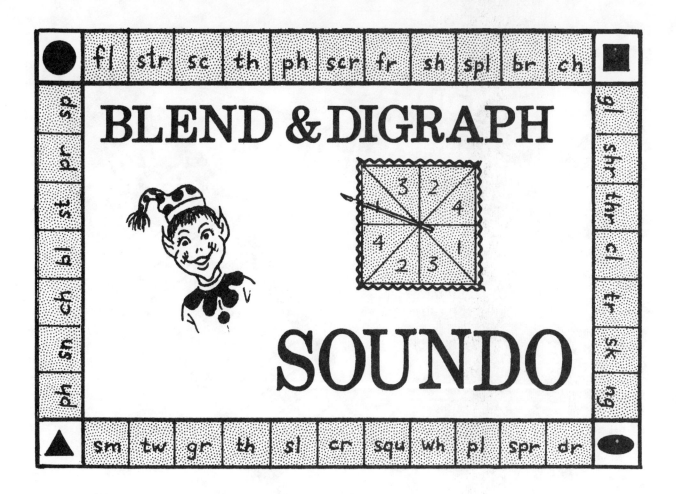

Skills: Consonant Blends & Vowel Sounds.

Materials: 12x18" white oaktag base boards
1x3" spinners (poster board)
brass fasteners
buttons for place markers

Directions: Produce the boards as illustrated, but
do not attach the spinners until the
boards have been covered with clear
contact paper. Use a brass fastener
to attach the spinners (be sure to use
a paper punch to make a hole in the
spinner--this helps to insure free
spinning). In Blend & Digraph Soundo,
each player begins in his own corner.
He spins the spinner and moves that
number of spaces in a clockwise direction
if he can pronounce the sounds correctly.
The first player to return home wins.
In Vowel Launch, the directions are the
same, except that players move upward
toward the rocket tip to win.

81

Skill: Long Vowel ($\overline{v}c\not{e}$ pattern) words

Materials: 16x22" poster board
50-75 2½x3" word cards (cut colored index cards in half)
buttons for place markers

Directions: Illustrate the game board with a bright purple dragon
and flaming orange breath. Cover the board with clear
contact paper. I use this game for practicing the
$\overline{V}C\not{E}$ pronunciation rule, but cards can be made for any
skill desired. (See the following page for examples).
In turn, each child picks up a card and reads the word.
If he is correct, he moves one space on the board.
More difficult words have a star on their card which
indicates a double-space move. When a player moves to
a dark space, he receives an extra turn.

Self Correction: (See arrows above indicating front and back sides
of playing cards). Place a picture illustrating
the word on the reverse side of each card or write
a simple phrase or sentence illustrating the usage
of the word.

Suggestions for additional card sets for "Dragon Hunt."
(Arrows point to the reverse, self-correcting side of
each card).

Short to Long
Vowel Sound Change

Pronounce the Consonant
Blend Sound. (Self-correct
with a picture on the reverse
containing the blend as
beginning sound).

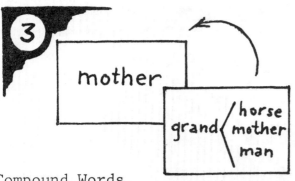

Compound Words
(which second word will
create a compound when combined
with the first word. (Self-correct
with answer on the reverse).

Contractions

Plurals
(regular "girl-girls" and
irregular forms "man-men").

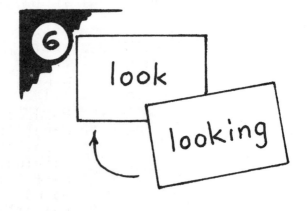

Identify the root.

Skill: Silent Consonant Combinations

Materials: 22x28" poster board base
             3" diameter circles (oaktag paper)
                make 50-100 of these "baseball" word cards.
             buttons for markers

Directions: Produce the game board as illustrated and
             cover it with contact paper. Print words
             illustrating the various Silent Letter
             Combinations on the back of each baseball
             card. Place the cards on the pitcher's
             mound. In turn, each player identifies
             the silent letter, reads the word and moves
             either 1 or 2 spaces as indicated on his
             card for correct answers. The first player
             to reach home wins.

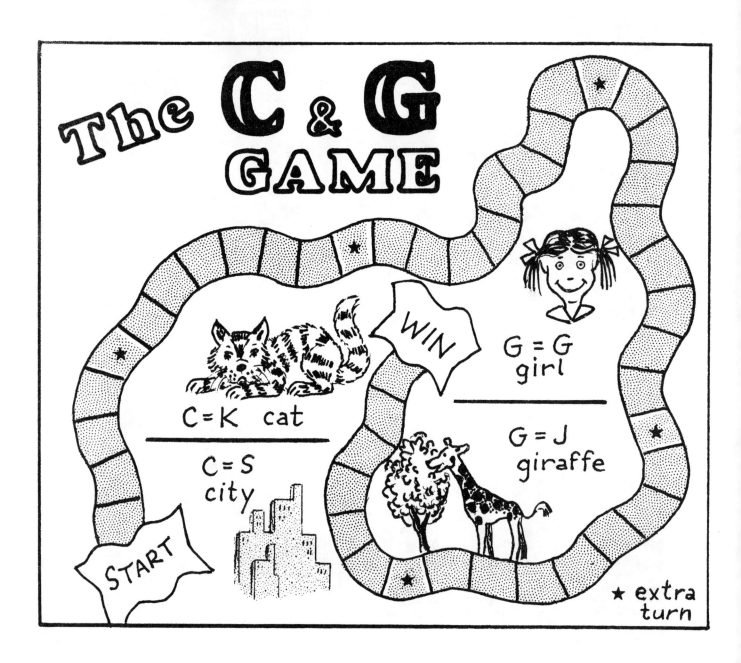

The C & G GAME

START

C = K cat
C = S city

WIN

G = G girl
G = J giraffe

★ extra turn

See directions on the
following page.

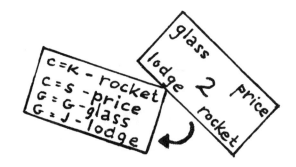

c = k - rocket
c = s - price
G = G - glass
G = J - lodge

glass — price
lodge 2 rocket

Skill: Variant Consonant Sounds C-G

Materials: 20x28" poster board (playing board)
                  7x11" poster board (spinner & card holder)
                  60 3x5" colored index cards
                  1x3" poster board spinner
                  brass fastener
                  4x6" poster board (for card holder)
                  buttons for place markers

Directions: Produce the game board as illustrated and
                  cover it with contact paper. Make the board
                  for the spinner and card holder by illustrating
                  the wheel and title (do not attach the spinner).
                  Cover the board with contact paper. Attach the
                  spinner using the brass fastener. Rule off the
                  4x6" poster board as illustrated, cut away the
                  X-ed squares and fold along the = lines. Place
                  the card holder on the spinner board as illus-
                  trated and staple the "back" sections to the
                  spinner board. On each playing card, print one
                  word which exemplifies each sound (c=k c=s g=g
                  g=j). In the center of each card print a 1, 2,
                  or 3 to indicate the number of moves to be made
                  for a correct response.

4x6" Card Holder

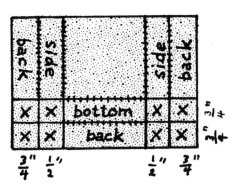

                  Children play by spinning the spinner to a sound,
                  drawing a card from the card holder, finding and
                  reading the word which exemplifies the sound spun.
                  If he is correct (self-correcting answers may be
                  printed on the reverse side of each card), he
                  moves the number of spaces indicated on his card.

Self Correction: Print the answer for each sound on the back
                  of each card. (See arrow on Page 86.)

87

Skills: Short and Long Vowel Sound Change, etc.

Materials: 16x22" poster board
             60 2x10" oaktag cards
             4½x6" poster board piece for the die
             4 - 1½x7" strips of contact paper (for wrapping die)

Directions: Design the playing board as illustrated and glue
             one blank playing card in each numbered position as
             shown. Cover the board with contact paper. Produce
             a die by ruling off the 4½x6" piece of poster board
             as illustrated. Write the numbers as indicated and
             cut away the blackened 1½" squares. Cover both sides
             with contact paper, fold along the lines between
             numbers to form a cube, and wrap the cube with the
             four strips of contact paper beginning each strip in
             a different direction.

             Print words on the playing cards--this game can be
             adapted to any skill. Place stacks of cards face-
             down on the playing board next to each numbered
             space. In turn, players toss the die and pick up
             a card from the correspondingly-numbered space on
             the board. If they correctly read the words,
             syllabicate, identify the prefix or suffix, etc. they
             score the number of points tossed.

88

Skill: Vowel Diphthongs   ou-ow

Materials: 12x18" oaktag board
              50 2½x3" word cards
              buttons for place markers

Directions: Illustrate the board as shown and cover
              it with contact paper. This game empha-
              sizes the "ow-ou" vowel diphthongs in
              sounding words, so select words containing
              the ou-ow sounds for the cards. Each
              player begins by placing his button on the
              clown's hammer. In turn, they select cards,
              read the words, and move up 10-points toward
              the bell for each correct response. If a
              child cannot read the word, he does not move.
              The first child to reach 100 wins.

b_sk_t   tr_ck_d   h_lp_r   m_g_c   c_rn_r

Skill: Decoding emphasizing consonant clues.

Materials: 16x22" poster board base
50-100 2x5" cards
colored buttons for markers (to match corner colors)

Directions: Illustrate the board as shown—coloring each corner differently, and cover with contact paper. Print word cards eliminating vowel letters (make sure the word can be "read" by sounding the consonant letters). Each player begins in his own color-matched corner and moves around the board clockwise. If he sounds out the consonants correctly and can give a real word which fits the consonant pattern, he can move a space. Reaching a starred space gives the player an extra turn. The first player to reach his home corner wins. Double moves can be indicated by starring more difficult words.

Self-correction: Print the entire word on the reverse side of each word card.

90

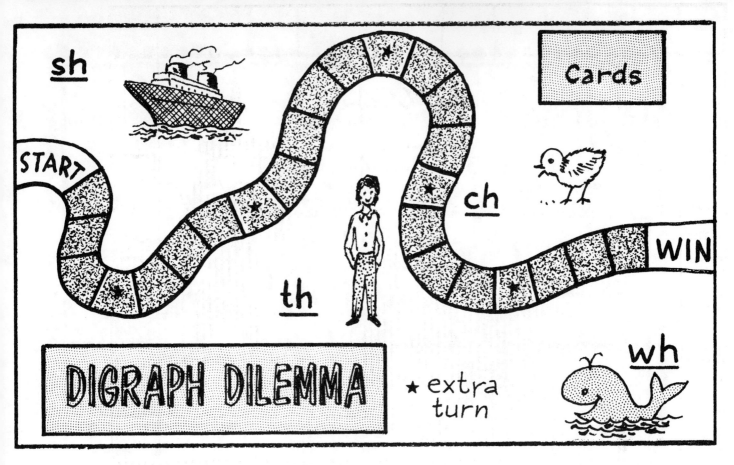

DIGRAPH DILEMMA

★ extra turn

Materials: 15x28" poster board
50 3x5" cards
1 2" diameter poster board circle

Directions: Illustrate the game board as shown. On the 2" diameter circle, write a 1 on the front and a 2 on the back. Cover the front and back of the circle with contact paper. Produce the cards by selecting the type desired (see above I or II). These cards are self-correcting and can be used in four different ways:

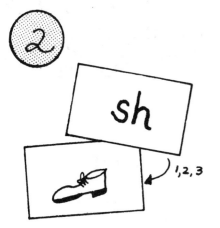

1) Look at the "sh" and pronounce its sound.

2) Look at the picture of the shoe and tell its beginning letters.

3) Look at the picture of the shoe and pronounce its beginning sound and spell its beginning sound.

4) Read the word "shoe" and self-correct by checking the picture answer on the back of each card.

Place the cards with the side to be used facing up on the board. In turn each player tosses the circle, selects his card, gives the desired response and moves the number of spaces tossed if he is correct.

91

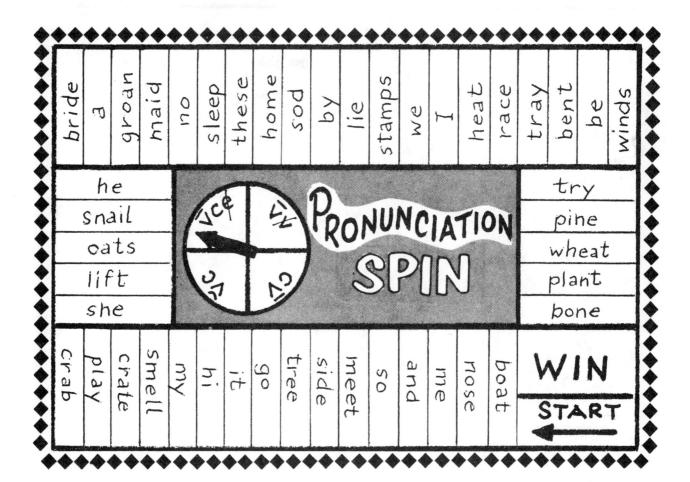

Skill: Vowel Pronunciation Rules: v̆c, v̄∜, v̄c∉, cv̄

Materials: 22x28" poster board
1 - 1/4" spinner (made from poster board)
water-base magic markers
buttons for markers (or attach clothespins
colored differently for each player, to the
spaces)

Directions: Produce the game board as illustrated, but
do not attach the spinner until the board
has been covered with contact paper. Attach
the spinner using a brass fastener. Play
begins by having all players place a button
marker on "start". In turn, play-spin the
spinner and move to the nearest word which
illustrates that pronunciation rule. If
they can find and pronounce the word correctly,
they leave their button marker on that space
until their next turn. If they do not answer
correctly, they must return to their previous
position on the board.

Self-Correction: Provide a list of words which follow each
rule—a child other than the one playing checks
the response.

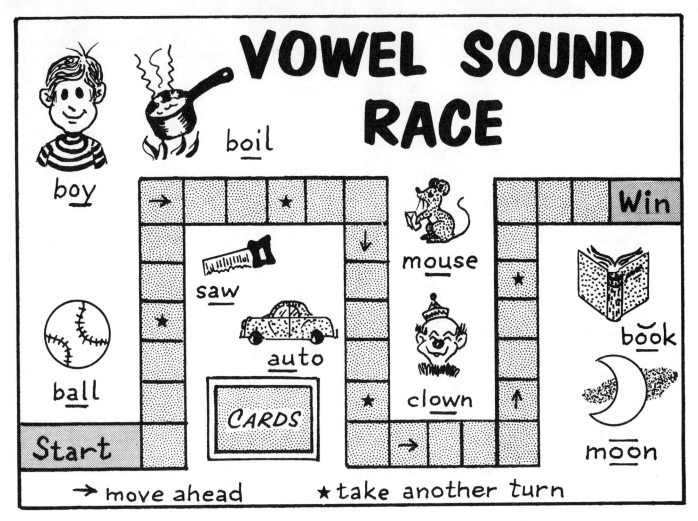

VOWEL SOUND RACE

boy

boil

mouse

Win

saw

book

auto

CARDS

clown

moon

ball

Start

→ move ahead   ★ take another turn

Skill:	Variant Vowels & Vowel Diphthongs
Materials:	22x28" poster board 100 3x5" playing cards water-base magic markers permanent black magic marker permanent red magic marker buttons or candy for place markers (they can eat candy treats as soon as they reach "WIN" - yummy!)

Directions: Illustrate the game board as shown above. Cover the board with clear contact paper. Print the cards by selecting 11 words for each sound-spelling indicated. The sounds being emphasized are printed in red, all other letters in the words are printed in black. In turn each child draws a card, pronounces the "red sound" in isolation (note: the illustrations are provided for the children's reference), and then pronounces the word. If he is correct, he moves either 1 or 2 spaces as indicated on each word card. Special moves are indicated on the game board.

Self-Correction: If desired, glue a picture or cartoon on the back of each word to identify it.

CARD COUPLES

Materials: oaktag or index paper
                   scissors
                   magic markers (water-base)
                   clear contact paper

Directions: Cut a set of 20-30 (2x4½") playing cards for each
game. Draw a heavy line down the center of each
playing card as illustrated. Next, hold two playing
cards so that the right side of "A" overlaps the
left side of "B" approximately ½" and cut a curved
or jagged line (see dots).

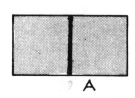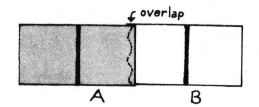

Place the cards on the table so that the cut lines
will fit together or "couple-up" as in a puzzle.
Write the desired skill information on the cards as
shown in the examples. Then pick up card "B" and a
new card "C" and overlap "B" and "C" as shown to cut
a new couple-up. (Use a different cut on each card).
Write on the next item and continue to complete the
set of cards. Be sure not to repeat or duplicate
any items--use different items for each card couple-up.

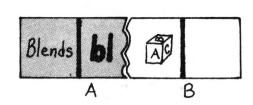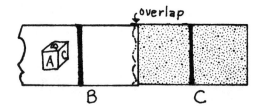

Play: Deal out the playing cards and place the "title" card
out to start play. Players place answer cards as soon
as they find corresponding answers. The first player
to use up all of his cards is the winner

Self-Correction: This is inherent since only the correct answer
card will "couple-up" or match by fitting.

94

CARD COUPLES

1. CONTRACTIONS

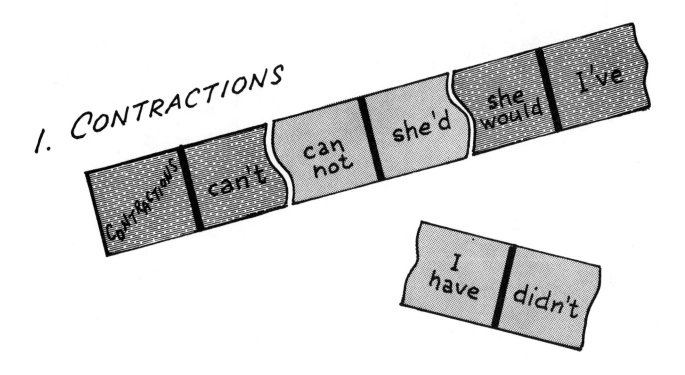

Contractions | can't | can not | she'd | she would | I've

I have | didn't

2. SYLLABICATION

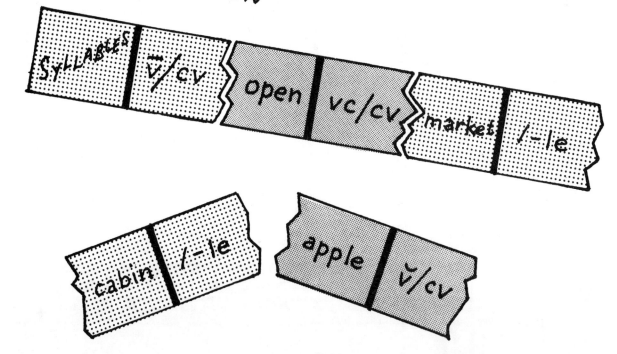

SYLLABLES | v/cv | open | vc/cv | market | /-le

cabin | /-le

apple | v/cv

3. Consonant Blends or Digraphs

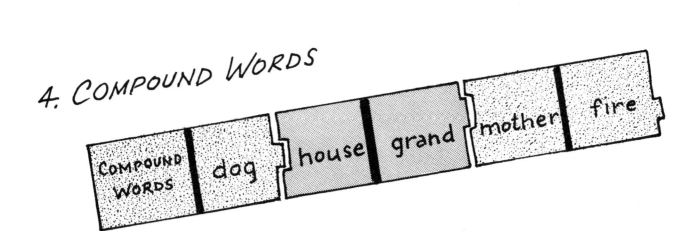

Blends & Digraphs | st | ☆ | wh | 🐋 | bl

4. Compound Words

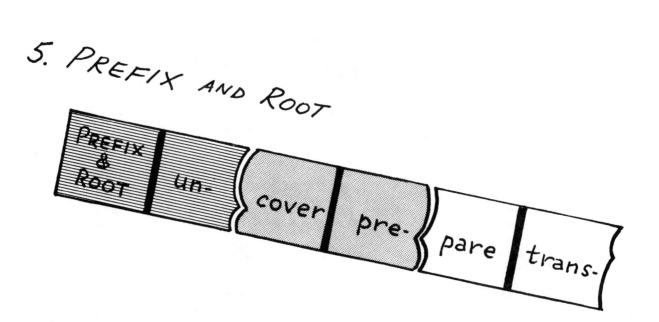

Compound Words | dog | house | grand | mother | fire

5. Prefix and Root

Prefix & Root | un- | cover | pre- | pare | trans-

6. SILENT LETTERS

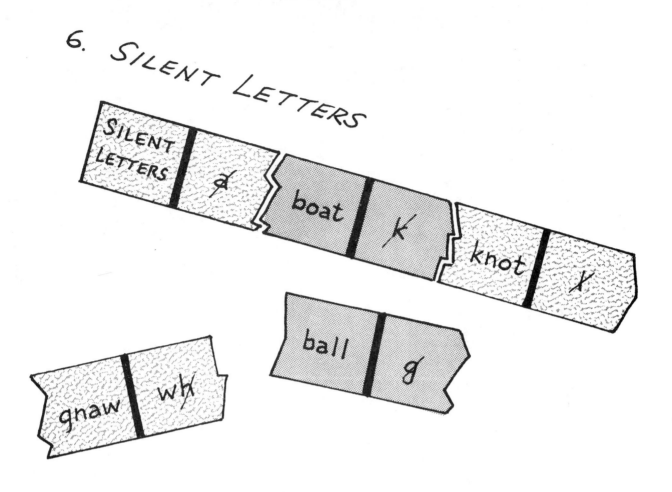

SILENT LETTERS | ~~d~~
boat | ~~k~~
knot | ~~t~~
gnaw | ~~w~~
ball | ~~g~~

7. HOMONYMS

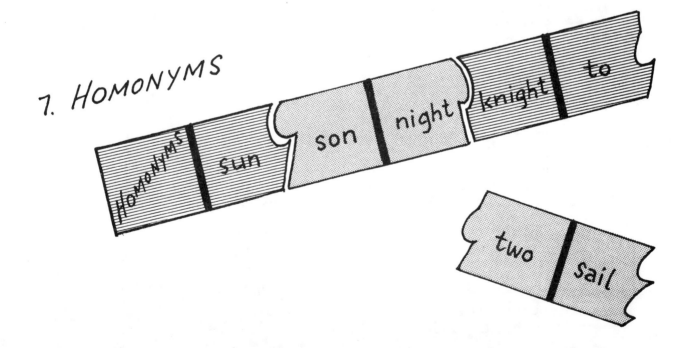

HOMONYMS | sun
son | night
knight | to
two | sail

TRIPLETTES

Materials: oaktag or index paper
        scissors
        magic markers (water-base)
        clear contact paper

Directions: Cut a set of 22 (2x4½") cards and 20 (2x2-3/4")
cards of a different color. Draw a heavy line
down the center of each 2x4½" card as illustrated.
Next hold one large card ("A") so the right side
overlaps the left side of one small card ("B")
approximately ½" and cut a curved or jagged line.
(See dots No. ①)

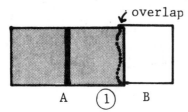 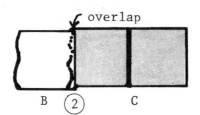

Then overlap the left side of another large card
under the right side of card B ½" and cut a new
jagged line. (See dots No. ②)

Place cards A-B-C together so they interlock and
print the desired skill information e.g.

 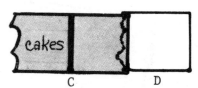

Next, overlap card C over another small card and
clip a jagged line. Continue this sequence of
alternating long and short cards and printing
the appropriate skill information.

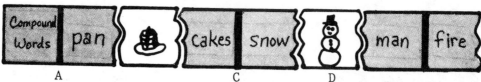

Play: Place the title card on the floor face-up. Deal
all the remaining large & small cards to the players.
Players place their cards in line as soon as they
see matches. The first player to use up all of
his cards is the winner.

Self-Correction: This is inherent since only the correct answer
cards will match by fit.

TRIPLETTES

1. COMPOUND WORDS

2. BEGINNING and ENDING SOUNDS

3. CONTRACTIONS

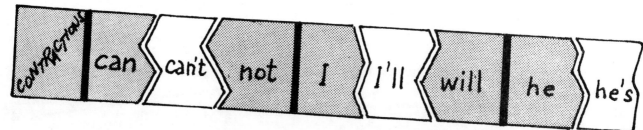

4. HOMONYMS IN THREES

Homonyms (3) | to | two | too | cent | scent | sent | pair | pare

5. SYLLABICATION

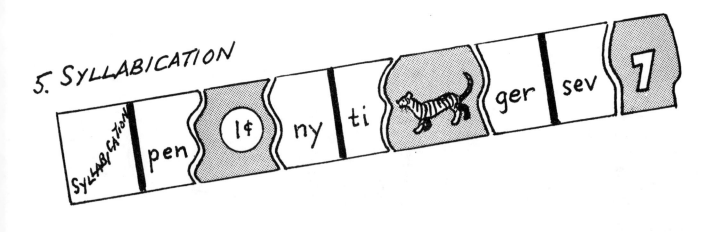

Syllabication | pen | 1¢ | ny | ti | ger | sev | 7

6. SYNONYMS & ANTONYMS

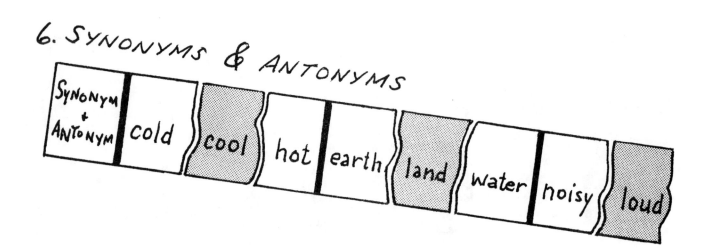

Synonym + Antonym | cold | cool | hot | earth | land | water | noisy | loud

7. RHYMING 3 PICTURES

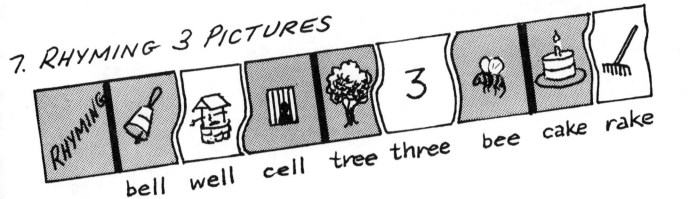

bell   well   cell   tree   three   bee   cake   rake

8. BEGINNING & ENDING CONSONANT BLENDS

9. PREFIX + ROOT + SUFFIX

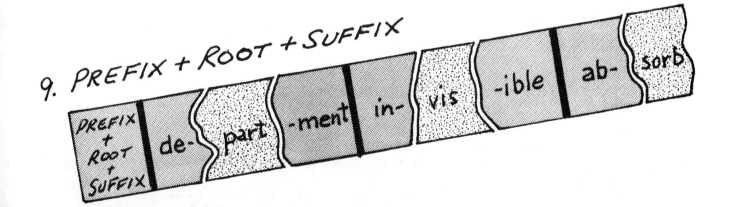

Materials: 4-ply poster board
water-base magic markers
clear adhesive contact paper
small pictures (where needed)
rug yarn (assorted colors - color-coded to the
        category or response which needs to be
        made. All identical responses as in all
        "short e" responses would use yellow, all
        "short i" responses would use blue, etc.)
yarn needle

Directions: Cut two pieces of poster board. Use a light shade
approximately 12x12" square, a 10x12" rectangle,
a 12" diameter circle, a 12" equilateral triangle
or a 9x18" oval for the top playing board. Cut
another piece ½" larger on all sides using a darker
shade for the back. Using Elmer's Glue, glue the
two pieces of poster board together. Next, using
water-base magic markers, print any titles, letters,
etc. I usually color-coordinate printed letters to
the yarn colors being used (eg. Long a and its
corresponding yarn is dark blue, Short a and its
corresponding yarn is light blue; Long e is dark
green, Short e is light green, etc.). Glue on any
pictures needed. Draw black lines ½" long next to
pictures or words on the dark back paper where the
slit for holding the yarn answers will be made.
Cover the board with clear contact paper overlapping
1½" to the back side. Now thread the yarn needle,
knotting the end several times. Insert the needle
at the back of the board and pull the needle and
yarn through to the front. Trim the yarn to a 14"
length and knot the tip to prevent fraying. Clip
½" slits into the board in the center of the black
lines where answers are to be made. Now work through
the excercise placing the correct yarns in the correct
slits to form a "yoke" and turn the board to the back
side. You can make the yarn yoke games self-correcting by cutting 1" pieces of yarn and gluing corresponding colors next to the answers as shown below.
In this way, when colors match, the child knows his
answers are correct. Finally, pull out the yarn
answer strings and cut a piece of contact paper 1"
smaller on all sides than the board. Use this piece
to cover the back of the board.

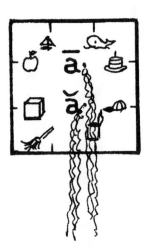

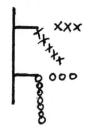

back of board
(self-correction)

xxx dark blue yarn
ooo light blue yarn

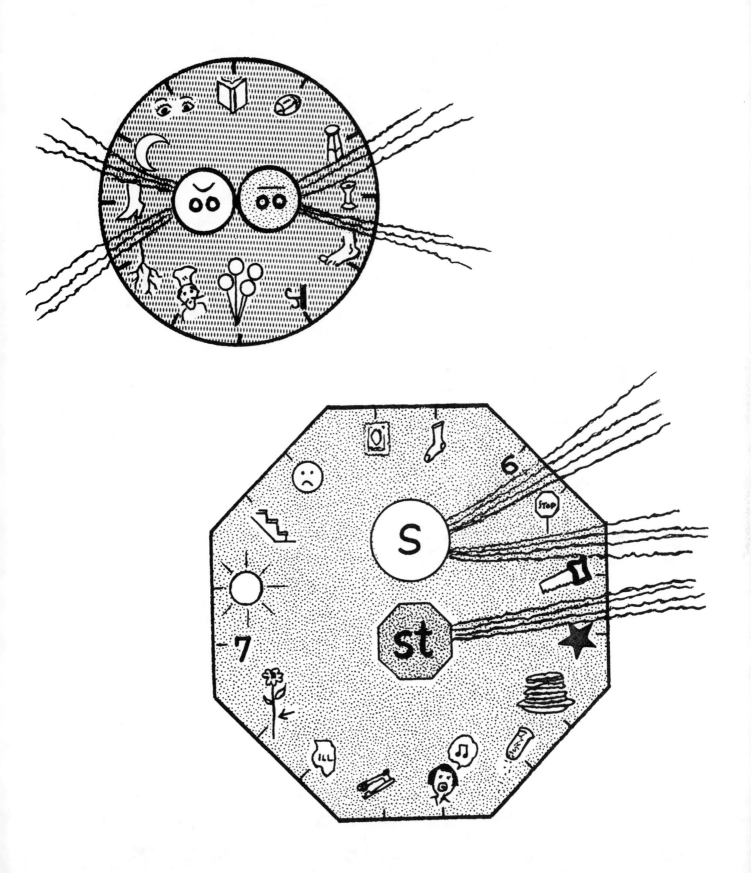

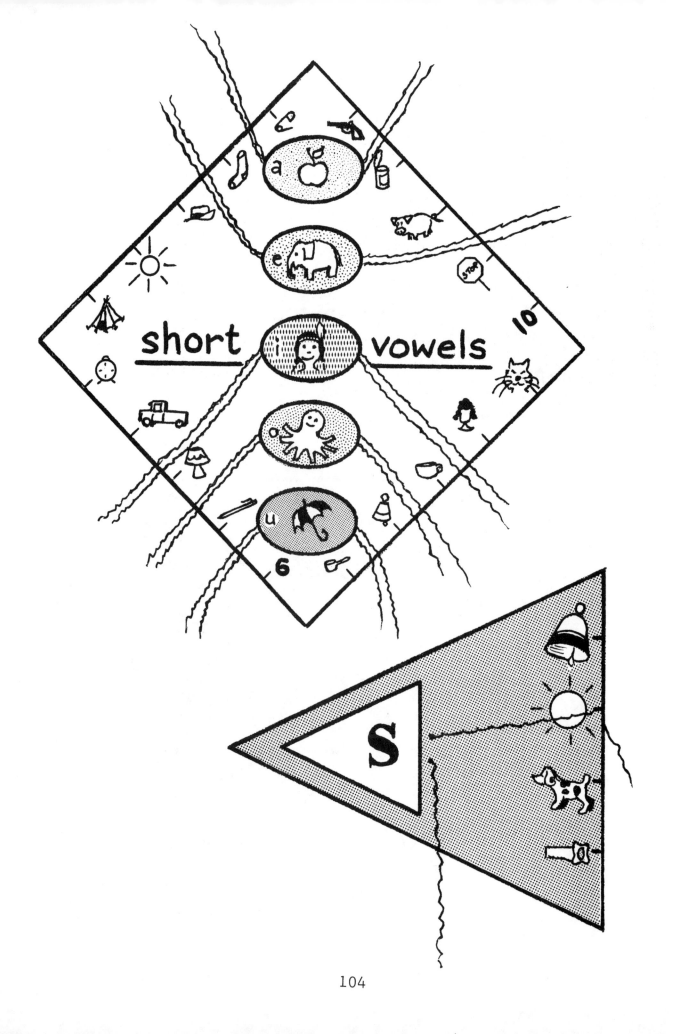

short vowels

104

COMPOUND WORDS

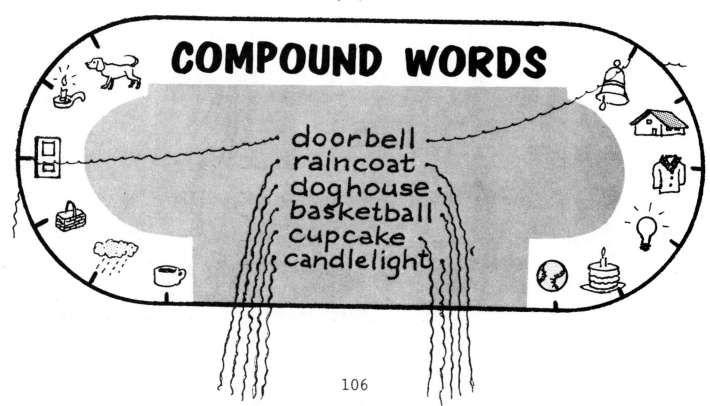

doorbell
raincoat
doghouse
basketball
cupcake
candlelight

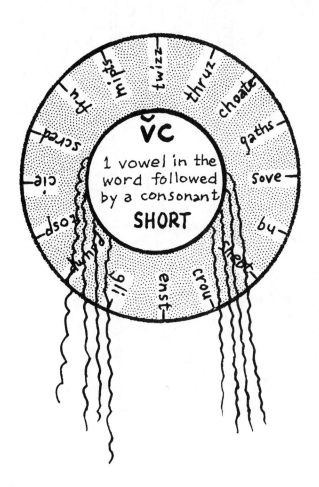

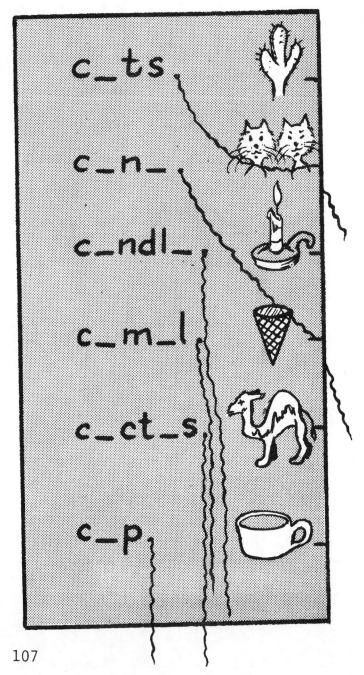

c_ts

c_n_

c_ndl_

c_m_l

c_ct_s

c_p

107

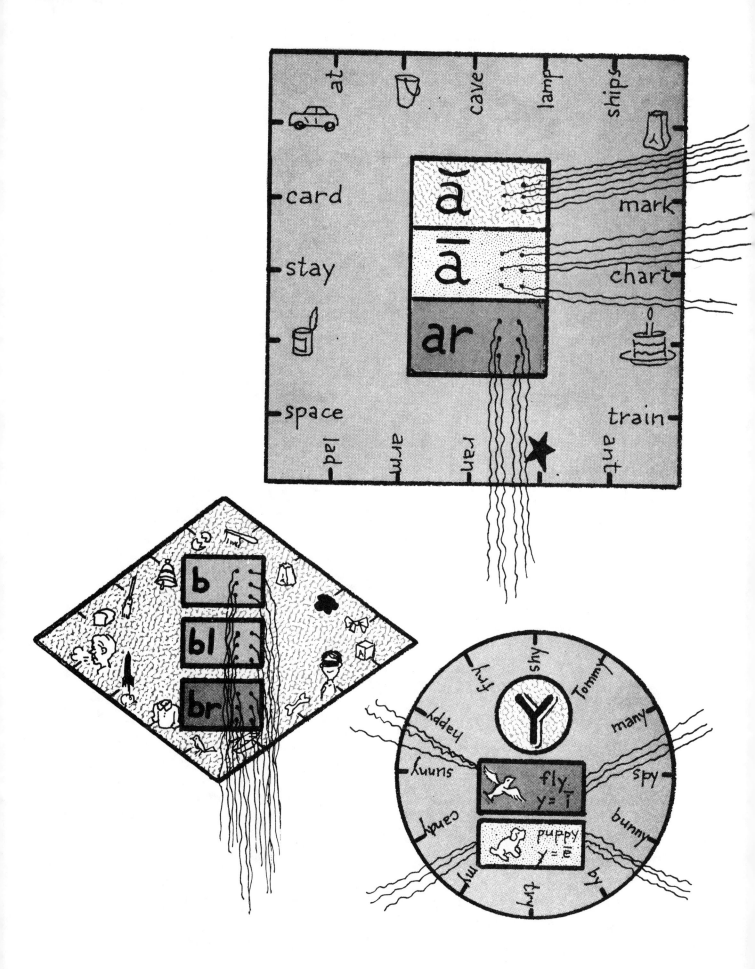

CARDS À LA CARTE

Materials: 4x6" or 3x5" plain index cards (assorted colors)
black permanent magic marker
red permanent magic marker

Directions: Words are printed on 3x5" index cards. Specific
skills such as Consonant Blends, Short Vowels, and
Affixes lend themselves to pairing and following
suit. Specific instructions for each game are given.

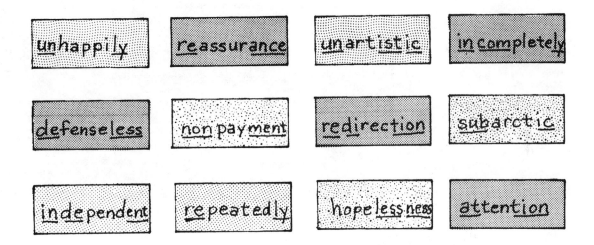

Affix Affinity - 100 - 2x6" colored index cards (divide 4x6" cards
in half)
black permanent magic marker (for printing words)
red permanent magic marker (for underlining affixes)

Directions: Select 100 words which contain prefixes and suffixes.
Print a word on each card using a black magic marker.
Underline the prefixes and suffixes using a red
magic marker. Place the cards in 12 stacks as illustrated. Two or three players compete, all playing
at once. The object is to find words which have a
prefix or suffix in common. When a pair is spotted,
the player pronounces the words and identifies the
common prefix or suffix; and if his fellow players
do not find a mistake, he keeps the two cards. At
the end of the game, the player who has the tallest
stack of cards wins.

A sample play would be to match "re-" in

"re as sur ance" and "re di rec tion"

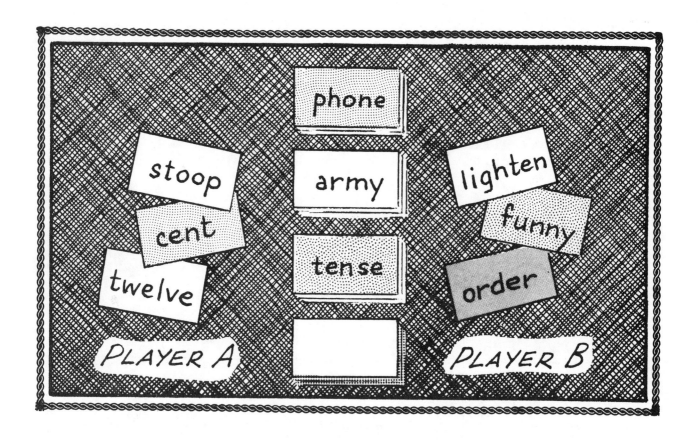

Skill: Matching & pronouncing consonant & vowel sounds

Soundbound - 140 - 3x5" index cards (assorted colors)

Directions: Print the words in the following list on the
3x5" colored cards (assorted colors make this
game very attractive). To play, give each
player three cards and place the remaining cards
in four stacks in the center of the table, three
face-up for matching, one face-down to replace
cards used from the players' hands. The object
of the game is to match any consonant or vowel
sound on one of the player's cards with a consonant or vowel sound on the card stacks. For
example, the A player could match the "t" sounds
in twelve and tense or the B player could match
the "ē" sounds in army and funny. Pairs are
placed face-down in front of each player. The
player replaces his used card with another from
the face-down stack so that he always has 3 cards
to play with. At the end of the game, the player
with the greatest number of cards wins. Players
must pronounce the sounds and the two words involved.

110

WORD LIST FOR SOUNDBOUND

graph	wrinkle	bloom
cartoon	sauce	shook
lunch	also	wood
giant	style	squint
royal	arm	yawn
yule	broil	scarf
scramble	scooter	knob
crumb	purse	flow
triangle	flush	queens
wax	whisper	frozen
jewel	circus	galaxy
glory	auto	dream
ginger	enjoy	glee
milk	hanger	joint
snuggle	goose	fly
swift	gown	clover
small	fault	phantom
prince	squirm	park
ounce	place	knock
yellow	spruce	plenty
phone	blouse	stamp
try	haze	halt
shrivel	clash	army
sign	worn	skinny
girls	quake	subject
throw	cause	wreath
spoil	tight	stitch
quail	slipper	child
rock	bomb	twilight
smooth	saddle	skull
wives	elbow	cowboy
nerve	prize	splendid
ford	fight	zipper
splurge	camel	screw
plaster	snooze	church
turkey	shrimp	foods
cloud	center	gnaw
brew	curve	tawny
straw	whirl	crook
sleeve	cube	voice
twelve	strung	power
quick	frown	spoke
thing	order	throat
oyster	gravy	drown
sprinkle	witch	hurtle
		few

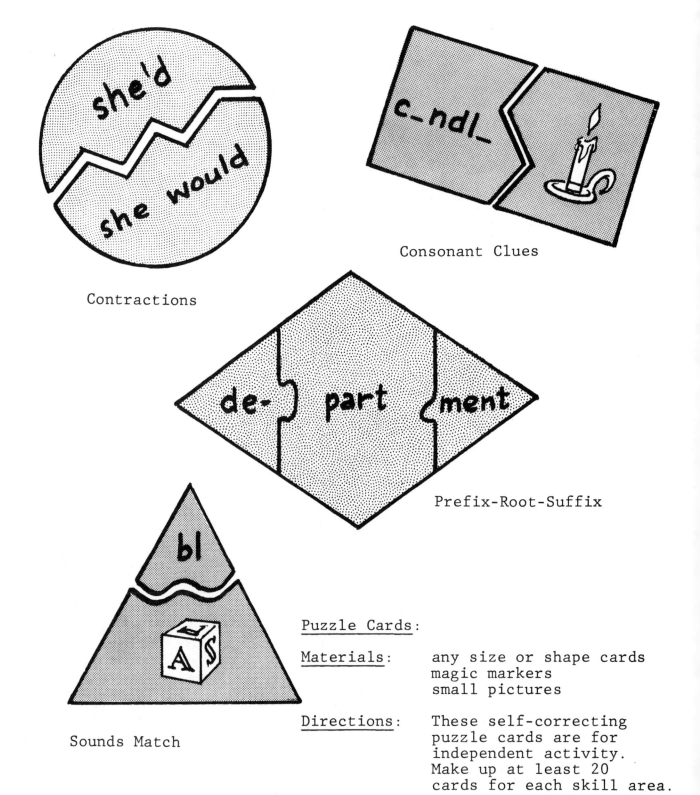

Contractions

Consonant Clues

Prefix-Root-Suffix

Sounds Match

Puzzle Cards:

Materials: any size or shape cards
              magic markers
              small pictures

Directions: These self-correcting
              puzzle cards are for
              independent activity.
              Make up at least 20
              cards for each skill area.

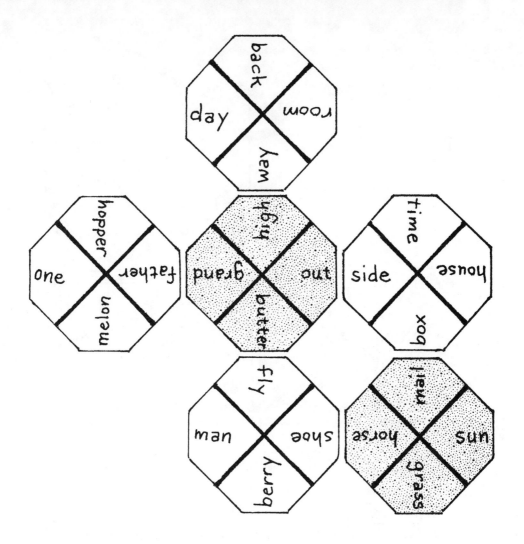

Skill: Compound Words

Octagon Quadrival - 40 oaktag cards approximately 4" in
                    diameter, shaped like octagons.

                    20 cards will have the first words in
                    compound word pairs. 20 cards will have
                    the second words in compound pairs.

Play: All cards except one will be dealt to the players. The
       withheld card is placed in the center of the table and
       in turn players attempt to form compound words by attach-
       ing one of their cards to one on the table. The first
       player to use up all his cards in making compound words
       wins.

Self-Correction: Provide the Compound Word List in the reference
                  section so children can check their words.

113

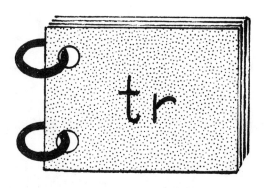

Skill: Sounding

Self-Teaching Sounds Flip

Materials: 10-30 3x4" poster board cards
             2 - 1¼"-1½" notebook rings
             paper punch
             permanent black magic marker
             pictures illustrating each sound

Directions: This self-teaching device can be adapted to any
            skill desired. For example, the cards could provide
            practice in Prefix, Root, or Suffix meanings.
            Another idea would be to print words on the front
            side and show the syllabication of that word on the
            opposite side.

            The device pictured is intended to help the child
            practice the consonant blend sounds.

Self-Correction: He says the sound out loud and then flips to
             see if the sound he made agrees with the beginning
             sound of the picture.

Pairing Card Games:

Materials: 3x5" colored index cards
              any size oaktag cards

Directions: Produce 40-60 cards per deck
              Color-code specific skill parts
              of words (e.g. the spr in the 3-Letter
              Blend game is colored red). Devise
              any type of card-playing rules desired:
              Old Maid, Rummy, etc.

Verb Forms

(40 cards - 10
different root words)

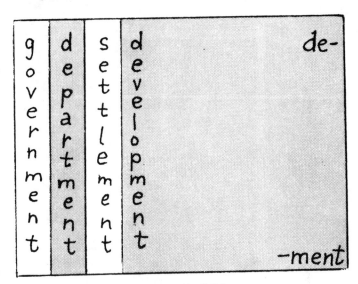

Prefixes & Suffixes

(60 cards - 4 for each prefix
& 4 for each suffix)

Antonyms

(60 cards, 30 pairs)

Rhyming Pictures

(40 cards to make 20 pairs
of rhyming pictures)

115

Silent Consonants

(60 cards - 3 pairs for each different silent letter combination)

Consonant Blends

(60 cards - 3 for each consonant blend)

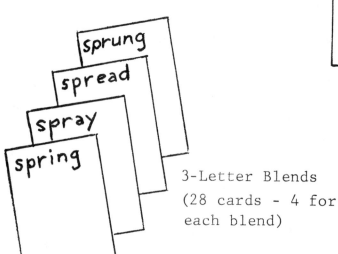

3-Letter Blends

(28 cards - 4 for each blend)

Short Vowel Change

Letter Sound +
Picture + Word Sets

(45 cards - 15 sets)

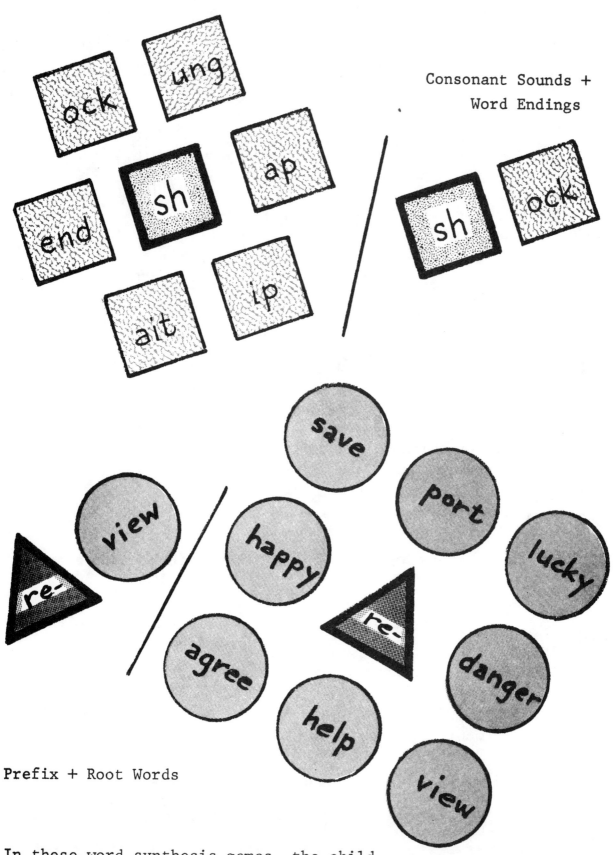

Prefix + Root Words

In these word synthesis games, the child
draws cards from stacks placed face-up
on the table to build words.

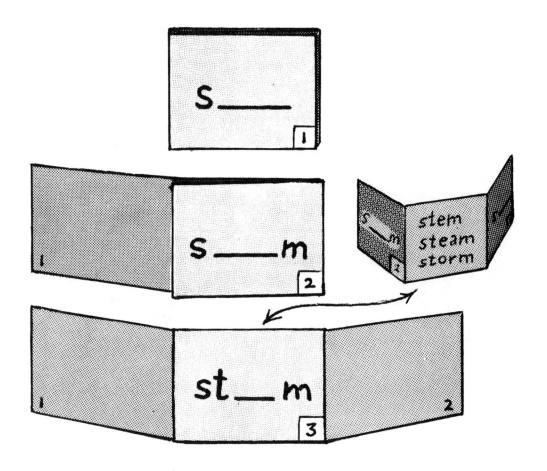

Skill: Word decoding using consonant clues

Word Guess

Materials: 25-50 3x9" oaktag cards
black magic marker

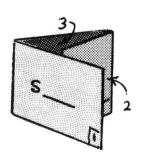

Directions: Fold each 3x9" oaktag card into three 3x3" areas.
Fold the right-hand area over the center and then
the left-hand area over the center. (1) On the
top of the card print the beginning letter of the
word you have in mind. (2) Open the card to the
second level and print the beginning and ending
sounds. (3) Finally, on the third level print all
the consonant letters in the word. Always show
the place-holding positions for vowel letters with
a line. A group of children play the game by look-
ing at the first level and each guesses a word which
would fit the beginning sound. The card is opened
to the second level and the children are permitted
to retain or change their guess. Finally, the third
level is exposed and any child who had previously
guessed the word wins the card. If not one had a
correct guess, all children compete to see who can
think of a word first.

Self-Correction: Turn the opened card over and print all the
words which could be correct answers. (See arrow.)

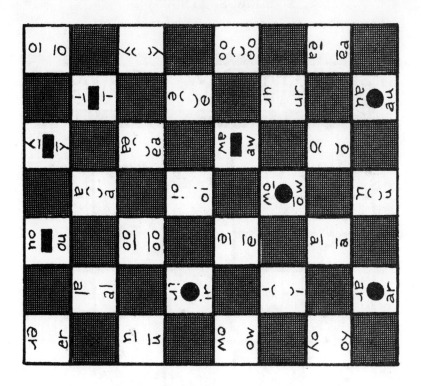

Sounding Checkers

Skill: Vowel Sound Review

Materials: 12x16 piece of light colored poster board
            28 - 2x2" black construction paper squares
            red magic marker
            green magic marker
            14 checkers: can use real checkers, poker
                          chips, or poster-board checkers
                          (Use 2 different colors of each)

Directions: Glue the 28 black squares to the poster
            board in checker-board fashion. The sounds
            printed at the bottom of each square are in
            red ink. The sounds at the top of each
            square (the ones facing the other player)
            are printed in green ink. This color-coding
            helps each player to read his side of the
            board more clearly. Each player in turn
            places his seven checkers on the board (on
            the bottom seven squares showing vowel sounds)
            by pronouncing the sounds being covered.
            When both players have all their checkers on
            the board, play continues by moving (as in
            the real game of checkers) and pronouncing the
            sounds being moved to. If a player makes a
            mistake, his opponent tells him the correct
            sound and the player must move his checker
            back (thus losing his play). Players are
            allowed to jump and capture the other player's
            checkers, but they must pronounce the sound
            jumped.

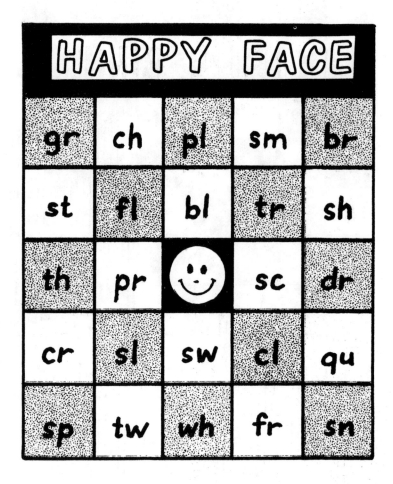

Skills: Variety (see adjoining pages)

Materials: Happy Face   10 - 7½ x 10" cards
             Rhyme-Around   10 - 6 x 8" cards

Directions: Produce ten playing cards for either
             game, making sure to vary the order
             and kinds of sounds and/or pictures
             used on each card. For example, in
             the Rhyme-Around game as many as 18-24
             different pictures can be used in
             various arrangements and combinations
             on the ten playing cards. Each child
             receives a card and several markers
             (paper, corn, etc.). The teacher calls
             the blend sounds or the rhyming word and
             the child puts a marker on his card if
             he has a correct response. The first
             child to fill either any row or his entire
             card wins--compare his responses to a
             record kept by the teacher of items called.

Additional sample playing cards for:

SOUNDS BINGO

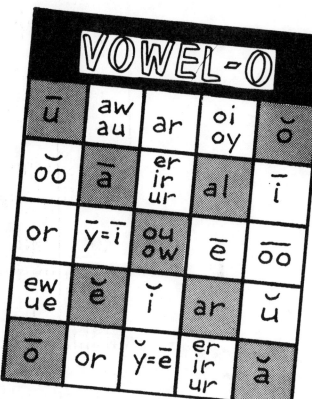

VOWEL-O

$\overline{u}$	aw au	ar	oi oy	$\breve{o}$
$\breve{oo}$	$\overline{a}$	er ir ur	al	$\overline{\imath}$
or	$\overline{y}=\overline{\imath}$	ou ow	$\overline{e}$	$\overline{oo}$
ew ue	$\breve{e}$	$\breve{\imath}$	ar	$\breve{u}$
$\overline{o}$	or	$\breve{y}=\overline{e}$	er ir ur	$\breve{a}$

Teacher pronounces words containing the sounds out loud.

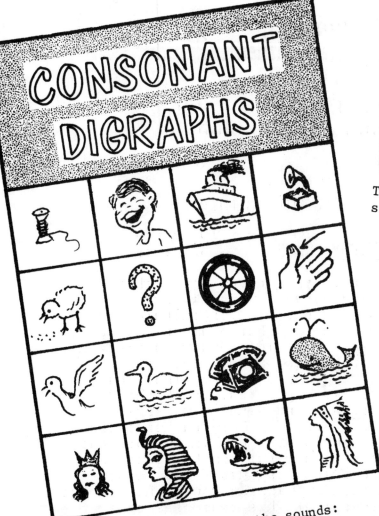

Teacher pronounces the sounds:
(sh-ch-th-wh-ph-qu-ng-gh-ck)
and the child marks the picture
containing the sound.

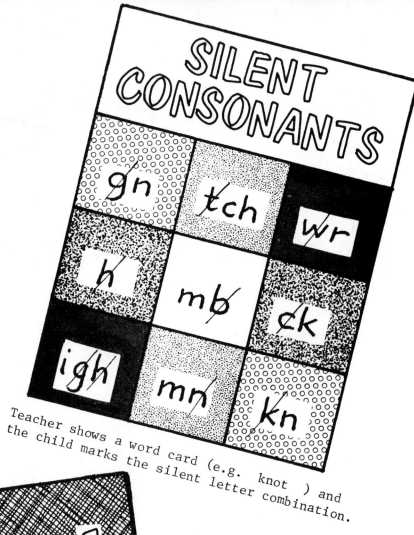

Teacher shows a word card (e.g. knot) and the child marks the silent letter combination.

Teacher shows a picture card or pronounces a word. The child marks the rhyming picture.

Matching numbers on the reverse sides
mean "<u>oy</u>-<u>boy</u>" are a pair.

Circles 'n' Squares

Materials: 20 - 2" diameter circles (1 color)
20 - 2" squares (another color)
water-base magic markers
clear contact paper

Directions: Print different variant vowel sounds on the front and
back of each circle. Glue different pictures of ob-
jects whose names contain the variant vowel sounds on
the front and back of each square. Code corresponding answers (e.g. "oy-boy") with the same number on
the reverse sides (see arrows). Cover both sides with
clear contact paper.

Play: Toss all the cards on the floor or on a table. Children play by picking up pairs (e.g. <u>oy</u> and <u>boy</u>)
and turning the cards over.

Self-Correction: If the numbers on the back sides of the cards
match (see arrows) the child has a correct pair and
may keep the cards.

Additional Sample Playing Cards for "Circles & Squares"

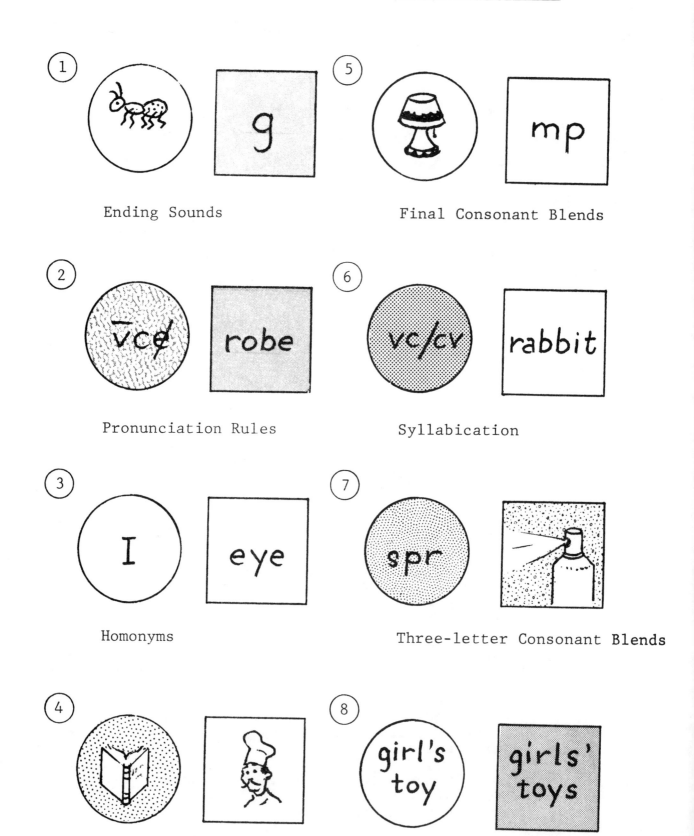

1. Ending Sounds

2. Pronunciation Rules

3. Homonyms

4. Rhyming

5. Final Consonant Blends

6. Syllabication

7. Three-letter Consonant Blends

8. Plural Possessives

$$\boxed{\text{PUZZLERS}}$$

Materials: Magazine pictures (at least 8x10")
              Rubber cement
              Magic Marker
              Ball Point pen
              Oaktag paper and 4-ply colored poster board
              Carbon paper (2 sheets)
              Contact paper (clear)

PLEASE READ THROUGH ALL DIRECTIONS BEFORE YOU BEGIN.

Directions: 1) Cut two pieces of oaktag two inches larger than
                the size of the magazine picture to be used on
                all four sides.

             2) Place the two sheets of carbon paper back-to-back
                so that the carbon sides are facing outward. Then
                place one oaktag sheet on top and one under the
                carbon sheets. Paper clip or staple the four
                corners to hold in place. Pressing very hard, use
                a ball point pen to outline the picture edges on
                the oaktag. Remove the picture and use the pen to
                design puzzle pieces.

             3) Remove the paper clips or staples and carbon paper.
                Using a black magic marker (water-base), trace over
                the carboned puzzle lines on both oaktag pieces.

ball point ink
on reverse side →

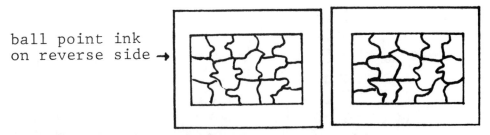

             4) Using rubber cement, apply one coat to the back of
                the picture and also the ball point side of the top
                oaktag sheet. Be sure to cover every speck of
                surface. Allow the rubber cement to dry a few

seconds. Carefully place the picture on the oaktag corresponding to the outside edge of the puzzle design. (Warning: once the picture touches the oaktag it is almost impossible to remove--I suggest asking someone to help you hold the four corners until correct placement is made).

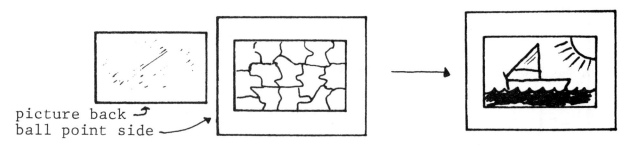

picture back
ball point side

5) Now place both pieces of oaktag as illustrated below and proceed to build your puzzle. Be careful to note that the right side of the pictured oaktag corresponds to the left side of the non-pictured oaktag (puzzles operate in reverse). Use water-base magic markers for printing or illustrating.

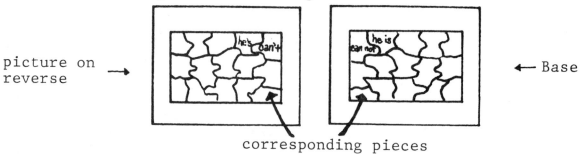

picture on
reverse

← Base

corresponding pieces

6) When the puzzle has been completed, trim around the outlined edge of each oaktag puzzle. Mount the base (non-pictured) oaktag on a larger piece of colored 4-ply poster board, print the puzzle title, and cover with clear contact paper. Then cover both sides of the pictured oaktag with contact paper and cut apart the pieces. Now the puzzle is completed. The child corresponds contractions and word combinations and places answers picture-side face-up.

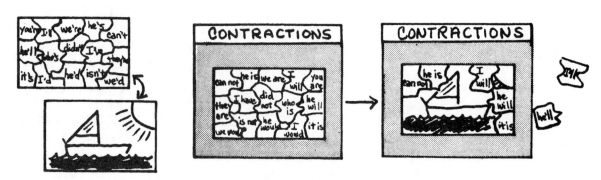

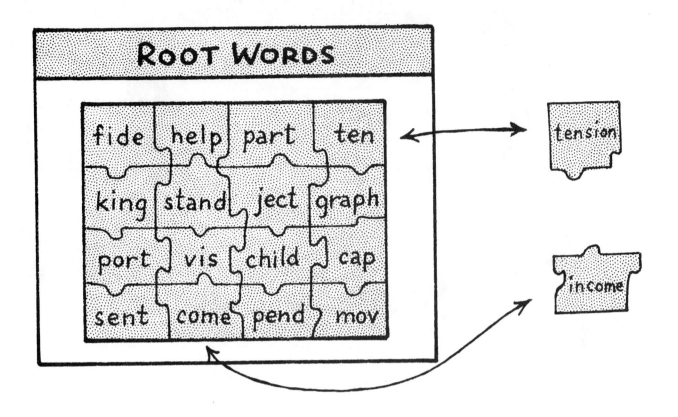

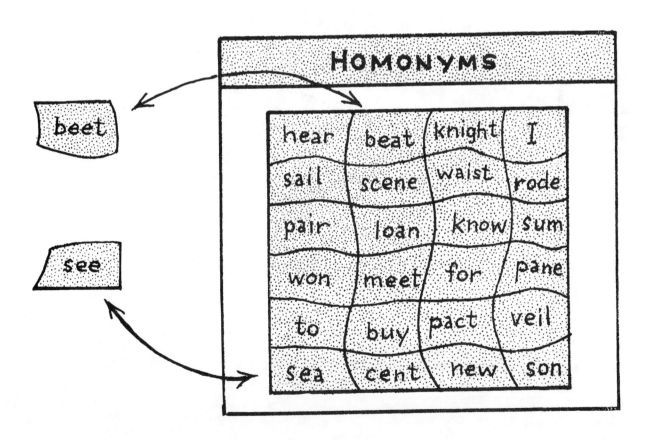

128

Consonant Blends

bl

Silent Letters

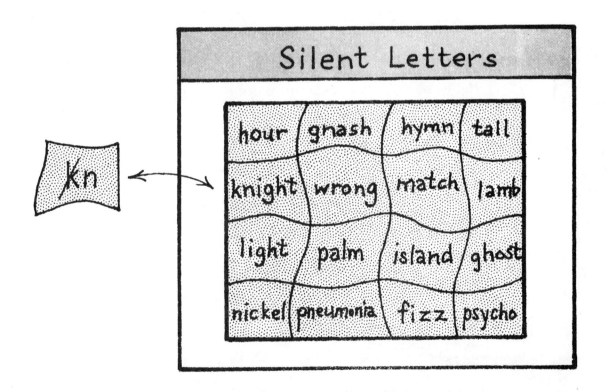

kn

hour	gnash	hymn	tall
knight	wrong	match	lamb
light	palm	island	ghost
nickel	pneumonia	fizz	psycho

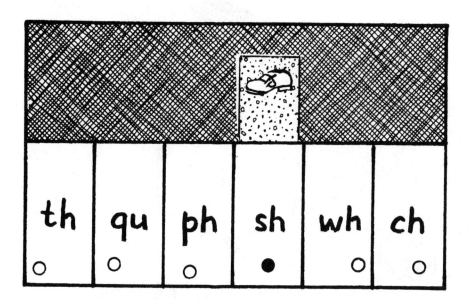 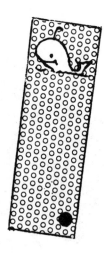

Consonant Digraphs

Materials: 12x18" oaktag or index paper
              additional oaktag for playing answer cards
              hole punch
              staples, glue or brass fasteners to secure pockets
              magic markers

Directions: Fold the oaktag or index paper to create a pocket
              folder measuring approximately 7½x18" in size.
              Mark pocket divisions using a magic marker. Print
              the desired "quiz items" on the front of each pocket
              section. Cover the front and back sides of the
              folder with clear contact paper if desired; use a
              razor blade to open the card-insertion areas. Use
              brass fasteners or staples to secure and separate
              the pockets. Next, punch holes in the areas along
              the bottom of each pocket section making sure that
              the holes are placed in a different location for
              each section (this is essential to self-correction).

              Cut a set of answer cards which are ¼" smaller in
              width than the pockets. The length should be 3 to 4"
              longer than the depth of the pocket. Insert an answer
              card into each pocket and print the desired answers
              on each card. Use a red magic marker to color in the
              area indicated on each playing card by the punched
              hole.

Self-Correction: If red dots show up in each punched area, the
                  child knows his answers are correct.

130

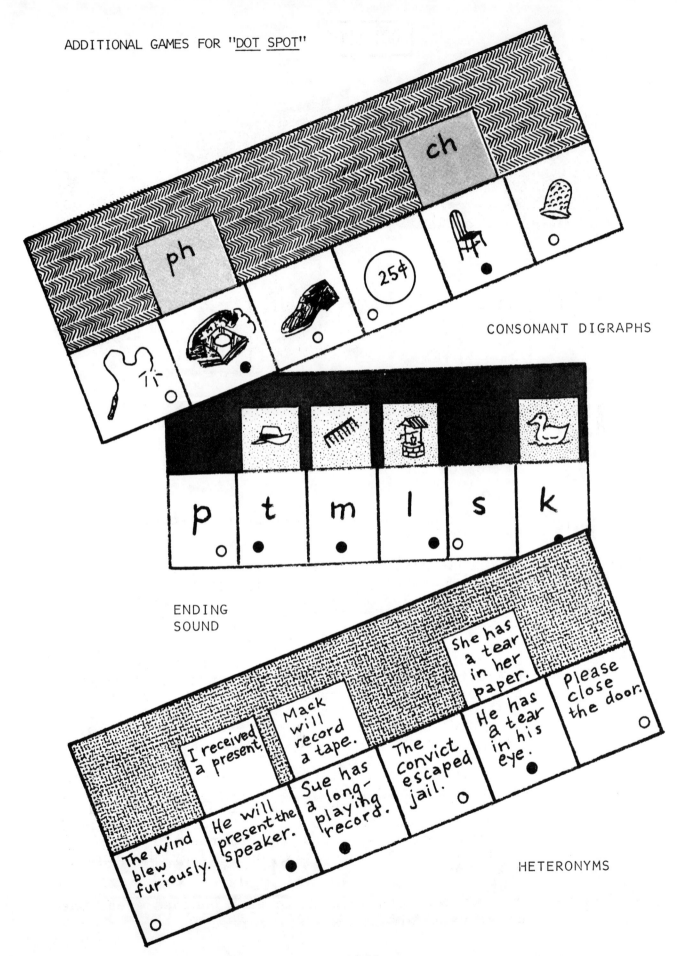

CONSONANT DIGRAPHS

ENDING
SOUND

HETERONYMS

131

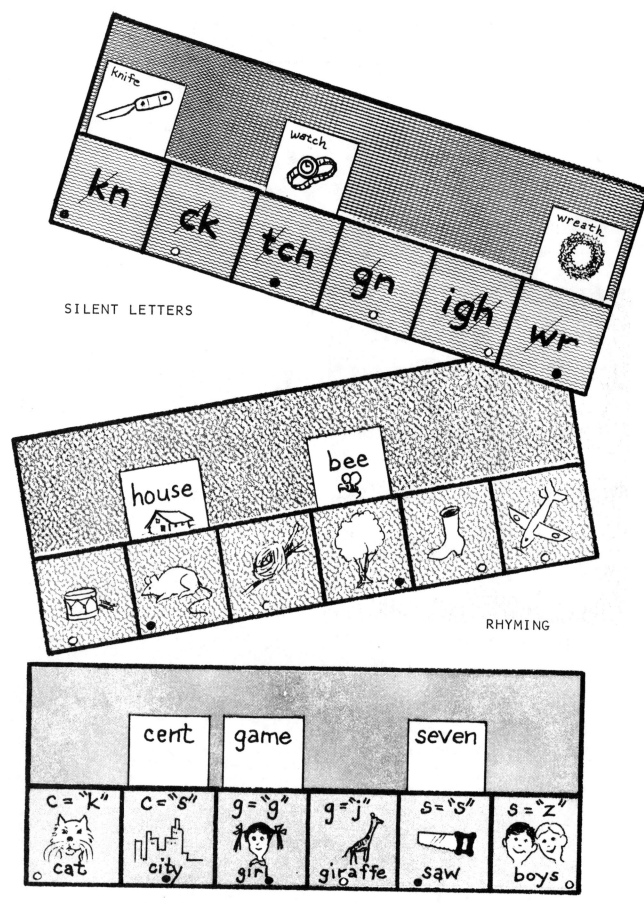

SILENT LETTERS

RHYMING

C - G - S VARIANT CONSONANT SOUNDS

132

Materials: 4-ply poster board (assorted colors)
white oaktag paper
water-base magic markers
small pictures (where needed)
permanent black magic marker
permanent red magic marker

Directions: Specific directions for each game are given. The
object of all games in this group is to match pairs.
At the end of each game, the child who has accumulated the greatest number of pairs or points wins.

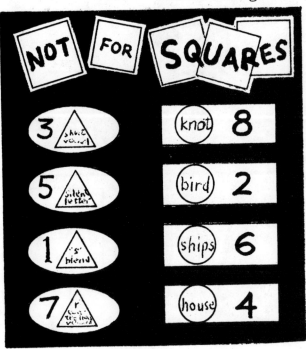

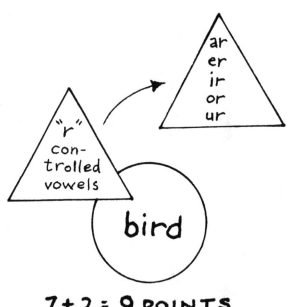

7 + 2 = 9 POINTS

Not For Squares - 22x22" square of black poster board
1½" x 1½" square block letters (title)
4 - 9" diameter yellow ovals
4 - 3½" x 9" green rectangles
40 3½" equilateral triangles (orange)
40 3½" diameter circles (pink)

Directions - Produce a game board as shown, except glue blank
triangles and circles on the base board to indi-
cate placement of word cards (triangles & circles).
Cover the board with contact paper. Now write
the word attack sounds to be matched on the triangles;
exemplifying words are printed on circles. Sort
triangles and circles face-up on the board as shown.
Children pair sounds and words and score points as
illustrated.

Self-Correction: The back of each triangular card gives the
possible answers.

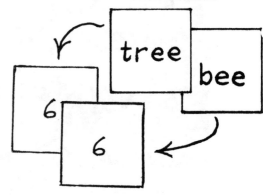

Skill: Rhyming

Mice on Ice - 20x28" light blue poster board
             40 - 2" squares (oaktag or poster board)
             Small pictures (if rhyming picture cards are desired)

Directions: Illustrate the game board as shown with 3" ice cubes
              (blue or white in color) and gaily-colored mice.
              Leave the fore area of each cube blank (do not show
              picture cards as they are illustrated for play).
              Cover the board with clear contact paper. Mice on Ice
              is a rhyming game, so print rhyming words or glue
              rhyming pictures to the 40 cards. To play, place a
              card face up on the fore area of each ice cube.
              Players take turns and hunt for rhyming word pairs.
              A sample play would be to pick up the picture cards
              "wig and pig".

Self-Correction: The back sides of rhyming pair cards have matching
                  numbers. (See arrows.)

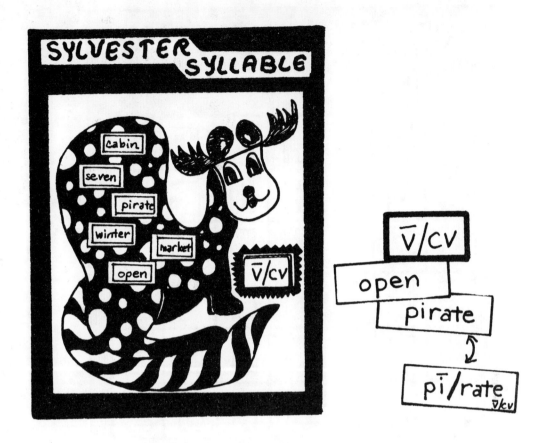

Skill: Syllabication

Sylvester Syllable - 20x22" orange poster board
                     22x28" black poster board
                     60 - 2x4" green word cards
                     40 - 3x5" red syllable rule cards

Directions: Illustrate the game board as shown, but place
              blank green cards where the words are to be placed
              on Sylvester's body and a blank red card in the
              "rule area". Cover the board with contact paper.
              Now print out ten syllable rule cards (red) for
              each rule (vc/cv, v̄/cv, v̆c/v and /_le). Prepare
              15 word cards (green) to exemplify each of the
              four rules. Shuffle the cards and place in stacks
              on the board as shown. Children take turns and are
              allowed to pick up as many face-up cards as they
              can find to match the rule card. At the end of
              the game, the child with the most green cards wins.

Self-Correction: See arrow indicating the front and back sides
                  of the green word cards.

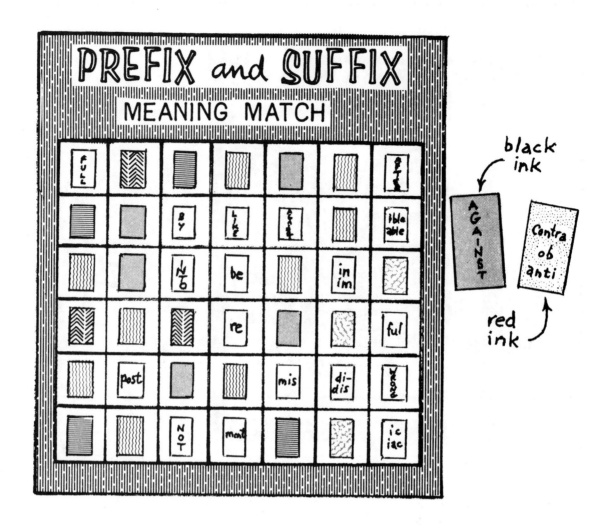

Skill: Affix Meanings

<u>Prefix and Suffix Meaning Match</u> - 22x28" poster board
                                    100 2x3" cards (50 pink, 50 blue)

Directions: Illustrate the game board by showing the title and
             ruling off the playing area into 2½ x 3½" rectangles
             (do not show cards as illustrated). Using the 50 pink
             cards, print prefixes horizontally on 25 and prefix
             meanings vertically on 25. Using the 50 blue cards,
             print suffixes horizontally on 25 and suffix meanings
             vertically on 25. To play, shuffle the cards all
             together and place one face-down on each rectangle.
             Players take turns turning one card face-up--as soon
             as any player spots an affix-meaning match, he calls
             out the affix and meaning. If he has a pair (e.g. **mis-/**
             wrong), he keeps the cards. The player who has the
             most pairs wins. As cards are removed, new cards are
             placed face-down from the deck of remaining cards.

Self-Correction: A master list of prefix and suffix meanings **should**
             be available to check responses.

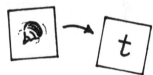

Skill: Beginning sound-letter correspondence

<u>Sound Spot</u> - 22" diameter 4-ply poster board circle
40 - 1½" oaktag squares
40 - small pictures illustrating beginning sounds
1 - 1" diameter "spot" or button

<u>Directions</u>: Illustrate the game board as shown, but do not indicate the pictured squares on the leopard's spots. Cover the playing board with contact paper. Glue pictures which exemplify the beginning consonant sounds on the 1½" oaktag squares. Picture cards are placed face-up on the leopard's spots. In turn, each child drops the 1" diameter "spot" or a button on the Sound Spot. If, for example, the spot falls on the letter <u>b</u>, the child looks on the leopard's spots for a picture whose name begins with the "b" sound. If he finds one, he picks it up and turns it over to see if the letter (self-correcting feature) matches the letter on the Sound Spot. If his answer is correct, he keeps the picture. At the end of the game, the child with the greatest number of pictures wins.

<u>Self-Correction</u>: Print the beginning sound letter on the back of each square.

137

Additional Skills for "Sound Spot":

Skill	Spot Area Contains	Sample Cards & Self-Correction back side
Long and Short Vowels	ă, ĕ, ĭ, ŏ, ŭ ā, ē, ī, ō, ū	→ ē
"R" Controlled Vowels	ar or er, ir, ur	→ ir
Final Consonant Blends	nt, lk sp, etc.	→ lk
Verbs and/or Adjectives	-ing, -ed, -s, -er, est	largest → -est
Silent Consonant Letters	k̸, c̸h̸, c̸k g̸, w̸, b̸ g̸h̸, l̸, n̸, etc.	lamb → b̸

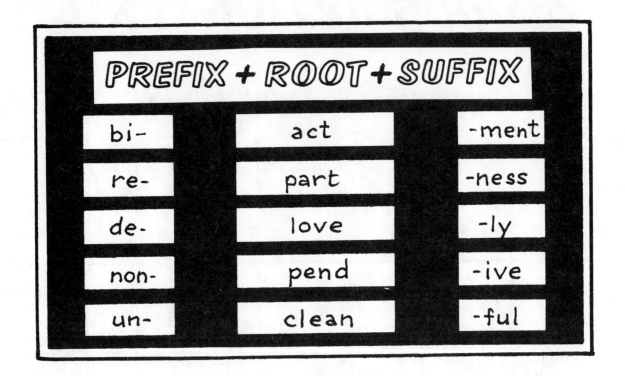

Skill: Affixation

Prefix + Root + Suffix - Black board 22 x 28"
                                            50   2x4½" yellow prefix cards
                                            75   2x8" blue root cards
                                            50   2x4½" pink suffix cards

Play: Stacks of prefix, root and suffix cards are placed on
the board as illustrated. Note: when producing the
game board, glue a plain colored card in place-holding
positions to correspond with the placement of prefix,
root and suffix cards--this will help the children
organize the cards for play. Words can be made by
combining any prefix with a root, any suffix with a
root, or preferably any prefix + root + suffix to form
a real word. Placing a number 1, 2, or 3 on the back
of each card will enable the children to add up the
points for each card used in obtaining a word point
score. A tally is kept and the winner is the child
who has accumulated the greatest number.

Self-Correction: A master list of possible combinations or a
dictionary can be used to check responses.

Skill: Long & Short Vowel Pronunciation Rules

<u>Pronunciation Prowl</u> - 28x20" white poster board
      30 - 1x2½" green cards
      30 - 1x2½" yellow cards
      1 spinner device & 1 brass fastener

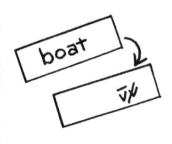

<u>Directions:</u> Illustrate the board as shown, making the second floor of the house yellow and the lawn and tree green. Sketch the pronunciation rules as shown but do not attach the spinner. In the four areas where you see word cards on the house, glue a plain yellow card. Glue plain green cards where you see word cards on the tree and lawn. Cover the board with contact paper. Punch the hole in the spinner and attach the spinner to the board with a brass fastener. Print words which exemplify the four pronunciation rules on the yellow and green cards and place these cards in stacks on the yellow and green blank cards on the board. Children spin the spinner, explain the rule, and pick up and read as many cards as they can find which follow that particular rule.

<u>Self-Correction:</u> The game can be made self-correcting by printing the corresponding rule on the back of each yellow and green word card. (see arrow.)

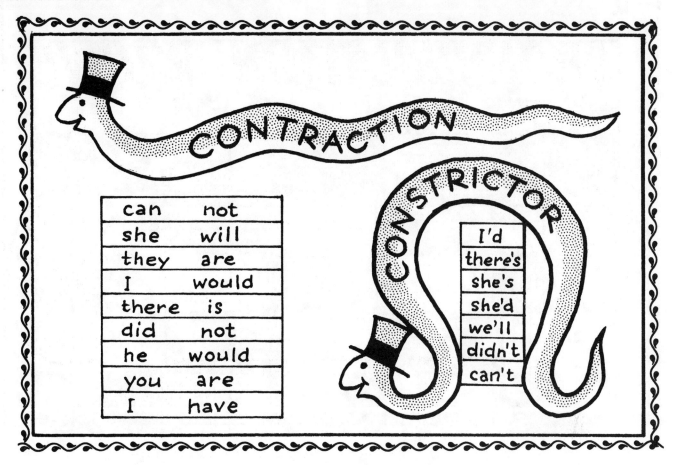

can	not
she	will
they	are
I	would
there	is
did	not
he	would
you	are
I	have

I'd
there's
she's
she'd
we'll
didn't
can't

she	would

16

she'd

16
*

Skill: Contractions

Contraction Constrictor - 18x28" poster board
              40 - 1x8" cards (oaktag or poster board)
              40 - 1x3½" cards (oaktag or poster board)

Directions: Illustrate the game board as above, but do not attach
              the printed cards as shown. To indicate the appropriate
              placement for cards, rule off a 9x12" area into 10 -
              9x1¼" rectangles (for non-contracted forms) and a
              4x8-3/4" area into 7 - 4x1¼" rectangles (for the con-
              tracted forms). Cover the completed board with contact
              paper. Now print the playing cards as illustrated with
              the non-contracted word forms on the long cards and the
              contractions on the short cards; continue until 40 pairs
              have been made. To begin play, place stacks of cards in
              the appropriate areas. Players take turns picking up
              pairs as illustrated.

Self-Correction: On the back of matching pair cards print matching
                   numbers. (see arrows) To keep player's scores, award
                   the number indicated on the card backs as points.*

Skills: Synonyms & Antonyms & Homonyms

<u>Synonym Antonym Homonym</u> - 22x28" 4-ply poster board
                                42 - 3x5" white oaktag cards

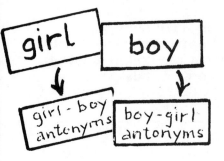

Directions: Produce a checker-board base as illustrated,
              but do not place any word cards on the board.
              Cover with clear contact paper. Now select
              seven homonym, seven synonym, and seven antonym
              pair words and print each word on a card (note:
              to make seven pair words will require 14
              individual cards). These cards are shuffled and
              placed in stacks as shown. Children take turns
              or all play at one time seeking Synonym, Antonym
              or Homonym pairs. The cards can be made self-
              correcting as illustrated. The child who finds
              the most pair cards wins.

Self-Correction: Cards reverse for self-correction.

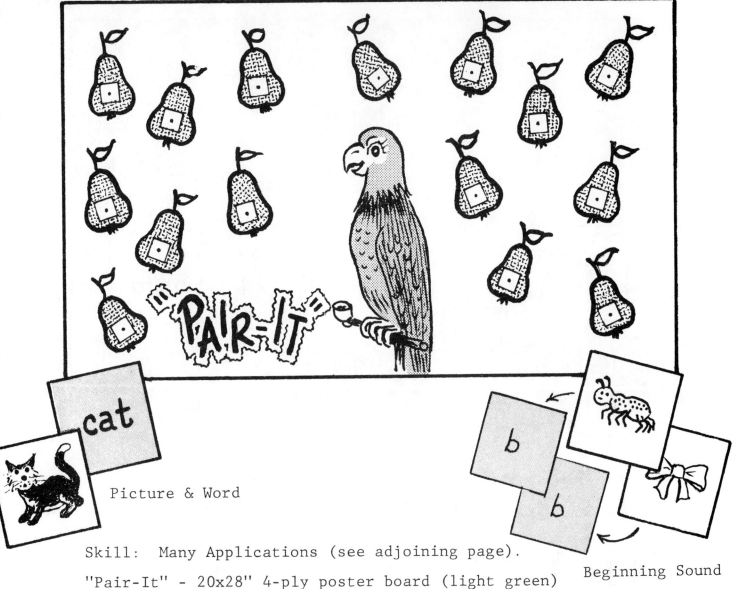

Picture & Word

Beginning Sound

Skill: Many Applications (see adjoining page).

"Pair-It" - 20x28" 4-ply poster board (light green)
20-60 1½" white oaktag squares
(pictures where needed)

Directions: Illustrate the game board as shown, giving the parrot
colorful yellow, green, red, blue and purple feathers.
The pears are shades of yellow and light green--draw
the pears without the small dotted squares. Cover the
board with contact paper. Next, decide on the skills
to be taught (this basic board can be used with a
variety of skill cards: rhyming pictures, pictures
with the same beginning sound, letters and pictures,
and words and pictures). On the 1½" oaktag squares,
glue the pictures or print the letters or sounds needed.
It is a good idea to make up four cards which can be
intermatched (e.g. four _at words). The cards are
placed face-up on each pear as shown by the dotted
squares. Children play by taking turns or all playing
at once always attempting to make "pairs" of related
cards. The child with the greatest number of pairs
wins.

Beginning
Letter-picture

Self-Correction: See arrows above indicating self-correction
matching letters.

ADDITIONAL PLAYING CARDS FOR "PAIR-IT"

1   BEGINNING LETTER AND PICTURE MATCH

2   SIGHT VOCABULARY PICTURE AND WORD

3   CONTRACTIONS

4   HOMONYMS

5   COMMON LETTER SOUND (ANYWHERE IN THE WORD — E.G. APPLE — LAMP)

6   PICTURE ANTONYMS

7   VARIANT CONSONANT SOUNDS C-G-S

8   PRONUNCIATION RULES

| horse | shoe | | any | one |

Skill: Compound Words

Compound Hound - 20x28" 4-ply poster board
                3/4 x 4" cards - 30 blue & 30 green
                water-base magic markers

Directions: Illustrate the board as shown except instead of
            showing words on the hound's body, glue blank
            blue cards on the front end, green cards on the
            back end. On the other blue cards, print the
            first words and on the green cards print the second
            words for the compound words you select. To begin
            play place blue and green cards on the hound as
            shown. Children attempt to make compound words
            by picking up cards and pronouncing the words.
            The child who makes the greatest number of compound
            words wins the game.

Self-Correction: A master list of possibilities will make the
            game self-correcting.

Cubed Pairs

Skill: Short or Long Vowel Sounds

Materials: 5-10 poster board pieces 4½x6"
                  5-10 colored poster board pieces 4½x6"
                  magic marker
                  small pictures illustrating sounds
                  clear contact paper 4-1½x6" strips for each die

Directions: Produce the cubes needed by ruling off each
                  poster board piece as illustrated. Glue
                  pictures on the white pieces and print sounds
                  on the colored pieces. Cover each piece with
                  contact paper and then cut away the blackened
                  areas. Fold along the lines between the sounds
                  or pictures to form a cube. Now wrap each cube
                  with four strips of 1½x6" contact paper, wrapping
                  each in a different direction.

                  Play involves tossing the cubes (sometimes tossing
                  from a container such as a shoebox is helpful)
                  and matching the sounds and pictures which are
                  face-up. A score is kept of the number of correct
                  pairs (eg. ŏ - top) which each player makes each
                  turn. At the end of the game, the player who has
                  the most points wins.

Self-Correction: Provide a sheet listing each vowel sound and
                  the pictures which correspond.

Materials: 50-100 wooden, spring-type clothespins
              4-ply poster board and/or corrugated cardboard
              water-base magic markers
              small pictures (where applicable)
              clear adhesive contact paper
              6 notebook rings (3/4")
              3/4" wide 3M plastic tape (colored)
              "Sharpie" permanent magic marker

Directions: Cut two or three pieces of 4-ply poster board to
              the desired board size (ranges from 6x12" to
              12x18" rectangles, 12" equilateral triangles, or
              12" diameter circles). Using quite a bit of
              Elmer's Glue, glue the two or three thicknesses
              together. On the surface, using water-base magic
              markers, illustrate, print the words and glue any
              needed pictures. Next wrap the heads of each
              clothespin with plastic tape. Print the letters
              or other answer information on the plastic tape
              using the "Sharpie" marker.

Now work through the clothespinning process, attaching correct answers to the appropriate items on the
board. Turn the board over to the reverse side and
develop a self-correcting scheme through color-coding,
letter matching or number matching as illustrated
below. Be sure to mark both the clothespins and board.
In cases where multiple clothespins have the same information printed on the front (eg. same syllabication
rule or same sound), be sure to code the backs in an
identical manner since such clothespins will be
interchangeable on the board. Now remove the clothespins and cover the board with clear contact paper
overlapping 1½" on the back side.

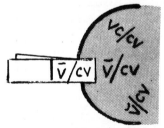 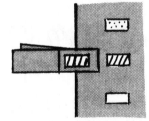 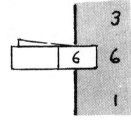

There are three methods of storing clothespins and
they are illustrated below. They are boxing, pinning
to a folder, or attaching to the back of the board
by a 5x12" strip of 4-ply poster board folded under
2" on the right and left hand sides and glued as
illustrated.

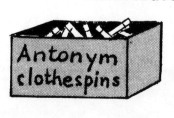  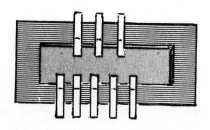

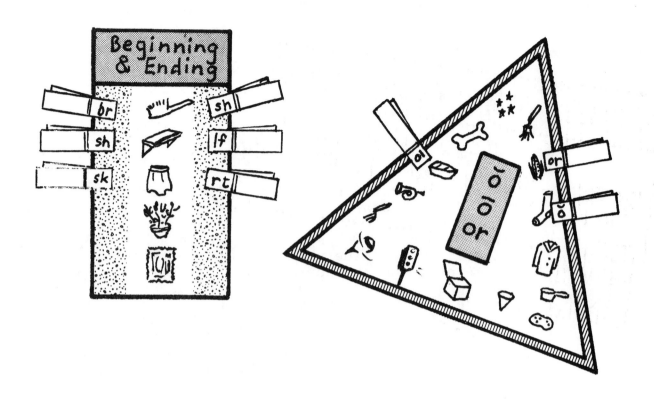

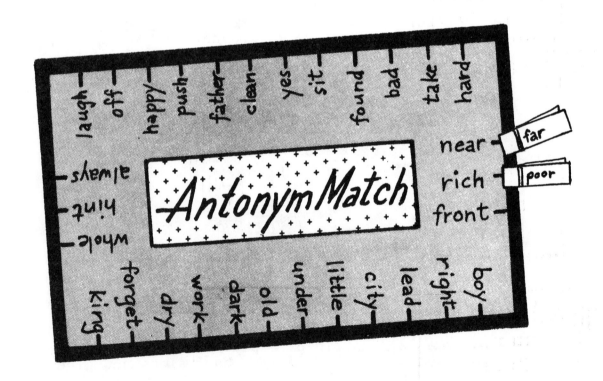

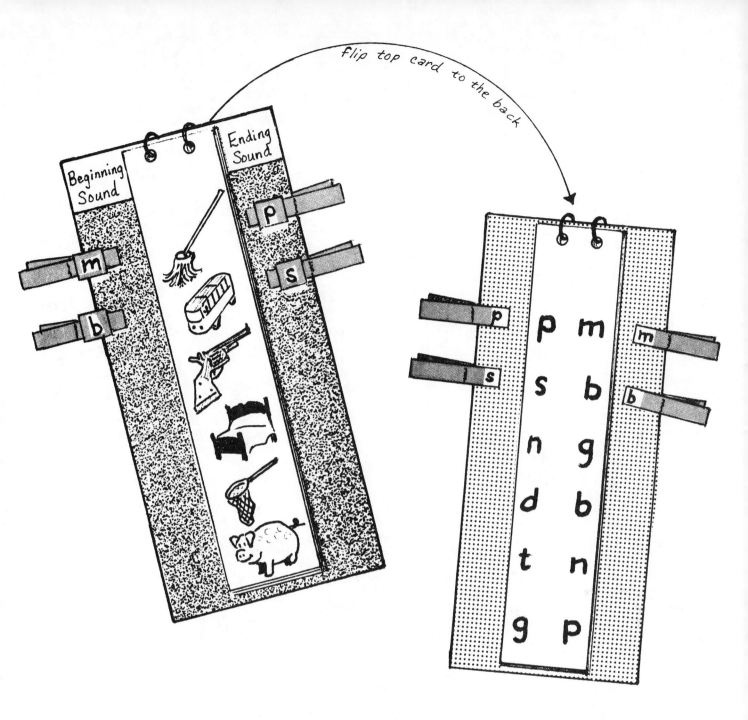

Skill: Beginning & Ending Sounds

Flip Pinning - You will need two sets of clothespins color-
coded for use as a beginning or as an ending sound.
Also note that beginning sounds and ending sounds are
printed on the clothespins differently, beginning
sounds have the depressed end of the clothespin to
the left--ending sounds have the depressed end to the
right (see illustration).

Self-Correction: The child flips the sheet just completed to
the back side and turns the board over to check his
answers.

151

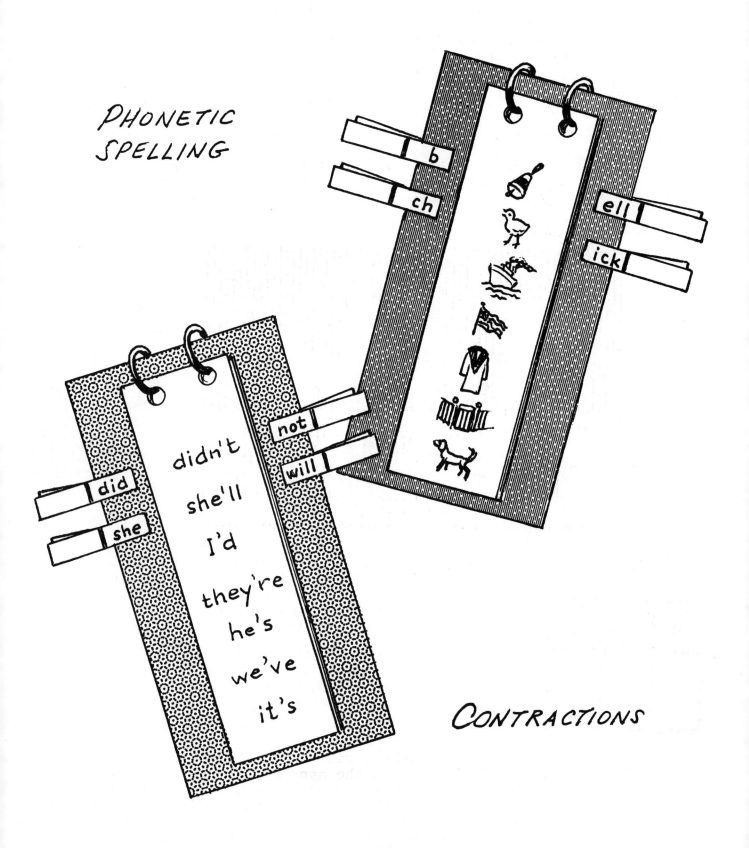

PHONETIC SPELLING

CONTRACTIONS

IT'S A CASE OF CATEGORIES

Materials: 12x18" white oaktag paper
4-ply poster board (assorted colors)
water-base magic markers
black permanent magic marker
razor blade
pictures (where needed)

Directions: Specific directions for each category case are given. In general, these are manipulatives to be used by a single child or a pair of children. Whether a board, folder or box approach is used, the object is to categorize example words or pictures. The materials can be made self-correcting if an answer-key card is provided listing which cards are to be placed in which folders.

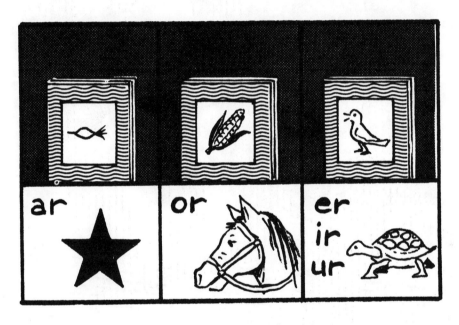 

"R" Controlled Vowel Sort - 12x18" piece of 4-ply poster board
40 - 3x7" cards (colored index cards or oaktag can be used)
water base magic markers
40 pictures exemplifying sounds

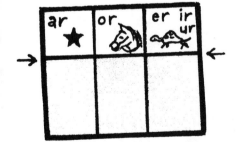

10 - ar   10 - or

20 - er, ir, ur

Directions: Using a black marker, rule the poster board off as illustrated and draw the appropriate sketches. Cover the board with contact paper on the front side only. Fold toward the back along the line indicated by arrows. Use glue or staples along the dividing lines and outside edges to form three pockets. Glue pictures to the cards which will be sorted into the appropriate pockets.

153

FINAL CONSONANT BLENDS

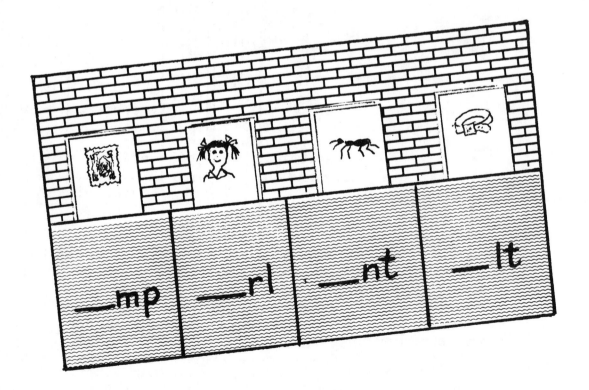

Root word cards (top folder):

fill	light	agree	side	port	color	turn	change	pay	press	heat	tract	love	capit
ent			ible	tor			less	ion		ble	tive		

Root Word Sort   make a 28x14" pocket folder
                  Cards are 1x8" oaktag

uncolorful

prepayment

disagreeable

PREFIX MATCH

| a- ab- |
| a- ad- |
| be- |
| con- com- |
| de- |
| e- ex- |
| in- im- |
| pre- |
| re- |
| un- non- |

comp

infilt

prep

retu

SUFFIX MATCH

| -able -ible |
| -er -or |
| -ful |
| -ize |
| -less |
| -ly |
| -ment |
| -ness |
| -ence -ance |
| -tion -sion |

orful

geless

vely

Prefix Match / Suffix Match   make two folders as suggested for
Root Word Sort Above (20x14"). Mount as illustrated
on 4-ply poster board for support. Play using same
set of cards as used for Root Word Sort.

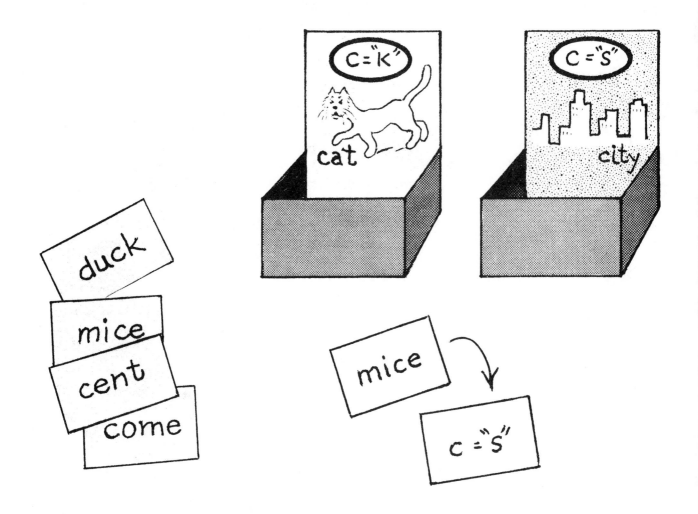

Skill: Variant Consonant Sounds C-G-S

<u>Sorting Boxes</u> - Each box requires a 9½ x 7½" piece of 4-ply poster board.

40 cards 2x3" in size

<u>Directions</u>: Rule off the poster board as illustrated and print the sounds being studied and key pictures for each as shown. Cover the piece with clear contact paper on both sides. Cut out the two pieces indicated. Cut slits along the lines indicated by x's. Fold along lines indicated by /'s. Use a stapler to secure the sides of the box. Make a set of 20 cards containing c="k" sound and 20 containing the c="s" sounds. The children play by sorting the cards into boxes.

xxx cut

//// fold

<u>Self-Correction</u>: The back of each card is marked with the correct sound (mice-c="s"). (see arrow)

156

Short Vowel Sort

Contraction Sort

Skill: Variant Consonant Sounds: C - G - S

Bouquet of Sounds - 22x28" 4-ply poster board (green)
                    6 - 3" diameter yellow circles
                    48 - 1½" petals (assorted colors-
                        each flower will have petals
                        of various colors).

Directions: The playing board is made by gluing the yellow
              circles to the board and outlining the positions
              where petals are to be placed. Print the sounds
              in the circles (any consonant or vowel sounds may
              be used) and cover the board with contact paper.
              Print words on the petals which exemplify the
              sounds being studied. Play involves placing
              petals so that the words written on them correspond
              to the sounds on the centers.

Self-Correction: Code the back of each petal with a K, S, G, J,
                   S, or Z for the sound of the variant consonant.
                   (see arrow)

158

Skill: Syllabication

Syllable Sort - 22x28" piece of 4-ply poster board is
                used for the game board
                Pockets are approximately 6x8" size
                and are cut from various colors of
                4-ply poster board and attached to the
                board along the sides and bottom, (leav-
                ing the top open)using brass fasteners.

                Cards - 50 2x6" oaktag cards

Directions: After the pockets are attached to the base
                board, use water-base magic markers to print
                "Syllable Sort" and the rules on each pocket.
                When the board is completed, cover with clear
                contact paper overlapping 1" to the back side.
                Use a razor blade to slit the top edge of
                each pocket so that cards may be inserted.
                Using a permanent black magic marker, prepare
                ten cards containing example words for each
                syllabication category. Play involves sorting
                the cards into the correct pockets.

Self-Correction: Draw the "pocket" shape which corresponds to
                the rule on the back of each game card.
                (see arrow)

159

SOUND STRIPS AND CARD FLIPS

Materials: 4-ply poster board (assorted colors)
12x18" white oaktag paper
razor blade
black permanent magic marker
notebook rings ½"-1" diameter

Directions: Sound Strips - The outside pockets are made by gluing two thicknesses of 4-ply poster board together leaving just enough unglued area to permit the strips to be inserted and moved up and down. Cut small "windows" using a razor blade to expose the letters to be changed (those on the sound strip). Illustrate the strip pocket and insert the blank oaktag strips. Gradually pull the blank strip through the pocket and print letters for completing words on the strip. Remove the strip and cover both the pocket and strip with clear contact paper. Now reassemble and begin play.

Envelopes range from 6-10"x4-8"
Strips range from 3-6" x 8-14"

Card Flips - The back board should be constructed of two layers of 4-ply poster board (dark color) glued together and covered with contact paper. Cards are cut from white oaktag paper or 3x5" index cards may be substituted. Using a black magic marker, print the letters and words as illustrated. See the sound lists and rhyming lists in the reference section. Punch holes in the cards and determine their placement on the back board. Punch appropriate holes in the back board at least ½" below the top edge of the board for greater resistance to tearing. Attach the cards using notebook rings and begin play by flipping any desired cards and pronouncing--nonsense words, as well as real words, provide great word-sounding practice.

Back boards range from 4-6" x 10-12"
Cards range from 2-6" x 3-3½"

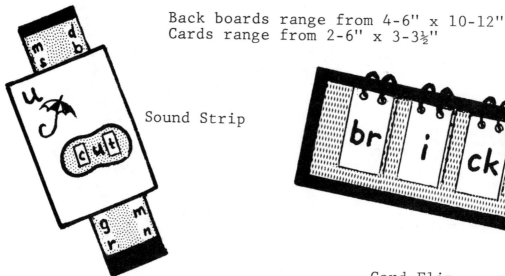

Sound Strip

Card Flip

160

Adjectives

clean er

r
sp
m

nd
t
th

ou

sh ou ts

cl
s
gr

d
nd
t

snack

Beginning &
Ending Word
Synthesis

Changing
Consonant Sounds
with
Consistent Vowel

look ed

Verb Forms

Short Vowel Change

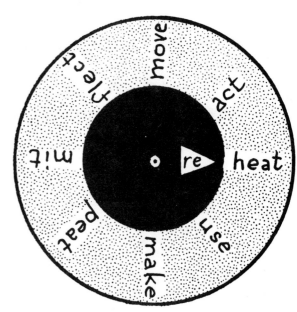

Prefix + Root Change

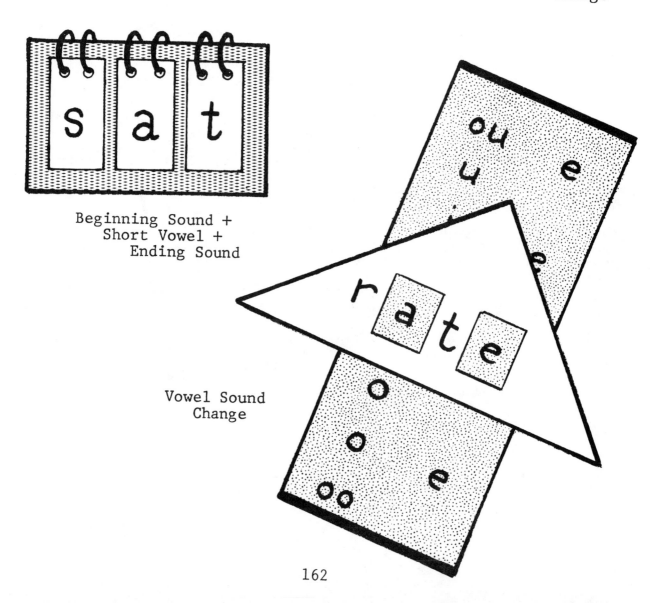

Beginning Sound +
Short Vowel +
Ending Sound

Vowel Sound
Change

INITIAL CONSONANTS

b	c	d	f	g
baby	cab	dad	face	gal
back	cabbage	dam	fact	game
bad	cabin	dance	factory	gang
bag	cage	danger	fail	garage
bake	cake	dark	fair	garden
ball	calf	date	fairy	gas
bank	call	day	fall	gate
bat	came	dead	family	gay
bath	camel	deep	fan	geese
be	camp	deer	far	gem
bear	can	dent	farm	get
bed	candle	dentist	fast	ghost
bee	candy	desert	fat	giant
beg	cane	desk	farther	gift
bell	cap	dew	feather	gill
bib	cape	dial	feel	girl
big	car	die	feet	give
bike	card	dig	fell	go
bird	carpet	dim	fence	goat
boat	carrot	dime	few	gold
bone	cat	dip	fight	golf
book	cave	dirt	fill	gone
boots	cent	dish	fin	good
bow	city	ditch	fine	goose
bowl	coat	dive	finger	gorilla
box	cob	do	fire	got
boy	coin	dock	first	gown
bug	cold	doctor	fish	guard
bunny	color	doe	fit	guess
burn	colt	does	five	guest
bus	comb	dog	fix	guitar
bush	come	doll	fog	gull
busy	cone	dome	food	gulp
but	cook	donkey	fool	gum
butter	cookie	don't	foot	gun
button	cool	door	for	guy
buy	cord	dot	fork	gym
buzz	corn	down	four	gypsy
by	corner	dozen	fox	
	cot	draw	full	
	cotton	duck	fun	
	country	dug	fur	
	cow	dump		
	cowboy	dust		
	cup	dye		
	cupboard			
	curl			
	curler			
	cut			

INITIAL CONSONANTS

h	j	k	l	m
hail	jacket	kangaroo	lace	machine
hair	jacks	keen	ladder	mad
half	jail	keep	lady	made
hall	January	keg	laid	magic
ham	jam	kennel	lake	magnet
hammer	jar	kept	lamb	mail
hand	jaw	ketchup	lame	make
happy	jay	kettle	lamp	man
hard	jeep	key	land	many
hat	jelly	kick	lap	map
hate	jet	kid	large	marble
hay	jewel	kill	last	march
he	job	kind	late	mash
head	join	king	laugh	mat
hear	joke	kiss	law	match
heart	jolly	kit	lawn	may
heat	joy	kitchen	lay	meal
heel	judge	kite	lazy	measure
hello	jug	kitten	leaf	meat
helmet	juice		leap	men
help	July		learn	mess
hen	jump		leather	met
here	June		leg	mice
hid	jungle		lemon	middle
high	junk		letter	mild
hill	just		library	mile
him			lick	milk
hip			lid	mind
his			life	mine
hit			lift	minute
hive			light	mirror
hockey			like	miss
hoe			lime	mist
hold			line	mitten
hole			lion	mix
home			lip	money
honey			list	month
hood			live	moon
hook			lock	mop
hop			log	more
hope			long	most
horn			look	mother
horse			lost	mouse
hose			lot	mouth
hot			loud	move
house			love	much
hug			low	mud
hunt			luck	mug
hurt			lunch	must
hum				my

INITIAL CONSONANTS

n	p	r	s	t
nail	pack	rabbit	said	table
name	page	race	sail	tail
nap	pail	radio	sale	take
napkin	paint	rag	salt	talk
navy	pair	rain	same	tall
near	pal	rake	sand	tap
neat	pan	ran	sang	tape
neck	paper	rat	sank	tar
need	parade	rattle	sat	task
needle	park	read	save	tax
neighbor	part	ready	saw	taxi
nest	pass	record	say	tea
net	past	red	sea	teacher
new	paste	rest	seal	team
news	path	rib	seat	teeth
next	paw	ribbon	see	telephone
nice	pay	rice	seed	television
nickel	pea	rich	seem	tell
niece	peach	riddle	sell	ten
night	peanut	ride	send	tent
nine	pear	ring	sent	test
nip	peep	rip	set	tie
no	pen	rise	seven	tiger
nod	penny	road	sew	time
noise	people	rob	sick	tin
none	pet	robin	side	tiny
noodle	piano	rock	sift	tip
noon	pick	rocket	sight	tire
north	pie	roll	silly	to
nose	pig	roof	sing	today
not	pin	room	sink	toe
note	pine	rope	sip	told
nothing	pink	rose	sit	ton
now	pipe	round	six	too
number	pizza	row	size	took
nun	poke	rub	so	tools
nurse	pony	rug	socks	tooth
nut	pond	rule	soft	top
	pony	ruler	sold	toss
	pool	run	soldier	touch
	pop	rush	some	towel
	pot	rut	son	town
	pull		song	toy
	pump		soon	tub
	pup		soup	tug
	purse		suit	tune
	push		sun	turkey
	puzzle		sunny	turn
			sunk	twin
				typewriter

INITIAL CONSONANTS

<u>v</u>	<u>w</u>	<u>x</u>	<u>y</u>	<u>z</u>
vacation	wag	**Xmas**	yacht	zeal
vacuum	wagon	x ray	yak	zebra
vain	wait		yank	zero
valentine	wake		yap	zest
valley	walk		yard	zigzag
valve	wall		yarn	zinc
van	want		yawn	zing
vane	war		yea	zinnia
vase	warm		year	zip
vegetable	was		yeast	zipper
veil	wash		yell	zone
vein	watch		yellow	zoo
vent	water		yelp	zoom
verb	wave		yes	
verse	wax		yesterday	
very	way		yet	
vest	we		yield	
view	wealth		yoke	
village	wear		yolk	
vine	web		yo-yo	
violet	wedding		you	
violin	weed		young	
visit	week		your	
voice	well		yours	
volcano	went		youth	
volume	were		yule	
vote	west			
vow	wet			
vulture	wide			
	wife			
	wig			
	wild			
	will			
	willow			
	win			
	wind			
	window			
	wine			
	wire			
	wise			
	wish			
	witch			
	with			
	wolf			
	women			
	wood			
	word			
	work			
	world			
	worm			
	would			

FINAL CONSONANTS

b	d	f	g	k
cab	bad	beef	bag	back
club	bed	brief	beg	book
cob	blood	calf	bog	chalk
cobweb	bread	chef	bug	chick
corncob	fad	chief	catalog	clock
crab	feed	cliff	chug	cook
crib	glad	cuff	clog	desk
cub	good	deaf	dig	duck
cube	had	dwarf	dog	hook
dab	head	elf	dug	ink
globe	hid	giraffe	egg	joke
grab	hood	golf	fig	lake
jab	kid	grief	flag	mark
job	laid	gulf	fog	mask
knob	lid	half	frog	neck
mob	load	herself	gag	oak
rib	loud	himself	hog	pack
rob	mad	hoof	hug	park
rub	maid	if	jig	pink
scrub	mud	knife	jug	quack
shrub	nod	leaf	keg	rack
snob	odd	life	lag	rake
sob	pad	loaf	leg	rock
stab	paid	mischief	log	sack
stub	pod	myself	mug	shake
suburb	proud	myself	nag	shark
superb	raid	off	peg	shock
tab	read	oneself	pig	shrink
tribe	red	puff	plug	sick
tub	rid	roof	rag	silk
tube	road	safe	rug	sink
wardrobe	rod	scarf	sag	skunk
web	sad	self	shag	smoke
	seed	shelf	shrug	snack
	shed	sheriff	snag	snake
	shred	sniff	snug	stick
	skid	staff	song	stork
	sled	stiff	tag	tank
	speed	stuff	tug	think
	stood	surf	twig	track
	wad	thief	wag	trick
	weed	wharf	wig	walk
	wood	whiff	zigzag	wick
		wife		wink
		wolf		work
		yourself		wreck

FINAL CONSONANTS

l	m	n	p	r
ball	aim	balloon	ape	bear
bell	arm	barn	bump	car
doll	broom	brown	camp	care
girl	clam	can	cape	cellar
grill	dam	corn	champ	chair
heel	dime	fan	chip	chapter
hotel	dream	green	chirp	cider
kill	drum	gun	chap	collar
nail	elm	iron	clap	color
nickel	film	kitten	clip	deer
oil	flame	lemon	creep	doctor
owl	from	lion	crisp	ear
pail	game	men	crop	fair
pearl	gum	mitten	cup	far
peel	gym	noon	damp	fear
pencil	ham	ocean	deep	fire
pool	hem	open	drape	flour
purple	jam	oven	drip	for
puzzle	lime	pan	drop	hair
rail	loom	pen	flap	hear
rifle	palm	plane	help	hour
royal	plum	queen	hip	letter
ruffle	program	question	hoop	mirror
saddle	ram	rain	hop	oar
sail	rhyme	ran	jeep	our
school	rim	robin	jump	pair
seal	roam	run	lamp	paper
shell	room	seven	lip	pear
shovel	same	sign	map	pepper
skull	scream	skin	mop	shore
small	seam	son	nap	snore
smell	seem	spin	pup	sore
smile	shame	spoon	rip	sour
snail	skim	stone	ship	star
soil	slam	swan	shop	stir
spell	slum	tan	skip	store
steal	some	ten	slap	sugar
stool	stadium	thin	sleep	summer
table	steam	thorn	soap	supper
tall	stem	tin	soup	sure
tile	stream	town	stamp	tar
toll	sum	train	step	tear
turtle	team	twin	stop	tire
veil	them	van	sweep	waiter
wall	time	violin	trap	water
well	trim	win	trip	wear
whale	warm	yarn	tulip	where
wheel	worm		whip	winter
	zoom		wrap	wire
				year

FINAL CONSONANTS

s	t	v	z
boots	ant	alive	amaze
bless	ate	brave	breeze
blouse	aunt	carve	bronze
cactus	basket	cave	buzz
chess	bat	curve	civilize
circus	blanket	dissolve	commercialize
close	boat	dive	daze
cross	bullet	dove	doze
dress	but	drove	freeze
else	cat	eve	froze
gas	coat	expensive	fuzz
geese	colt	forgive	gauze
glass	cost	give	individualize
goose	count	glove	itemize
grass	cut	grave	jazz
guess	dirt	grieve	maze
horse	east	grove	memorize
house	eat	have	ooze
kiss	eight	hive	organize
less	fast	improve	paralyze
mess	fat	leave	penalize
miss	fight	live	prize
nurse	foot	move	quiz
paints	forest	native	realize
pants	fruit	negative	recognize
plus	gift	nerve	seize
press	goat	olive	size
promise	hat	pave	sneeze
purse	heart	positive	snooze
sense	hot	preserve	socialize
tennis	jet	prove	squeeze
us	kite	relative	sterilize
waitress	meat	remove	summarize
walrus	nest	reserve	symbolize
yes	net	serve	trapeze
	paste	shave	waltz
	pet	slave	whiz
	plate	sleeve	
	pocket	solve	
	rat	starve	
	rent	stove	
	skate	survive	
	skirt	twelve	
	state	valve	
	street	wave	
	sweet	weave	
	test		
	ticket		
	toast		
	vote		
	wet		

INITIAL CONSONANT BLENDS (2-letter)

bl	br	cl	cr	dr
black	brace	claim	crab	drab
blackboard	bracelet	clam	crack	draft
blacksmith	brad	clamp	cracker	drag
blade	brag	clang	crackle	dragon
blame	braid	clank	cradle	drain
bland	brain	clap	craft	drama
blank	brake	clarinet	cramp	drank
blanket	branch	clash	crane	drape
blare	brand	clasp	crank	drapery
blast	brass	class	crash	drastic
blaze	brave	classify	crate	draw
bleach	bread	classroom	crater	drawer
bleak	break	claw	crawl	drawing
bled	breath	clay	crayon	dread
bleed	breathe	clean	crazy	dream
blemish	bred	cleanser	creak	dreary
blend	breed	clear	cream	drench
bless	breeze	clearing	crease	dress
blest	breezy	clerk	create	dresser
blew	brew	clue	creative	dressing
blimp	briar	click	creature	dribble
blind	bribe	cliff	credit	drier
blindfold	brick	climate	creek	drift
blink	bride	climax	creepy	driftwood
blizzard	bridge	climb	crescent	drill
block	brief	climber	crest	drink
blood	bright	cling	crew	drip
bloodhound	brim	clinic	crib	drive
bloom	bring	clip	cricket	driver
blossom	brisk	clipper	crime	drizzle
blot	Britain	clock	crisp	drool
blouse	brittle	close	crocodile	drop
blow	broad	closet	crooked	drown
blue	broccoli	clot	crop	drowsy
bluff	broil	cloth	cross	drug
blunt	broke	clothes	crow	druggist
blur	bronze	clothespin	crowd	drugstore
blush	brood	cloud	crown	drum
bluster	brook	clover	crumb	drunk
	broom	clown	crunch	dry
	brother	club	crush	
	brought	cluck	crust	
	brow	clump	crutch	
	brown	clumsy	cry	
	brownie	cluster		
	browse	clutter		
	bruise			
	brush			

INITIAL CONSONANT BLENDS (2-letter)

fl	fr	gl	gr	pl
flag	fraction	glacier	grab	place
flake	fracture	glad	graceful	plaid
flame	fragile	glamorous	grade	plain
flamingo	fragment	glance	graduate	plan
flannel	fragrance	glare	grain	plane
flap	frail	glass	grammar	planet
flash	frame	glaze	grand	plank
flashlight	freak	gleam	grandmother	plant
flat	freckle	glee	grandfather	planter
flavor	free	glide	grant	plaster
flea	freedom	glimpse	grape	plastic
flesh	freeze	glitter	grapefruit	plate
flew	freight	globe	graph	platform
flexible	frequent	gloomy	grasp	platter
flight	fresh	glory	grass	play
flip	friction	gloss	grasshopper	playful
flirt	friend	glossary	grave	playground
float	frighten	glove	gravel	playhouse
flock	frill	glow	gravity	plaza
flood	fringe	glue	gravy	plead
floor	frisky		gray	pleasant
flop	frog		graze	please
florist	from		grease	pleasure
flour	front		great	pleat
flow	frontier		greedy	pledge
flower	frost		green	plentiful
fluid	frosting		greet	plenty
flush	frown		greeting	pliers
flute	froze		grew	plot
flutter	fruit		greyhound	plow
fly	fry		grief	pluck
			grill	plug
			grim	plum
			grime	plumber
			grin	plumbing
			grind	plume
			grip	plump
			gripe	plural
			grizzly	plus
			groan	plush
			grocery	
			groom	
			grouch	
			ground	
			group	
			grow	
			growl	
			grumble	

pr	sc	sl	sm	sn
practice	scab	slam	smack	snack
praise	scale	slang	small	snag
prance	scalp	slant	smart	snail
pray	scamper	slap	smash	snake
preach	scar	slate	smear	snap
precious	scarce	slave	smell	snapshot
predict	scare	slavery	smile	snare
prefer	scarecrow	sled	smirk	snatch
prepaid	scarf	sleek	smock	sneak
prepare	scatter	sleep	smoke	sneeze
prescription	scene	sleepy	smooth	sniff
present	scenery	sleet	smother	sniffle
president	scent	sleeve	smudge	snip
press	science	sleigh	smug	snob
pressure	scientist	slender	smuggle	snoop
pretend	scissors	slept		snooze
pretty	scold	slice		snore
pretzel	scoop	slid		snort
prevent	scooter	slide		snout
preview	scorch	slight		snow
price	score	slim		snowball
priceless	scout	sling		snowdrift
pride	sculpture	slip		snowfall
priest	scum	slipper		snowflake
prince		slippery		snowplow
princess		slit		snowy
print	sk	sliver		snug
printer		slogan		snuggle
printing	skate	slope		
prison	skeleton	sloppy		
prisoner	sketch	slot		
privacy	ski	slouch		
private	skid	slow		
prize	skill	slug		
problem	skillet	slum		
produce	skim	slumber		
product	skin	slump		
professor	skinny	slur		
profit	skip	sly		
program	skirt			
progress	skull			
prohibit	skunk			
project	sky			
projector	skyline			
promise	skyscraper			
prompt				
pronounce				
proof				

INITIAL CONSONANT BLENDS (2-letter)

sp	st	sw	tr	tw
space	stable	swallow	trace	tweed
spaceship	stack	swam	track	tweet
spade	staff	swamp	tractor	tweezers
spaghetti	stage	swan	trade	twelve
spaniel	stain	swarm	tradition	twenty
spank	stair	swat	traffic	twice
spanking	stall	sway	tragic	twig
spare	stamp	swear	trail	twilight
spark	stand	sweat	trailer	twin
sparkle	staple	sweater	train	twine
sparrow	star	sweep	training	twinkle
spasm	start	sweet	tramp	twirl
spatter	starve	sweetheart	trample	twist
speak	state	sweetness	transfer	twister
speaker	station	swell	translate	
spear	statue	swept	trap	
special	stay	swerve	trapeze	
speck	steak	swift	trash	
speech	steal	swim	travel	
speed	steam	swing	tray	
speedometer	steel	swirl	treasure	
spell	steep	switch	treat	
spelling	stem	swollen	treatment	
spend	step	sword	tree	
spent	stereo	swung	tremble	
sphere	stick		trembling	
spice	still		trench	
spider	sting		trial	
spike	stir		triangle	
spill	stitch		tribe	
spin	stock		trick	
spinach	stocking		tricky	
spine	stomach		tried	
spiral	stone		trim	
spirit	stood		trimming	
spit	stool		trip	
spite	stop		triple	
spoil	store		troop	
spoke	storm		trot	
spoken	story		trouble	
sponge	stove		trout	
spook	stuck		truck	
spool	student		true	
spoon	studio		truly	
sport	study		trunk	
spot	stuffing		trust	
spotlight	stumble		truth	
spout	stump		truthful	
spy	stupid		try	
	style			

INITIAL CONSONANT BLENDS - (3-letter)

scr	shr	spl	spr
scram	shrank	splash	sprain
scramble	shred	splatter	sprang
scrap	shrew	spleen	spray
scrapbook	shrewd	splendid	sprawl
scrape	shriek	splendor	spread
scratch	shrill	splice	spree
scrawl	shrimp	splint	sprig
scream	shrine	splinter	spring
screech	shrink	split	springy
screen	shrinkage	splotch	sprinkle
screw	shrivel	splurge	sprite
scribble	shrub		sprout
script	shrubbery		spruce
scroll	shrug		sprung
scrub	shrunk		
scrunch			

squ	str	thr
squabble	straight	thrash
squad	strainer	thread
square	strand	threat
squash	strange	threaten
squat	stranger	three
squaw	strangle	thresh
squawk	strap	thrift
squeak	straw	thrifty
squeal	strawberry	thrill
squeamish	stream	thrive
squeeze	streamer	throat
squid	street	throb
squint	stretcher	throne
squirm	strike	through
squirrel	string	throughout
squirt	strip	throw
	stripe	thrown
	strong	thrust
	struggle	

FINAL CONSONANT BLENDS

ct	ft	ld	lf	lk
collect	cleft	bald	delf	bulk
connect	craft	bold	elf	calk
correct	deft	build	golf	chalk
detract	draft	child	gulf	elk
duct	drift	cold	myself	hulk
effect	gift	field	self	milk
elect	graft	fold	shelf	silk
exact	heft	gild	wolf	sulk
fact	left	gold	yourself	
impact	lift	held		
inject	loft	hold		
inspect	raft	mild		
instruct	shaft	mold		
perfect	shift	old		
predict	sift	rebuild		
project	soft	scald		
react	swift	sold		
reflect	theft	told		
reject	thrift	weld		
select	tuft	wield		
subject	waft	wild		
suspect		yield		

lm	lt	lp	mp	nce
balm	adult	alp	blimp	advance
calm	belt	gulp	bump	announce
elm	bolt	help	camp	bounce
film	colt	kelp	champ	chance
helm	consult	pulp	clamp	convince
overwhelm	dealt	scalp	cramp	dance
realm	fault	whelp	damp	dunce
whelm	felt	yelp	dump	fence
	guilt		hump	finance
	halt		jump	France
	insult		lamp	glance
	jolt		limp	lance
	kilt		lump	once
	knelt		plump	ounce
	lilt		pump	pounce
	malt		ramp	prance
	melt		shrimp	prince
	occult		slump	pronounce
	pelt		stamp	romance
	quilt		stump	since
	result		swamp	trance
	salt		tramp	wince
	silt			
	smelt			
	spilt			

175

FINAL CONSONANT BLENDS

nch	nd	nk	nt	pt
bench	band	bank	ant	abrupt
branch	bend	blank	bent	accept
brunch	blend	blink	cement	adapt
bunch	bound	bunk	cent	adept
cinch	found	crank	dent	adopt
clench	friend	drink	faint	apt
crunch	fund	frank	front	concept
drench	grand	honk	glint	corrupt
French	ground	ink	haunt	crept
hunch	hand	junk	hunt	crypt
inch	hound	link	lint	disrupt
launch	land	pink	mint	Egypt
lunch	mend	sank	paint	erupt
munch	pound	shrink	plant	except
pinch	round	skunk	print	intercept
punch	sand	spank	rent	interrupt
quench	send	stink	scent	kept
ranch	sound	tank	sent	opt
scrunch	spend	thank	spent	script
stench	stand	think	squint	swept
trench	tend	trunk	tent	wept
wrench	wind	wink	vent	

rb	rg (rge)	rk	rl	rm
absorb	barge	ark	barley	alarm
adverb	burg	bark	Carl	arm
barb	dirge	clerk	curl	charm
blurb	emerge	cork	darling	dorm
curb	enlarge	dark	earl	farm
disturb	forge	fork	early	firm
garb	gargle	hark	furl	form
harbor	George	jerk	garland	germ
herb	gorge	lark	garlic	harm
orb	iceberg	mark	girl	inform
perturb	immerge	park	gnarl	norm
suburb	large	perk	hurl	perform
superb	Marge	pork	marlin	reform
turban	merge	quirk	parlor	squirm
urban	splurge	shark	pearl	storm
verb	submerge	shirk	sirloin	swarm
	surge	spark	snarl	term
	urge	stark	swirl	therm
	verge	stork	twirl	uniform
		Turk	unfurl	warm
		work	whirl	worm

FINAL CONSONANT BLENDS

rn	rp	rs
adorn	burp	coarse
barn	carp	converse
born	chirp	course
burn	harp	curse
churn	sharp	disperse
corn	slurp	endorse
darn	tarp	horse
earn	twerp	immerse
fern	twirp	inverse
horn	usurp	Norse
intern	warp	nurse
learn		purse
morn		rehearse
return		reverse
scorn		sparse
stern		submerse
thorn		terse
torn		universe
turn		verse
worn		worse
yarn		

CONSONANT DIGRAPHS

ch	sh	th (voiced)	th (voiceless)	wh
chain	shack	than	thank	whack
chair	shade	that	thankful	whale
chalk	shadow	the	Thanksgiving	wharf
champ	shaggy	their	thaw	what
chance	shake	theirs	theater	whatever
change	shallow	them	theft	wheat
chapter	shame	themselves	theme	wheel
charcoal	shampoo	then	thermometer	wheelbarrow
charge	shape	there	thermos	wheeze
charm	shark	therefore	thick	when
chart	sharp	these	thicken	whenever
chase	sharpen	they	thief	where
chat	shatter	this	thimble	wherever
cheap	shave	those	thin	whether
cheat	shawl	though	thing	which
check	she	thus	think	whiff
checkerboard	shed		third	while
cheek	sheep		thirst	whimper
cheep	sheer		thirteen	whine
cheerful	sheet		thirty	whip
cheese	shelf		thorn	whirl
cherry	shell		thought	whirlpool
chess	shepherd		thousand	whirlwind
chest	sherbet		thread	whisk
chew	sheriff		threat	whisker
chewing	shift		throat	whisper
chick	shin		through	whistle
chicken	shine		throw	white
chief	shiny		thumb	whittle
child	ship		thunder	whiz
children	shirt		Thursday	whopper
chilly	shoe			why
chime	shoot			
chimney	shop			
chimpanzee	shore			
chin	short			
china	shorten			
chip	shot			
chirp	shoulder			
chocolate	shout			
choke	shove			
choose	shovel			
chop	show			
chopsticks	shower			
chore	shown			
chubby	shudder			
chuckle	shut			
church	shutter			
	shy			

CONSONANT DIGRAPHS

ph ("f")

phantasy
phantom
Pharaoh
pharmacist
pharmacy
pharynx
phase
pheasant
phenomenon
philanthropy
Philip
philosopher
philosophy
phlegm
phobia
phoenix
phone
phoneme
phonetics
phonics
phonograph
phosphate
photo
photogenic
photograph
photographer
photographic
photography
phrase
physic
physical
physician
physics
physiology
physique

ck ("k")

back
black
block
brick
broomstick
candlestick
check
chick
clock
cluck
crack
dock
drumstick
duck
jack
kick
knock
lick
lipstick
lock
luck
neck
pack
pancake
peacock
pick
prick
quack
quick
rack
rock
shack
shamrock
shock
sick
smack
smock
smokestack
snack
sock
stick
thick
tick
toothpick
track
truck
wreck

qu

quack
quadrangle
quadruplet
quail
quaint
quake
qualification
qualify
quality
quantity
quarantine
quarrel
quarrelsome
quarry
quart
quarter
quartet
quartz
queasy
queen
queer
quell
quench
query
quest
question
questionnaire
quibble
quick
quicken
quicksand
quiet
quill
quilt
quintet
quintuplets
quit
quite
quiver
quiz
quota
quotation
quote
quotient

gh ("f")

cough
enough
laugh
rough
tough
trough

ng

awning
bang
bring
ceiling
clang
cling
drawing
duckling
earring
evening
fang
gang
greeting
handwriting
hang
inning
king
long
lung
meeting
morning
opening
painting
pudding
railing
reading
ring
sang
saying
setting
sewing
sing
sling
song
spelling
spring
sting
stocking
string
strong
stuffing
swing
thing
wedding
wing
wrong
young

FINAL CONSONANT DIGRAPHS

ch	ck	sh	th
beach	block	brush	bath
church	lock	crash	cloth
couch	luck	dish	death
each	pick	fish	fifth
much	quack	fresh	growth
perch	quick	rash	mouth
reach	sack	splash	south
such	tock	swish	tooth
touch		trash	

ph	gh	ng
autograph	cough	bang
epitaph	enough	bring
graph	laugh	flung
hieroglyph	rough	gong
Joseph	slough	long
phonograph	tough	lung
telegraph	trough	sing
		swing
		wrong

VARIANT CONSONANT SOUNDS C - G - S

c = "k"	c = "s"	g = "g"	g = "j"
cab	cedar	gain	gelatin
cabin	ceiling	gallery	gem
cage	celery	galaxy	gene
cake	cell	gallon	general
calf	cellophane	gamble	generalization
camel	cemetery	game	generalize
camp	cent	gang	generally
can	center	gangster	generate
candy	centimeter	garden	generation
cap	centipede	gas	generator
car	central	gauze	generosity
card	century	gay	generous
carrot	cereal	gear	genial
cat	ceremony	geese	genie
cave	certain	get	genius
coach	certificate	gift	gentle
coal	cider	girl	gentleman
coast	cigar	glass	genuine
coat	cinnamon	globe	geography
cobra	citizen	glue	geometry
cobweb	city	goat	George
coconut	cylinder	gobble	Georgia
cocoon	cymbal	goblin	geranium
coffee	Cynthia	goggles	German
coin	cypress	gold	gesture
cold	dice	goldfish	giant
collar	face	golf	gigantic
collie	fence	gone	gin
color	ice	good	ginger
comb	juice	goose	gingerbread
cook	lace	gopher	gingersnap
cookie	mice	gorilla	giraffe
corn	nice	got	gym
couch	niece	gourd	gymnasium
cow	piece	guess	gymnastics
cube	place	guest	gyp
cup	race	guilt	gypsy
curb	twice	gulf	gyrate
curl	voice	gull	gyro
curtain		gum	
cushion		gumdrop	
cut		gun	
cute			

VARIANT CONSONANT SOUNDS
C - G - S

s = "s"	s = "z"	Words with both the hard & soft sounds:	
sack	adds	circle	ourselves
sad	as	circuit	
saddle	bears	circus	screams
safe	blames	civic	seas
sail	boys	cycle	season
sailor	brings	cyclops	sees
saint	bugs		smiles
salad	chains	garage	stars
sale	chairs	garbage	stories
salt	cheese	geography	strings
sandwich	cookies	gigantic	
sang	daisies		
sat	dogs		
satin	dreams		
saw	drives		
sea	ears		
seal	elves		
seat	ends		
second	eyes		
seed	fairies		
sell	families		
send	frogs		
set	girls		
seven	has		
sick	his		
silk	homes		
silver	jobs		
sing	learns		
sister	miles		
six	names		
so	oars		
soap	planes		
sock	please		
soda	rains		
sofa	smiles		
some	tails		
song	tease		
soup	trees		
suit	wars		
sun	whales		

SILENT CONSONANT LETTERS

wr	ck	igh	tch
wrack	block	bright	batch
wrangle	brick	daylight	blotch
wrangler	bucket	delight	catch
wrap	buckle	eight	catcher
wrapper	check	fight	ditch
wrapping	chick	freight	etch
wrath	click	fright	fetch
wreath	clock	headlight	hatch
wreck	cluck	high	hatching
wreckage	crack	highlight	hitch
wrecker	cricket	height	itch
wren	deck	highway	ketchup
wrench	duck	light	latch
wrestle	fleck	lighter	match
wretch	flick	lighthouse	notch
wriggle	freckle	lightning	patch
wring	kick	might	pitch
wringer	knock	moonlight	pitcher
wrinkle	lock	neigh	scotch
wrist	luck	neighbor	scratch
wristwatch	neck	nigh	sketch
write	nick	night	sketching
writer	nickel	nightgown	snatch
writhe	package	nightmare	snitch
writing	pick	right	splotch
written	pickle	sigh	stitch
wrong	quack	sleigh	stretch
wrote		slight	stretcher
wrought		straight	swatch
wrung		sunlight	switch
wry		thigh	twitch
		tight	watch
		tighten	witch
		tightrope	wretch
		weigh	

SILENT CONSONANT LETTERS

mb

bomb
climb
comb
crumb
dumb
honeycomb
lamb
limb
numb
plumber
plumbing
succumb
thumb
tomb

l

alm
almond
balk
balm
calf
calk
calm
chalk
embalm
folk
folklore
folktale
half
halfway
kinfolk
palm
psalm
qualm
stalk
talk
walk
yolk

gn

align
assign
benign
campaign
champagne
consign
design
designer
feign
foreign
gnash
gnarl
gnat
gnaw
gnome
gnu
lasagne
malign
realign
reign
resign
sign

p

psalm
pseudo
pseudonym
pshaw
psyche
psychiatrist
psychiatry
psychic
psychology
psycopathic
ptomain

h

aghast
ghastly
gherkin
ghetto
ghost
ghostly
ghoul
ghoulish
homage
honest
honor
honorable
honorary
hour
hourglass
hourly
oh
pharaoh
rhapsody
rhetoric
rheumatism
Rhine
rhinestone
rhinoceros
rhododendron
rhubarb
rhyme
rhyming
rhythm
thyme

mn

autumn
column
condemn
hymn
solemn

kn

knack
knapsack
knave
knead
knee
kneel
knelt
knew
knickers
knife
knight
knit
knob
knock
knocker
knoll
knot
knotty
know
knowing
knowledge
known
knuckle

s

aisle
Arkansas
corps
debris
Illinois
Iroquois
island
isle
lisle

SHORT VOWELS (V̆C pattern)

ă	ĕ	ĭ	ŏ	ŭ
add	bed	bib	blob	brush
ant	beg	brick	block	bud
ax	bell	bridge	blond	bug
back	belt	chick	Bob	bump
bag	bench	chin	bomb	bun
band	bend	clip	bond	bus
bat	bread	crib	box	club
bath	cell	dig	chop	crumb
black	cent	dish	clock	crust
calf	check	drink	cob	cub
cap	chef	fin	sop	cuff
calf	chess	fish	cot	cup
catch	chest	inch	crop	drum
crab	desk	ink	dock	duck
crack	dress	inn	dot	dust
dad	egg	itch	drop	fudge
dance	elf	kick	flock	gull
fan	fence	king	flop	gulp
fat	head	knit	fox	gum
flag	hem	lick	gold	gun
gas	hen	list	job	hub
glass	jet	milk	John	hug
half	left	mitt	jot	hut
ham	leg	mix	knob	judge
jacks	melt	pick	knock	jug
jam	neck	pig	knot	jump
lamb	nest	pink	lock	mud
lash	net	rich	lodge	muff
latch	pet	ring	lot	mug
mad	press	ship	mob	nun
man	red	sift	mod	plug
mat	shelf	sink	mop	plum
match	shell	spit	notch	punch
math	sled	split	odd	pup
pad	smell	spring	plot	rub
patch	stem	sting	pod	rug
plaid	step	swim	pond	run
quack	stretch	swing	pot	scrub
raft	sweat	switch	rob	shrub
rag	ten	thin	rock	shrug
rat	thread	twig	rod	shut
sack	twelve	twins	Scotch	such
sad	vest	whip	shock	suds
sag	web	wick	shop	sun
scab	well	wig	shot	thumb
scratch	wet	wink	sob	truck
spank		witch	sock	tub
splash			sod	tug
stab			stop	
tacks			top	
tag			trot	
van				

LONG VOWELS (c$\bar{\text{v}}$ pattern)

ā	ē	Ī	ō	ū
a	be	hi	fro	flu
	he		go	gnu
	me		ho	Lu
	she		Jo	tabu
	we		lo	
	ye		no	
			pro	
			so	
			yo-yo	

a̅ɪ	a̅y̶	e̅a̶	e̅e	e̅y̶
afraid	ashtray	beach	bee	abbey
ail	away	beak	beef	alley
aim	bay	beam	beet	bailey
bail	betray	bean	bleed	barley
bait	clay	beat	cheek	dickey
braid	day	bleach	cheese	donkey
brain	decay	cheap	chimpanzee	galley
chain	delay	cheat	creek	hackney
claim	dismay	clean	deep	hockey
contain	Friday	creak	eighteen	honey
drain	gay	cream	feed	jockey
explain	gray	crease	fourteen	journey
fail	halfway	dream	free	key
faith	hallway	east	freeze	kidney
frail	hay	eat	geese	medley
gain	highway	feast	greed	money
gait	hurray	flea	Greek	monkey
grain	inlay	freak	green	mopey
hail	jay	gleam	greet	motley
jail	Kay	grease	greeting	parsley
laid	lay	heal	heel	pokey
lain	may	heap	jeep	pulley
maid	mislay	heat	knee	Shelley
mail	Monday	jean	kneel	trolley
main	okay	leak	meet	turkey
Maine	pay	leap	parakeet	valley
mermaid	play	meal	peek	volley
nail	portray	meat	queen	
paid	pray	neat	screen	
pail	ray	pea	see	
pain	relay	peach	seed	
plain	say	pleat	sheet	
raid	slay	scream	sleep	
rail	spray	seal	sleeve	
rain	stay	seat	sneeze	
raise	stairway	sneak	speed	
regain	stray	speak	squeeze	
retail	subway	squeak	street	
sail	sway	steal	sweep	
snail	Thursday	steam	sweet	
Spain	today	streak	teeth	
sprain	tray	stream	three	
stain	Tuesday	tea	tree	
straight	way	teach	weed	
strait	Wednesday	teacher	week	
tail		team	wheel	
trail		treat		
wail		wheat		
wait		wreath		

LONG VOWELS

$\overline{i}\cancel{e}$	$\overline{o}\cancel{a}$	$\overline{o}\cancel{e}$	$\overline{u}\cancel{i}$	$\overline{u}e$
applied	approach	doe	bruise	avenue
complied	bloat	floe	bruit	barbecue
cried	boast	foe	cruise	blue
defied	boat	goes	fruit	cue
denied	charcoal	hoe	fruitful	due
die	cloak	Joe	juice	flue
died	coach	mistletoe	juicy	glue
dried	coal	Moe	nuisance	hue
fried	coast	Poe	pursuit	pursue
implied	coat	roe	recruit	residue
lie	croak	soe	sluice	revenue
lied	float	toe	suit	revue
magnified	foam	woe	suitor	subdue
modified	gloat			sue
multiplied	goal			Sue
occupied	goat			true
pie	groan			
pried	load			
purified	loaf			
qualified	loan			
relied	moan			
replied	moat			
spied	oaf			
supplied	oak			
terrified	oat			
tie	oath			
tied	poach			
tried	roach			
untie	road			
vie	roam			
	roast			
	soak			
	soap			
	throat			
	toad			
	toast			

LONG VOWELS (v̄c¢·pattern)

ā_¢	ē_¢	ī_¢	ō_¢	ū_¢
age	athlete	bike	awoke	abuse
bake	Cantonese	bride	bone	altitude
base	cede	dice	broke	assume
brake	Chinese	dime	choke	chute
cage	compete	dive	close	consume
cake	complete	file	coke	costume
cane	concede	fine	cone	crude
case	concrete	fire	dome	cube
cave	convene	hide	doze	cute
chase	eve	hike	drove	duke
crane	excrete	ice	explode	dune
date	extreme	kite	expose	exclude
drape	gangrene	knife	froze	excuse
face	gene	like	globe	execute
flake	impede	lime	hole	flute
flame	intervene	line	home	fume
frame	Irene	mice	hope	fuse
game	Japanese	mile	hose	huge
gate	kerosene	mine	joke	include
grape	obese	nine	mole	introduce
hate	obscene	pile	nose	intrude
lace	Pete	pine	note	June
lake	precede	pipe	phone	minute
make	pyrene	pride	poke	molecule
name	recede	prize	pole	mule
page	replete	rice	promote	mute
pale	scene	ripe	quote	nude
place	scheme	rise	robe	parachute
plane	secrete	shine	rode	produce
plate	serene	side	role	protrude
race	Siamese	slice	rope	reduce
rake	stampede	slide	rose	refuge
same	Steve	smile	shone	rude
scale	supreme	spice	slope	rule
scrape	theme	strike	smoke	salute
shade	these	tide	sole	seclude
shave	trapeze	tile	spoke	solitude
skate	Zeke	time	stole	spruce
snake		tribe	stone	substitute
space		twice	stroke	tube
stage		vine	throne	tune
state		white	tone	use
tape		wide	vote	yule
vase		wife	whole	
wake		wine	woke	
wave		wipe	yoke	
whale		wise	zone	
		write		

SHORT AND LONG VOWEL CHANGE

v̆c	cv̄	v̄∅	v̄c∉
am	a (letter)	aim	
at	a		ate
back			bake
bet	be	beet-beat	
bit			bite
bled		bleed	
bran		brain	
bred		breed	
can		cain	cane
clam		claim	
cot		coat	
cub			cube
cut			cute
den		dean	
dim			dime
fad			fade
fill			file
fin			fine
glob			globe
got	go	goat	
hat			hate
hep	he	heap	
hid	hi		hide
hit	hi		
hop	ho		hope
hug			huge
kit			kite
lid		lied	
mad		maid	made
man		main	mane
met	me	meat	mete
not	no		note
pad		paid	

v̆c	cv̄	v̄v̸	v̄ce̸
pal		pail	pale
pan		pain	pane
pet		peat	Pete
pill	pi		pile
pin	pi		pine
plan		plain	plane
ran		rain	
rip			ripe
rod		road	rode
run		ruin	
set		seat	
shell	she		she'll
shin			shine
sit			site
slid			slide
slop			slope
sop	so	soap	
stem		steam	
tap			tape
ten		teen	
them	the		theme
till			tile
Tim			time
tub			tube
us	u (letter)		use
van		vain	vane
wet	we		
win			wine

191

PRONUNCIATION RULES - EXCEPTIONS

$\underline{\breve{v}c}$	$\underline{\breve{v}c}$	$\underline{\breve{v}c}$	$\underline{c\bar{v}}$	$\underline{\bar{v}\cancel{v}}$	$\underline{\bar{v}\cancel{v}}$	$\underline{\bar{v}c\cancel{e}}$
bass	log	wild	do	again	laugh	approve
bind	long	wind	fe	ahead	lead	are
bold	loss	won	re	air	lei	aye
bolt	lost	yolk	se	aisle	lief	axe
boss	malt		si	apiece	lien	bare
broth	might		ski	appear	near	bathe
child	mild		the	area	neigh	beige
Christ	mold		to	bay	niece	caste
climb	molt		who	bear	pear	come
cloth	month			beau	piece	crepe
cold	most			been	pier	dare
colt	myth			beige	plaid	done
comb	night			bey	plaque	dove
cost	of			brae	prayer	eye
cross	oh			bread	pray	fare
dog	old			breast	prey	give
don't	pint			brief	priest	glove
droll	polk			build	queer	grease
fight	poll			built	rear	hare
find	post			buy	rein	have
flight	prof			cay	rough	hear
floss	right			cheer	said	live
fog	roll			chief	shriek	love
fold	Ruth			cough	sieve	matte
frog	scold			dead	skein	move
from	scroll			deaf	sleigh	none
frost	sigh			dear	square	one
ghost	sight			door	stair	pare
gold	sign			dread	steak	prove
gong	slosh			eight	tear	rare
gosh	smog			fear	their	scare
gross	sold			feud	they	seize
gym	song			field	thief	shove
high	strong			fierce	tier	some
hind	swamp			flair	touch	spare
hog	swatch			freight	veil	sphere
hold	thigh			great	view	stare
honk	tight			grey	wealth	suede
host	told			grieve	wear	tease
hymn	toll			guest	weigh	there
I'd	tomb			guild	weird	were
I'll	troll			guy	whey	where
I'm	'twas			hay	yea	
Job	wand			head	year	
John	was			health	you	
jolt	wasp			heir		
kind	watch			hey		

"R" CONTROLLED VOWELS

ar	er	ir	or	ur	(Special: ar="air" sound)
alarm	alert	affirm	afford	blur	air
arch	amber	aspirin	airport	burglar	aware
argue	anger	birch	before	burn	bare
arm	baker	bird	born	burp	beware
armor	banner	birth	chlorine	burr	blare
army	beaver	birthday	chore	burro	care
art	butter	chirp	chorus	burst	chair
artist	camper	circle	cord	church	compare
barber	chapter	circuit	core	churn	dare
bark	clerk	circus	corn	curb	declare
barn	cracker	confirm	divorce	curdle	eclair
car	dessert	dirt	door	current	fair
card	expert	dirty	dorm	curse	fare
carpet	fern	fir	explore	curtain	flair
cart	germ	firm	floral	curve	flare
cartoon	her	first	for	disturb	glare
charm	herd	flirt	force	flurry	hair
chart	iceberg	girdle	ford	fur	hare
dark	insert	girl	fork	furnace	impair
dart	jerk	irk	form	furniture	pair
farm	jeweler	Irving	fort	gurgle	pare
garage	kerchief	Kirk	forth	hurl	prepare
garbage	kernel	quirk	glory	hurry	rare
garden	merge	shirk	horn	hurt	repair
gargle	murder	shirt	horse	hurtle	scarce
guard	nerve	sir	lord	murder	scare
harbor	northern	skirt	meteor	nurse	share
hard	number	smirk	more	occur	snare
harm	perch	squirm	morning	perturb	spare
harp	perk	squirt	normal	purchase	square
jar	person	stir	north	purple	stair
large	prefer	stirrup	oral	purr	stare
marble	reverse	swirl	ore	purse	ware
march	scatter	third	perform	return	welfare
margin	serve	thirst	porch	scurry	
mark	swerve	thirteen	pork	sturdy	
marshal	term	thirty	port	suburb	
park	thermos	twirl	resort	surf	
parsley	tiger	whirl	score	surface	
partner	transfer		shore	surgeon	
shark	verb		short	turban	
smart	verse		snore	turbine	
spark	whisper		sore	turkey	
sparkle	worker		sort	turn	
star	zipper		sport	turtle	
starch			store	urban	
target			stork	urge	
varnish			storm	urgent	
war			story	urn	
			support		
			sword		

MISCELLANEOUS VOWEL SOUNDS

ȳ	y̆	ōw	ow	ou
apply	angry	below	allow	about
by	army	bellow	anyhow	aloud
bye	battery	billow	bowwow	announce
cry	beauty	blow	brow	blouse
cycle	berry	borrow	brown	bounce
cyclist	bunny	bow	chowder	bound
cyclone	canary	bungalow	clown	cloud
cypress	candy	crossbow	cow	couch
dry	carry	crow	cowboy	count
dynamite	cherry	elbow	crowd	crouch
eye	city	fellow	crown	doubt
fly	cloudy	flow	down	douse
fry	dirty	follow	downhill	foul
hybrid	dizzy	glow	downpour	found
hydrant	dusty	grow	downstairs	gouge
hydrogen	easy	Halloween	downtown	grouch
hyper	factory	know	drown	ground
hyphen	fairy	low	drowsy	hound
July	funny	marshmallow	eyebrow	house
lye	fuzzy	meadow	flower	joust
my	galaxy	minnow	fowl	loud
nylon	gravy	mow	frown	lounge
paralyze	happy	narrow	gown	louse
pry	heavy	overflow	how	mound
python	hungry	pillow	howl	mount
rhyme	icy	pillowcase	now	mouse
rye	ivy	rainbow	owl	mouth
shy	jelly	row	plow	ouch
sly	jewelry	rowboat	pow	ounce
spy	juicy	scarecrow	powder	out
sty	lady	shadow	power	outlet
style	lucky	shallow	powwow	pouch
styrofoam	marry	show	prowl	pound
supply	muddy	slow	shower	pout
terrify	navy	sorrow	snowplow	pronounce
try	penny	sow	somehow	round
type	pony	sparrow	towel	route
typist	pretty	stow	tower	scout
why	puppy	swallow	town	shout
	rusty	throw	vow	slouch
	sandy	tomorrow	vowel	sound
	shiny	tow	wow	south
	sleepy	wallow	yowl	spout
	snowy	willow		sprout
	tardy	window		trout
	thirsty	yellow		voucher
	tiny			without
	ugly			wound
	wavy			
	windy			

MISCELLANEOUS VOWEL SOUNDS

ō͞u	ough	o͞u	ew	oi
boulder	cough	bayou	blew	appoint
dough	enough	coup	brew	asteroid
doughnut	rough	couth	chew	avoid
doughy	tough	ghoul	crew	boil
mould	trough	pouf	crewel	broil
moulder		rouge	dew	choice
moult		slough	drew	coil
poultice		through	few	coin
poultry		wound	flew	Detroit
soul		you	grew	disappoint
soulful		youth	hew	doily
thorough			jewel	embroidery
			knew	exploit
			mew	foil
			new	groin
			newt	hoist
			pew	Illinois
			preview	join
			review	joint
			screw	loiter
			shrew	moist
			skew	needlepoint
ē͞i	ei=(ā)		slew	noise
			spew	oil
ceiling	beige		stew	oink
conceive	chow mein		steward	point
deceive	eight		stewardess	poise
either	feign		strew	poison
leisure	feint		strewn	rejoice
neither	freight		threw	sirloin
perceive	lei		view	soil
protein	neigh		whew	spoil
receive	reign		withdrew	tenderloin
seize	rein		yew	toil
seizing	skein			toilet
seizure	sleigh			viewpoint
sheik	veil			voice
Sheila	vein			void
	weigh			voile
	weight			

195

MISCELLANEOUS VOWEL SOUNDS

oy	au	aw	oo	oo̮
alloy	applaud	awe	balloon	book
annoy	applause	awful	bloom	booklet
boy	assault	awning	boot	brook
buoy	astronaut	bawl	broom	cook
convoy	audit	brawl	caboose	cookbook
corduroy	Audrey	brawn	cartoon	cookie
cowboy	August	claw	choose	crook
coy	auto	coleslaw	cocoon	driftwood
decoy	because	crawl	cool	fatherhood
destroy	caught	dawdle	cuckoo	firewood
employ	cause	dawn	food	fishhook
employee	Claude	draw	goose	foot
enjoy	clause	drawer	groom	good
foyer	default	drawl	hoof	goody
joy	defraud	drawn	igloo	hood
Joyce	distraught	fawn	kangaroo	hook
joyful	exhaust	flaw	loom	look
loyal	fraught	gnaw	loop	motherhood
oyster	fault	hawk	loose	plywood
ploy	flaunt	heehaw	moon	pocketbook
Rolls Royce	fraud	jaw	moose	rookie
Roy	haul	law	noon	shook
royal	haunt	lawful	pool	soot
soy	jaunty	lawn	raccoon	stood
tomboy	launch	Lawrence	rooster	took
toy	laundry	mother-in-law	school	withstood
Troy	maraud	outlaw	scoop	wood
voyage	Maude	pawn	scooter	wooden
	maul	raw	shampoo	woof
	Milwaukee	saw	shoot	wool
	naughty	scrawl	smooth	
	overhaul	scrawly	snooze	
	Paul	scrawny	soon	
	pause	seesaw	spook	
	Santa Claus	shawl	spool	
	sauce	sprawl	spoon	
	saunter	squaw	tattoo	
	somersault	straw	teaspoon	
	taught	tawny	too	
	taunt	thaw	tooth	
	taut	tomahawk	troop	
	trauma	withdraw	zoo	
	vault	yawn		

MISCELLANEOUS VOWEL SOUNDS

ēₐ	ĕₐ	ₑā	īₑ	īē
beach	bread	break	applied	achieve
bead	breast	great	cried	apiece
beagle	breath	steak	die	babies
beak	dead		died	bakeries
bean	deaf		dried	belief
beast	death		fried	believe
beat	dread		lie	berries
beaver	feather		lied	brief
bleach	gingerbread		modified	buggies
cheap	head		necktie	canaries
clean	health		pie	candies
cream	heather		pliers	carries
deal	heaven		pried	chief
dream	homestead		relied	cities
eagle	instead		replied	cookies
east	jealous		satisfied	fairies
feast	lead	**al**	specified	field
flea	leather		spied	grief
gleam	leaven	all	tie	grieve
grease	meant	almost	tied	groceries
heal	measure	already	tried	handkerchief
heat	peasant	alright	vie	hygiene
jeans	pheasant	also		ladies
league	pleasant	altar		niece
lean	pleasure	alter		parties
leap	read	altogether		pennies
leave	ready	always		piece
meal	spread	bald		priest
meat	stealthy	balk		rabies
peach	sweat	ball		relief
peak	thread	baseball		relieve
please	threat	basketball		retrieve
pleat	tread	call		siege
read	treasure	enthrall		shield
scream	wealth	exalt		shriek
sea	weather	fall		spiel
seal	widespread	false		wield
seat	zealous	football		yield
speak		hall		
squeak		halt		
steal		malt		
steam		recall		
stream		salt		
tea		scald		
teach		small		
team		snowball		
weak		snowfall		
wheat		stall		
wreath		squall		
		wall		
		waltz		
		waterfall		

RHYMING WORDS

ā	ād	āj	āk	āl	ām
bay	aid	age	ache	fail	aim
clay	braid	cage	bake	jail	blame
day	fade	gauge	break	mail	came
gay	grade	page	cake	nail	fame
hay	laid	rage	lake	pale	flame
jay	made	sage	make	sale	game
lay	paid	stage	rake	scale	name
pay	raid	wage	snake	snail	same
play	shade		steak	tail	shame
ray	trade		take	whale	
say			wake		
tray					

ān	āp	ās	āt	āv	āz
brain	ape	base	date	brave	blaze
chain	cape	brace	eight	cave	glaze
crane	crepe	chase	gate	crave	graze
drain	drape	face	great	gave	haze
gain	grape	lace	hate	pave	phase
lane	scrape	place	late	save	phrase
main	shape	race	plate	shave	praise
pain	tape	space	skate	slave	raise
plane		trace	straight	wave	
rain		vase	wait		
train					

ăch	ăd	ăg	ăk	ăm	ămp
batch	add	bag	back	am	camp
catch	bad	brag	black	clam	champ
hatch	dad	drag	crack	dam	clamp
latch	glad	flag	jack	ham	damp
match	had	gag	pack	jam	lamp
patch	mad	nag	quack	lamb	ramp
scratch	plaid	rag	rack	ram	stamp
snatch	sad	sag	sack	slam	tramp
		snag	snack	swam	
		wag	tack		

ăn	ănd	ăng	ănk	ăp	ăs
can	and	bang	bank	cap	bass
fan	band	clang	blank	clap	brass
man	brand	gang	clank	flap	class
pan	grand	hang	crank	lap	gas
plan	hand	rang	rank	map	glass
ran	land	sang	sank	nap	grass
tan	sand	slang	spank	snap	lass
van	stand		tank	tap	mass
			thank	trap	pass
				wrap	

RHYMING WORDS

ăsh	ē	ēd	ēf	ēl	ēm
ash	bee	bead	beef	deal	beam
cash	fee	bleed	brief	feel	cream
crash	he	feed	chief	heel	dream
dash	key	lead	grief	kneel	gleam
flash	knee	need	leaf	meal	scheme
gash	me	plead	reef	peel	scream
lash	sea	read	thief	seal	seem
mash	she	seed		squeal	steam
rash	tea	weed		steal	theme
smash	we			wheel	
splash					

ēp	ēs	ēt	ēz	ĕd	ĕk
cheap	cease	beat	breeze	bed	check
creep	crease	cheat	cheese	bread	deck
deep	geese	eat	freeze	fed	fleck
jeep	grease	feet	please	fled	neck
keep	lease	greet	seize	head	peck
leap	niece	heat	sneeze	led	speck
sheep	peace	meat	squeeze	red	wreck
sleep	piece	neat	tease	said	
sweep		sheet	these	sled	
weep		street		spread	
		sweet		thread	

ĕl	ĕn	ĕnd	ĕs	ĕst	ĕt
bell	den	bend	bless	best	bet
fell	hen	blend	chess	blessed	get
sell	men	end	dress	chest	jet
shell	pen	friend	guess	guest	let
smell	ten	lend	less	nest	met
spell	then	mend	mess	pest	net
tell	when	send	press	quest	pet
well	wren	spend	stress	rest	set
yell		tend	yes	test	wet
				west	yet

ī	īd	īl	īm	īn	īnd
buy	bride	aisle	climb	dine	bind
die	cried	file	crime	fine	blind
guy	hide	mile	dime	line	dined
high	lied	pile	grime	mine	find
lie	pride	smile	I'm	nine	grind
my	ride	style	lime	pine	kind
pie	side	tile	rhyme	shine	mind
sky	tide	while	time	spine	signed
spy	wide			vine	wind
tie				wine	
why					

199

RHYMING WORDS

īs	īt	ĭch	ĭd	ĭg	ĭk
dice	bite	ditch	bid	big	brick
ice	fight	hitch	did	dig	chick
mice	kite	itch	hid	fig	kick
nice	light	pitch	kid	jig	lick
price	might	rich	lid	pig	pick
rice	night	stitch	rid	sprig	quick
slice	sight	switch	skid	twig	sick
spice	white	witch	slid	wig	thick
twice	write				trick

ĭl	ĭlt	ĭm	ĭn	ĭng	ĭnk
bill	built	dim	been	bring	blink
chill	guilt	gym	chin	cling	clink
fill	kilt	him	fin	fling	drink
hill	quilt	limb	in	king	ink
ill	spilt	rim	pin	ring	link
kill	stilt	skim	skin	sing	mink
pill	tilt	slim	spin	spring	pink
spill	wilt	swim	thin	string	shrink
still		trim	twin	thing	sink
will			win	wing	think

ĭnt	ĭp	ĭst	ĭt	ō	ōd
flint	dip	fist	bit	crow	code
glint	drip	hissed	fit	dough	crowed
hint	flip	kissed	hit	flow	load
lint	lip	list	kit	go	mowed
mint	rip	missed	knit	low	road
print	sip	mist	mitt	mow	slowed
quint	skip	twist	pit	no	snowed
splint	slip	wrist	quit	oh	strode
squint	trip		sit	row	toad
tint	zip		split	so	
				throw	

ōk	ōl	ōld	ōm	ōn	ōp
broke	bowl	bold	chrome	lone	cope
choke	coal	cold	comb	cone	dope
croak	goal	fold	dome	flown	hope
folk	hole	gold	foam	groan	pope
joke	mole	hold	gnome	loan	rope
poke	poll	mold	home	moan	scope
smoke	role	old	roam	own	slope
soak	scroll	scold		phone	soap
stroke	troll	sold		stone	
	whole	told		throne	

RHYMING WORDS

ōst	ōt	ōz	ŏb	ŏg	ŏk
boast	boat	chose	blob	bog	block
coast	coat	clothes	cob	dog	clock
dosed	goat	doze	job	fog	dock
ghost	note	goes	knob	frog	flock
host	oat	hose	mob	hog	knock
most	quote	nose	rob	jog	lock
post	throat	rose	slob	log	rock
roast	vote	those	snob	smog	sock
toast	wrote	toes	sob		

ŏl	ŏp	ŏt	ū	ūl	ūm
ball	chop	blot	blue	cool	boom
call	drop	cot	chew	drool	broom
crawl	flop	dot	do	fool	gloom
fall	hop	got	glue	pool	groom
hall	mop	hot	new	rule	loom
shawl	pop	knot	shoe	school	plume
small	shop	lot	too	spool	room
tall	stop	pot	who	stool	tomb
wall	top	shot	you	tool	zoom
		tot			

ūn	ūp	ūs	ūt	ūz	ŭb
dune	coop	goose	boot	bruise	club
June	hoop	juice	chute	choose	cub
moon	loop	loose	flute	cruise	hub
noon	scoop	moose	hoot	lose	rub
prune	snoop	spruce	loot	news	scrub
soon	soup	truce	root	ooze	shrub
spoon	swoop	use	shoot	shoes	snub
tune	troop		toot	snooze	stub
				whose	sub
				zoos	tub

ŭch	ŭf	ŭg	ŭk	ŭm	ŭmp
clutch	bluff	bug	cluck	bum	bump
crutch	cuff	chug	duck	come	dump
Dutch	fluff	dug	luck	crumb	hump
hutch	huff	hug	pluck	drum	jump
much	muff	jug	stuck	dumb	lump
such	puff	lug	suck	gum	plump
touch	rough	mug	truck	hum	pump
	scuff	rug	tuck	plum	stump
	stuff	shrug		some	
	tough	rug		thumb	

201

RHYMING WORDS

ŭnch	ŭng	ŭnk	ŭsh	ŭst	ŭt
brunch	clung	bunk	blush	bust	but
bunch	flung	chunk	brush	crust	cut
crunch	hung	drunk	crush	dust	gut
hunch	rung	dunk	flush	gust	hut
lunch	sprung	flunk	gush	just	jut
munch	strung	junk	hush	rust	mutt
punch	stung	monk	mush	thrust	nut
scrunch	tongue	skunk	rush	trust	rut
	young	sunk	slush		shut
		trunk	thrush		what

oil	ou	ouch	oun	ound	out
boil	bough	couch	brown	bound	doubt
broil	brow	crouch	clown	found	out
coil	chow	grouch	crown	ground	pout
foil	cow	ouch	down	hound	scout
oil	how	pouch	drown	mound	shout
soil	now	slouch	frown	pound	snout
spoil	plow	vouch	gown	round	spout
toil	vow		noun	sound	sprout
voile	wow		town	wound	trout

al	aw	ar	er	or	orn
all	claw	air	cheer	core	born
ball	draw	bear	clear	door	corn
call	flaw	care	dear	floor	horn
crawl	jaw	chair	ear	four	scorn
fall	law	fair	fear	more	shorn
hall	paw	hair	here	oar	thorn
shawl	raw	pear	near	pour	torn
small	saw	scare	peer	roar	worn
tall	straw	share	queer	score	
wall	thaw	square	spear	snore	
		there	tear	store	

ur	urk	urs
blur	clerk	curse
fur	irk	hearse
her	jerk	nurse
purr	lurk	purse
sir	perk	terse
slur	smirk	verse
stir	work	worse
were		

COMPOUND WORDS

afternoon
afterthought
aircraft
airplane
airport
anteater
anybody
anyhow
anyone
anything
anywhere
archway
armchair
backbone
backfield
backfire
background
backhand
backstroke
backward
bagpipe
bareback
barnyard
baseball
baseboard
basketball
bathrobe
bathroom
battlefield
battleship
bayberry
bedclothes
bedrock
bedroom
bedside
bedspread
bedtime
beefsteak
beehive
beeline
beeswax
billboard
birdbath
birdhouse
birthday
birthplace
blackberry
blackbird
blackboard
blackout
blacksmith
blindfold
bloodhound

blueberry
bluebird
blueprint
boathouse
bombshell
bookcase
bookkeeper
bookmark
bookworm
boxcar
breakdown
bridegroom
bridesmaid
broadcast
broomstick
buckshot
buckwheat
bulldog
bullfight
butterfly
buttermilk
buttonhole
campfire
candlelight
candlestick
cardboard
carload
chairman
checkerboard
chopsticks
classmate
classroom
clothespin
collarbone
cornbread
corncob
corncrib
cornfield
courthouse
courtyard
cowboy
crossword
daydream
daylight
daytime
doghouse
doorbell
doorstep
doorway
doughnut
downfall
downhill
downstairs

downtown
dragonfly
driveway
drugstore
drumstick
earache
eardrum
earphone
earthquake
evergreen
everybody
eyeball
eyebrow
eyelash
eyelid
eyesight
farmhouse
firecracker
firefly
fireman
fireplace
firewood
fisherman
flashlight
football
footprint
footstep
gingerbread
goldfish
grandmother
grapefruit
grapevine
grownup
gumdrop
hairpin
handcuff
handkerchief
headache
headlight
headline
highway
homemade
homesick
honeybee
honeymoon
horseback
horseshoe
houseboat
housewife
housework
jackknife
jellyfish
keyboard

keyhole
landscape
lifetime
lighthouse
lookout
milkman
moonlight
motorboat
motorcycle
mousetrap
necklace
necktie
newspaper
nightgown
notebook
outdoor
outfield
outside
overcoat
overhand
overlook
overnight
overtime
overweight
pancake
patrolman
pickpocket
pillowcase
pitchfork
playground
playhouse
pocketbook
pocketknife
policeman
popcorn
postman
rainbow
raindrop
rainfall
roadside
roommate
rosebud
rosebush
rowboat
runaway
salesman
sandpaper
saucepan
sawdust
scarecrow
schoolbook
schoolroom
schoolteacher

COMPOUND WORDS

schoolyard	spaceship	teacup	watchman
seashore	springtime	teakettle	waterfall
seaweed	staircase	teaspoon	watermelon
shopkeeper	starfish	textbook	weekday
sidewalk	steamboat	thunderstorm	wildcat
skyline	stepladder	tightrope	wildlife
skyscraper	storeroom	tomcat	windmill
smokestack	storybook	toothache	windowpane
snapshot	strawberry	toothbrush	wishbone
snowball	sunburn	toothpaste	wintertime
snowfall	Sunday	toothpick	without
snowflake	sunflower	tugboat	workday
snowplow	sunlight	undershirt	workman
snowshoe	sunshine	underwear	wristwatch
somebody	sweetheart	upstairs	
someone	tablespoon	wallpaper	
something	taxicab	watchdog	

CONTRACTIONS

not	have	will	is
aren't	I've	he'll	he's
can't	they've	I'll	here's
couldn't	we've	she'll	it's
didn't	you've	they'll	one's
doesn't		we'll	she's
don't		you'll	that's
hadn't			there's
hasn't			what's
haven't			when's
isn't			where's
mustn't	would	are	who's
shouldn't			
wasn't			
weren't	he'd	they're	
won't	I'd	we're	
wouldn't	she'd	you're	
	they'd		
	we'd		
	you'd		

PLURAL FORMS

Note: (→ change to)   (+ add)

root + s

acorn-acorns
angel-angels
animal-animals
apple-apples
bag-bags
ball-balls
barn-barns
bat-bats
bed-beds
book-books
boy-boys
cat-cats
chair-chairs
cow-cows
desk-desks
dog-dogs
duck-ducks
egg-eggs
fan-fans
flag-flags
frog-frogs
gift-gifts
hand-hands
hat-hats
idea-ideas
job-jobs
kite-kites
lamp-lamps
lion-lions
marble-marbles
meat-meats
mitten-mittens
nail-nails
pan-pans
pin-pins
plate-plates
queen-queens
shoe-shoes
table-tables
tent-tents
tire-tires
tree-trees
umbrella-umbrellas
vine-vines
wagon-wagons
wall-walls
weed-weeds

y → i + es

army-armies
baby-babies
bakery-bakeries
battery-batteries
berry-berries
body-bodies
bunny-bunnies
canary-canaries
candy-candies
cherry-cherries
city-cities
company-companies
cooky-cookies
daisy-daisies
enemy-enemies
family-families
galaxy-galaxies
grocery-groceries
injury-injuries
lady-ladies
money-monies
multiply-multiplies
party-parties
penny-pennies
puppy-puppies
salary-salaries
sky-skies
spy-spies
story-stories
study-studies
treaty-treaties
victory-victories

s + es

address-addresses
boss-bosses
bus-buses
business-businesses
campus-campuses
circus-circuses
class-classes
compass-compasses
cross-crosses
dress-dresses
gas-gases
genius-geniuses
glass-glasses
grass-grasses
guess-guesses
kiss-kisses
mass-masses
miss-misses
moss-mosses
pass-passes
princess-princesses
process-processes
sickness-sicknesses
sinus-sinuses
stewardess-stewardesses
success-successes
thermos-thermoses
trespass-trespasses
virus-viruses
waitress-waitresses
witness-witnesses
yes-yeses

Note: (—→ change to)   (+ add)

sh + es

ash-ashes
brush-brushes
bush-bushes
dish-dishes
finish-finishes
fish-fishes
flash-flashes
galosh-galoshes
gash-gashes
leash-leashes
marsh-marshes
mesh-meshes
polish-polishes
rash-rashes
relish-relishes
rush-rushes
sash-sashes
slash-slashes
splash-splashes
wish-wishes

ch + es

arch-arches
batch-batches
beach-beaches
bench-benches
bleach-bleaches
branch-branches
church-churches
couch-couches
crutch-crutches
ditch-ditches
hatch-hatches
hutch-hutches
inch-inches
latch-latches
march-marches
match-matches
patch-patches
peach-peaches
pinch-pinches
pitch-pitches
punch-punches
ranch-ranches
reach-reaches
rich-riches
scratch-scratches
search-searches
sketch-sketches
speech-speeches
stitch-stitches
stretch-stretches
torch-torches
touch-touches
watch-watches
witch-witches

x + es

affix-affixes
annex-annexes
appendix-appendixes
ax-axes
box-boxes
duplex-duplexes
fox-foxes
index-indexes
mailbox-mailboxes
mix-mixes
prefix-prefixes
sandbox-sandboxes
sex-sexes
six-sixes
suffix-suffixes
wax-waxes

PLURAL FORMS

Note: (→ change to)   (+ add)

z + es	f, fe → ve + s	or retain f + s
buzz-buzzes	calf-calves	belief-beliefs
fizz-fizzes	dwarf-dwarves	bluff-bluffs
frizz-frizzes	elf-elves	brief-briefs
fuzz-fuzzes	half-halves	chef-chefs
jazz-jazzes	hoof-hooves	chief-chiefs
quiz-quizzes	knife-knives	clef-clefs
razz-razzes	leaf-leaves	cliff-cliffs
waltz-waltzes	life-lives	cuff-cuffs
whiz-whizzes	loaf-loaves	fluff-fluffs
	oaf-oaves	goof-goofs
	ourself-ourselves	gulf-gulfs
	scarf-scarves	huff-huffs
	self-selves	kerchief-kerchiefs
	sheaf-sheaves	motif-motifs
	shelf-shelves	muff-muffs
	thief-thieves	puff-puffs
	wife-wives	rebuff-rebuffs
	wolf-wolves	reef-reefs
	yourself-yourselves	relief-reliefs
		riff-riffs
		roof-roofs
		skiff-skiffs
		sniff-sniffs
		staff-staffs
		stiff-stiffs
		tiff-tiffs
		whiff-whiffs

Irregulars

binoculars
clothes
deer
fish
grapefruit
locust
moose
pajamas
pants
scissors
sheep
shorts
shrimp
tongs
trousers
tweezers
analysis-analyses
axis-axes
basis-bases
cactus-cacti
child-children

crisis-crises
datum-data
foot-feet
formula-formulae
fungus-fungi
goose-geese
hippopotamus-hippopotami
locus-loci
man-men
medium-media
memorandum-memoranda
mouse-mice
nucleus-nuclei
oasis-oases
ox-oxen
phenomenon-phenomena
radius-radii
stimulus-stimuli
tooth-teeth
woman-women

POSSESSIVES

's	's	'	'
(nouns, names & irregular plurals)	(monosyllabic singular nouns ending in -s)	(regular plurals)	(plurals of proper nouns)
bee's	bass's	arms'	Appalachian Mountains'
boy's	boss's	babies'	Bahamas'
cat's	bus's	bats'	Barkers'
children's	chess's	boys'	Black Hills'
coat's	class's	cats'	Browns'
deer's	cross's	chairs'	Carsons'
dog's	dress's	cows'	Great Lakes'
flower's	floss's	dogs'	Hawaiian Islands'
geese's	glass's	elves'	Indiana Dunes'
girl's	grass's	enemies'	Johnsons'
goat's	mass's	fairies'	Joneses'
horse's	miss's	families'	Kennedys'
Jill's	Ross's	fingers'	Morgans'
John's	Russ's	girls'	Peabodys'
Karen's	sis's	glasses'	Rocky Mountains'
lamp's		heads'	Smiths'
Mary's		hills'	Smoky Mountains'
men's		islands'	Thompsons'
mother's		ladies'	United States'
nail's		lambs'	Virgin Islands'
oxen's		nurses'	West Indies'
Pat's		plates'	Whites'
pony's		ponds'	
queen's		puppies'	
rat's		rabbits'	
sheep's		shelves'	
Sue's		snakes'	
tree's		thumbs'	
women's		turkeys'	
		turtles'	
		wolves'	

IRREGULARS

her
hers
his
its
mine
my
our
ours
their
whose
your
yours

208

```
                    ┌─────────────────────┐
                    │    VERB FORMS       │
                    │ PRESENT TENSE ( -s ) │
                    └─────────────────────┘
```

① root alone with   ② add -s with   ③ add, -es after
  I, we, or they   he, she, or   x, z, ch & sh
                            it

bake   bakes
cough   coughs
drink   drinks
eat   eats
fold   folds
give   gives
grow   grows
help   helps
jump   jumps
laugh   laughs
look   looks
paint   paints
play   plays
rain   rains
ride   rides
run   runs
sing   sings
tell   tells
thank   thanks
walk   walks
write   writes
attach   attaches
bleach   bleaches
brush   brushes
buzz   buzzes
catch   catches
dash   dashes
finish   finishes
fizz   fizzes
flash   flashes
hatch   hatches
march   marches
match   matches
mix   mixes
punch   punches
scratch   scratches
search   searches
splash   splashes
teach   teaches
touch   touches
watch   watches

209
```
```

```
┌─────────────────────────────────┐
│         VERB FORMS              │
│  PRESENT PARTICIPLE ( -ing )    │
└─────────────────────────────────┘
```

① -ing to a root word ending in any vowel except silent e in v̄c¢ pattern

② -ing to the "vvc" pattern

③ -ing to the vcc pattern

agree-agreeing	aim-aiming	back-backing
be-being	bleed-bleeding	bark-barking
blow-blowing	clean-cleaning	bend-bending
cry-crying	coast-coasting	check-checking
delay-delaying	drain-draining	crack-cracking
do-doing	dream-dreaming	farm-farming
fray-fraying	fail-failing	jump-jumping
fry-frying	feed-feeding	knock-knocking
know-knowing	keep-keeping	lock-locking
look-looking	need-needing	melt-melting
mow-mowing	paint-painting	park-parking
pay-paying	rain-raining	rent-renting
play-playing	read-reading	ring-ringing
pray-praying	roar-roaring	send-sending
pry-prying	roast-roasting	snack-snacking
say-saying	sail-sailing	spring-springing
see-seeing	scream-screaming	stamp-stamping
snow-snowing	sneak-sneaking	stand-standing
stay-staying	speed-speeding	tick-ticking
throw-throwing	steal-stealing	wink-winking
try-trying	weep-weeping	

④ drop final silent e and add -ing

⑤ v̆c double final consonant and add -ing

bake-baking	beg-begging
close-closing	blur-blurring
dive-diving	dot-dotting
drive-driving	fog-fogging
fade-fading	grab-grabbing
freeze-freezing	hop-hopping
grease-greasing	hug-hugging
hope-hoping	jog-jogging
ice-icing	kid-kidding
paste-pasting	mop-mopping
poke-poking	pop-popping
race-racing	rub-rubbing
score-scoring	run-running
share-sharing	stir-stirring
shine-shining	swap-swapping
time-timing	top-topping
type-typing	trot-trotting
use-using	
waste-wasting	
weave-weaving	

```
                    ┌─────────────────────┐
                    │   VERB FORMS        │
                    │ PAST TENSE ( -ed )  │
                    └─────────────────────┘
```

① double final consonant and add -ed

beg-begged
chip-chipped
chop-chopped
drop-dropped
fib-fibbed
grin-grinned
jam-jammed
knit-knitted
plan-planned
scrub-scrubbed
sip-sipped
sob-sobbed
stir-stirred
stun-stunned
trot-trotted

② in cy pattern change y to i and add -ed

apply-applied
bury-buried
cry-cried
deny-denied
dry-dried
ferry-ferried
fry-fried
marry-married
muddy-muddied
occupy-occupied
pry-pried
reply-replied
spy-spied
tidy-tidied
try-tried

③ in vowel + y pattern add -ed

annoy-annoyed
convey-conveyed
delay-delayed
destroy-destroyed
dismay-dismayed
employ-employed
enjoy-enjoyed
key-keyed
okay-okayed
play-played
pray-prayed
relay-relayed
stay-stayed
stray-strayed
survey-surveyed

④ final silent e add d

bake-baked
bounce-bounced
choke-choked
dine-dined
guide-guided
live-lived
pile-piled
pledge-pledged
score-scored
slice-sliced
smile-smiled
smoke-smoked
time-timed
trade-traded
wipe-wiped

⑤ Exceptions

are-were
bend-bent
bind-bound
bring-brought
build-built
buy-bought
can-could
catch-caught
cling-clung
come-came
creep-crept
deal-dealt
dig-dug
dream-dreamt
feed-fed
feel-felt
fight-fought
find-found
flee-fled
fling-flung
grind-ground
hang-hunt
have-had
hear-heard
hold-held
is-was
keep-kept
kneel-knelt

lay-laid
lead-led
leave-left
lend-lent
light-lit
lose-lost
make-made
mean-meant
meet-met
pay-paid
read-read
say-said
seek-sought
sell-sold
send-sent
shoot-shot
sleep-slept
slide-slid
sling-slung
spend-spent
spin-spun
stand-stood
stick-stuck
sting-stung
strike-struck
string-strung
sweep-swept
swing-swung

teach-taught
tell-told
think-thought
weep-wept
win-won
wind-wound
wring-wrung

211

Prefix	Meaning	Examples
a- ab-	away from	apart absent above abstract
a- ad- ap- at-	to, toward	advance adhere advertise attend appall apparatus appoint attach
amphi- ambi-	around	amphitheater amphibian ambidextrous ambition ambiguous
ante-	before	anteroom antecedent antedate
anti-	against, oppose	antifreeze antitrust antiwar
be-	by	beside between behave beneath
bi-	two, twice	bicycle biplane bifocal biweekly
circum-	around	circumstance circumspect circumference
co- com- cor- con- col-	with, together	cooperate coeducation combat combine commercial common correct correspond conflict conduct congress collect
contra-	against	contradict contrast contravene
de-	away, against	depart decay decease defend deform
dia-	around, through	diameter diagonal diagram diaphragm
dis- di-	apart, not	digest dimension divide disagree discourage dishonest dispose
en- em-	in, into	enforce envelope emphasis embark
epi-	upon	epidermis epidemic epigram
e- ex-	out of	emit evict event exit export expose
hetero-	different	heteronym heterogeneous
homo-	same	homonym homogeneous homogenize
in- im-	in, into	incision incline incorporate indent impress improve impulse
in- im- il- ir-	not	inactive indefinite imperfect illegal immortal irregular irresponsible
inter-	between	intermission international interrupt
intra- intro	inside	intramural intravenous introduce
mis-	wrong	mistreat misspell mistake misread
mono-	one, single	monotone monograph monopoly monorail
non-	not	nonconformist nonsense nonfiction
ob- of- op-	against	obstacle object offense opposition
pan-	whole	panorama pantomime pantheon
per-	through, fully	persecute permit perfect persist
peri-	around	perimeter periscope period

Prefix	Meaning	Examples
post-	after, behind	postscript postpone posterior
pre-	before	prefix preview predict prevent
pro-	in front of	profuse profit produce project
re-	again, back	repeat report retract return
se-	aside	secure segregation secret
semi-	half, partly	semicircle semimonthly semiprivate
sub-	under	submarine subtract substitute
super-	over	supernatural superintendent supervise
syn-	with, together	synonym synchronize synthesize
trans-	across, beyond	transport transfer transparent
tri	three	tricycle tripod triangle trinity
ultra-	beyond	ultraviolet ultramodern ultraism
un-	not	uncertain unhappy uncomfortable

COMMON ROOT WORDS (for affixation)

Root	Meaning	Root	Meaning
agon	struggle	cede, ceed,cess / to go, yield	
agra	field	celer	fast
all	other	cell	to hide, room
alt	high	cent	hundred
am	to love	centr	center
ambul	to walk	cern,cert	to make certain
andr	man	charge	to load
angel	messenger, angel	chrom, chro	color
angul	angle	chron	time
anima	spirit	-cide, cis	to kill, cut
ann, enn	year	circul	round
annel,annul	ring	civ	citizen
anthrop	man	clam, claim	to shout
apt, ept	to adjust, fit	clar	clear
aqua	water	clean	clean
arch	first, to rule	cleav	to split, stick
are	space	clin, climat	to lean, slope
arithm	number	cloth	cloth
arm	weapon, arm	clud,clus,close / to close	
art	skill, craft	cogn	to know
aster, astr	star	coll	glue
athl	contest, prize	color	color
atm	breath	come	to come
audi	to hear	cord	heart
avi	bird	corp	body
		cover	cover, hide
back	back	creat	to make
bak	to bake	cred	to believe
ball	ball	crease	to grow
ban	proclaim, banish	cri	to judge
barr	to obstruct	crimin	charge, crime
bat	to strike	cumul	heap
bell	beautiful / war	cur	care
bid, bead	to ask, pray	cur, course	to run
bide	to stay	cuss	to strike
bind (bin)	to bind	cycl	circle
bio	life		
brac	arm	day	day
brek, ea o	to break	dei, div	God
brev	short	del	to destroy
burn, bran	to burn	dem	to judge
		demo	people
cad,cid,cas	to fall, happen	dent	tooth
camp	field	derm	skin
can, cyn	dog	desire	to want
cap	cape	dict	to speak
cap,cip,cept,ceive / to take		doc	to teach
capit	head	dom	home
carn	flesh, meat	domin	master
cav	hollow	dos, dot	to give

Root	Meaning	Root	Meaning
drif	to drive	graph,gram	to write
drink	to drink	grat	thankful, free
duc	to lead	grav	to dig, to weigh
dur	hard, lasting	greg	flock
ego	self	hab	to have
electr	electric	hald (hold)	to hold
empt	to buy, take	hav	to have
equ	equal (horse)	her	to hear
erg, urg	work, power	her, hes	to stick
err	to wander	homo	man
ess, ent	to be	hum	liquid
eth	character, custom	hunt	to pursue,seize
fa, fess	to speak	ident	same
fac,fic,fect / to do, to make		integr	whole
fac	face	it	to go
fall, fals	to deceive		
femin	woman	ject, jac	to throw
fend	to strike	journ	day
fer	to carry	jud	judge
fid	faith	junct,jug,join / to join	
fin	end, limit	jur	swear
firm	strong		
fix	to fasten	kin	to beget
fla (flate)	to blow	know	to know
flam	flame		
flect, flex	to bend	lab, lep	to take,seize
flict	to strike	labor	to work
flu, flux	to flow	lapse	to slip
foc	focus	lat	to carry/wide
for	door, outdoors	later	side
form	shape	lax	loose,allow
fort	strong	led	to lead
frag,fract	to break	leg,lig,lect	to choose/read
frater	brother	leg	law
fric	to rub	learn	to teach
frig	cold	lev	to raise
front	forehead	liber	free/weigh
fug	to flee	lid, lis	to damage
fum	smoke	lif	life, to live
funct	to perform	lig	to bind
fund,found	to base, establish	light	light
fus,fund,found / to pour		like	similar
		line	line
gam	marriage	liter	letter
ge	earth	loc	place
gen	cause, birth	log	word
gest, ger	to bear, carry	long	long
get	to get	luct	to struggle
gif (give)	to give	lud, lus	to play
gnos, gnom	to know		
god	God	mak	to make
grad, gress	to step	mal	bad
		man	man, human
		man	to stay

Root	Meaning	Root	Meaning
mand	to command,entrust	par, part	to bear
mania	craving	par	equal/to prepare
manu	hand	part	part
mar	sea	pat, pass	lie open/suffer
mark	sign, boundary	pater	father
mascul	man	path	feeling / path
mater	mother	ped	child / foot
mechan	machine	pel, puls	to push
med	to attend to	pend, pens	to hang, weight
med	middle	per	to try out
membr	limb, member	physi	nature
memor	to remember	pict	to paint
mend	fault	plac	to please
mens	to measure	plain	to lament
ment	mind	plaud	to strike,applaud
mer	to earn	plex,plic	to fold
merg, mers	to dip	plor	to cry
meter, metr	measure	plus, plur	more
migra	to wander	pod, pus	foot
milit	to fight	popul	people
mim	to imitate	port	to carry / gate
mit, miss	to send	pot, poss	to be able
moni	to advise	prehend	to take
mort	death	press, print	to press
mov,mot,mob	to move	prim, prin	first
mut	to change	put	prune / correct
nam	name	qual	what kind
nect	to knot	quant	how much
nerv	nerve	quest,quir,quis	/ to ask/seek
noc, nox	injure / night		
nom	order	rad	ray
nomin, nom	name	rap	to seize
norm	rule	ras,rad	to scrape
nov	new	rat	reckon, reason
numer,	number	rect, reg	to rule, right
nunc,nounce	to announce		
nutri	to nourish	rode, ros	to gnaw
		roll, rol	to roll
ocul	eye	run	to run
od, hod	road	rupt	to break
onym, onoma	name		
op	sight, eye	san	healthy
oper	work	sat	enough
opt	to choose	say	to declare
optim	best	scend, scent	to climb
orb	circle	scop	to look
ordin	order	scrib,script	to write
organ	instrument	sect, sec	to cut
orn	to decorate	sed,sid,sess	to sit
own	to have	see	to see
		sell	to sell
pact	to agree, fasten	sens, sent	to feel
par	to appear	sequ, sec	to follow
		ser	series

Root	Meaning	Root	Meaning
serv	to serve	tourn (turn)	to go around
shape	form	tox	poison
side	side	tract	to drag, draw
sign	sign	trib	to share, bestow
simil	like	trud, trus	to thrust
sist	to stand	turb	to agitate
sit, set	to sit	typ	model
soci	companion		
sol	alone / sun	ultim	last
solv, solu	to free	urb	city
son	sound	us, ut	to use
sort	chance		
spec, spic	to look	vac	empty
spell	to recite	vad, vas	to go
sper	to help	vag	to wander
spir	breath, life	val	to be strong
spond, spons	to pledge	var	diverse
sta, stit	to stand, set	veh, vect	to carry
stall	place	ven	to come
stasis, stat	standing	vend	to sell
stead	place	verb	word
stig, sting, stinct / to mark		verg	to lean
stil	a drop	vert, vers	to turn
string, strict / to tie		vest	to dress
struct	to build	vid, vis	to see
suad, suas	to advise, persuade	vinc, vict	to conquer
sum, sumpt	to take	vir	man / poison
		vita	life
tail	to cut	viv	to live
tang, tact	to touch	voc, voke	to call, voice
tard	late, slow	volv, volu	to roll
tax, tact	arrangement	vot	to vow
teg, tect	to cover	vuls	to tug
tell, tal	to count, relate		
temper	proper mixture	wak	to be awake
tempor	time	war	aware
tempt	to try	ward	to protect
ten, tin, tain / to hold		warn	to protect
tend, tens, tent / to stretch		wit, wis	to know
tenu	thin	worth	value
termin, term	end, limit		
terr	earth/to frighten	zeal	fervor
test	witness		
text	to weave		
the, theo	God		
thes, thet	to place, put		
think	to appear		
tim	to fear / honor		
ting, tinct	to dye		
tol	to raise, support		
tom, tme	to cut		
tor	to twist		
tot	entirely		

AFFIXED FORMS OF SOME COMMON ROOTS

ROOT	EXAMPLES
agon	agonize, agony, agonistic
agra	agrarian, agriculture, agronomy
alt	altimeter, altitude, alto
am	amicable, amiable, enamor
ambul	amble, ambulatory, ambulance
andr	androgen, androgyny
angel	angelic, angel
angul	angular, angulate, angulation
anima	animate, animation, animus
ann, enn	annual, anniversary, centennial
annel, annul	annular, annulate, annulet
anthrop	anthropology, philanthropy, anthropomorphic
apt, ept	adapt, aptitude, inept
aqua	aquatic, aquarium, aqueduct
arch	anarchy, monarch, patriarch
arithm	arithmetic, logarithm
arm	armor, army, armament, armada, armadillo
art	artisan, artistic, artist
aster, astr	asteroid, asterisk, astronaut, aster, astrology
athl	athlete, athletic
atm	atmosphere, atmospheric
audi	audible, audit, audience, audition, auditorium
avi	aviation, aviary, aviator

ROOT	EXAMPLES
back	backer, background, backward
bak	bake, bakery, baker
ball	balloon, ballot
ban	banish, ban
barr	barrier, barricade, barring
bat	batter, battle, battery
bell	belle, embellish, belligerent, bellicose
bid, bead	forbid, bidder, bidding
bide	bide, abide
bind	binding, bindery, binder
bio	biology, biography, biopsy
brac	bracelet, brace
brek (ea, o)	breakfast, breaker, breakage
brev	brevity, brief, abbreviate
burn, bran	burner, brand, burst
cad, cid, cas	casualty, cadaver, cadence, casual
camp	encampment, camper, campus
can, cyn	canine, cynic, cynical, cynosure
cap, cip, cept, ceive	caption, capture, capable, accept, except, deception
capit	capital, decapitate, capitulate, capitol
carn	carnal, carnival, carnivore, carnation
cav	cave, cavern, cavity
cede, ceed, cess	concede, precede, succeed, exceed, success, process
celer	accelerate, decelerate

ROOT	EXAMPLES
cell	cellar, cellular, cellophane
cent	centimeter, percentile, centipede, centigrade
centr	central, centrifugal, centrosphere
cern, cert	discern, disconcert
charge	chargeable, discharge, recharge
chrom, chro	chromatic, chrome, dichromatic
chron	chronology, chronic, synchronize
cide, cis	suicide, homicide, pesticide, incision, incisor
circul	circle, circulate, circulation
civ	civil, civilization, uncivil
clam, claim	exclaim, proclaim, clamorous
clar	clarify, clarity, clarion, declare
clean	cleanse, cleaner
cleav	cleave, cleavage, cleaver
clin, climat	recline, incline, decline
cloth	clothes, cloth, clothing
clud, clus, close	include, seclude, conclusion
cogn	recognize, prognose, cognizant, incognito
coll	collate
color	colorful, coloration, discolor
come	income
cord	cordial, core
corp	corpuscle, corporal, corpse
cover	discover, recover, uncover

ROOT	EXAMPLES
creat	create, creative, creation
cred	creed, credit, incredible
crease	increase, decrease
cri	critic, criterion, criticize
crimin	incriminate, criminal, discriminate
cumul	accumulate, cumulative
cur	curator, cure, curative
cur	current, cursive, cursory, curt
cuss	concussion, discuss, repercussion
cycle	cyclone, cycle, cyclist
day	daily, holiday, daylight
dei, div	divine, deity, deify
dem	condemn
demo	democracy, democrat, demagogue
dent, dont	dentist, denture, orthodontist
derm	epiderm, dermatology, dermatologist
desire	undesirable, desirable
dict	dictation, dictate, diction, dictionary
doc	doctrine, indoctrinate, document
dom	domicile, kingdom, domestic
domin	dominate, predominate, domineer
dos	dosage, dose
duc	deduct, product, reduce, induction, educate
dur	duration, endure, durable

ROOT	EXAMPLES
ego	egotism, egocentric, egotistic
electr	electricity, electrical, electronic
empt	exempt, pre-empt
equ	equal, equator, equation, equestrian
erg, urg	urge, urgent, urgency
err	error, erratic, errant
ess, ent	essence
eth	ethnic, ethic, ethical
fa, fess	confess, profess
fac, fic, fect	factory, facilitate, infect, defective
fac	facade, facial, facet
fall, fals	fallacy, falsify, false
femin	feminine, effeminate
fend	defend, offend
fer	fertile, suffer, transfer
fid	confide, fidelity
fin	finish, infinite, confine
firm	confirm, firmly
fix	affix, transfix, fixation
fla (flate)	inflate, deflate
flam	flammable, flamingo, flame
flect, flex	flexible, deflect, reflector
flict	conflict, inflict
flu, flux	fluctuate, flush, fluid
foc	focal, focus

ROOT	EXAMPLES
for	forest, forestry
form	formula, conform, reform
fort	force, forte, fortitude
frag, fract	fracture, fragment, fraction
frater	fraternity, fraternal
fric	friction, fricative
frig	refrigerate, frigid, refrigerator
front	confront, frontier, frontage
fug	fugitive
fum	fume, fumigate
funct	function, defunct
fund, found fus, fund,	foundation, fundamental, fund, fuse, fusion
gam	polygamy
ge	geography, geology
gen	gender, generate, general
gest, ger	gesture, congest, digest
get	beget, forget
gif (give)	gift, gifted, forgive
gnos, gnom	agnostic, gnome, prognosis
god	goddess, godly
grad, gress	gradual, progress, aggressive, digress
graph, gram	autograph, mimeograph, telegram
grat	congratulate, grateful, gratitude
grav	grave, aggravate, gravity

ROOT	EXAMPLES
greg	congregate, gregarious
hab	habit, inhabit, rehabilitate
hav	haven, have
her, hes	adhere, cohere, cohesion
homo	Homo sapiens, homonym, homogenous
hum	humid, humidity
hunt	hunter, hunting
ident	identical, identify
integr	integral, integrate
it	exit, itinerant, itinerary
ject, jac	inject, objection, project, reject
journ	journey, adjourn, journal
jud	judicial, judge, judgment
junct, jug, join	disjoint, juncture, conjunct
jur	jury, adjust, jurisdiction
kin	kinship, kindred, kinfolk
know	knowledge, knowing
labor	laboratory, laborious, labor
lapse	relapse, collapse
lat	latitude, latitudinal
later	lateral, unilateral, bilateral
lax	relax, laxative, lax
led	leader, led, mislead
leg, lig, lect	select, neglect, collect
leg	legal, legitimate, legislate
learn	relearn, learner, learning

ROOT	EXAMPLES
lev	level, lever, alleviate
liber	liberation, liberal, liberty
lid, lis	collide, collision
lif	life, lifeless, lifelike
lig	ligament, ligature
light	delight, alight, lightning
like	alike, likeness, likely
line	linear, liner, line
liter	literate, literature, literal
loc	location, relocate, locality
log	logic, catalog, logo, dialog, monolog
long	longitude, along, belong
luct	fluctuate, reluctant
lud, lus	lusty, ludicrous, lust, luster
mak	remake, maker, make, makeshift
mal	malfunction, malice, malign
man	human, manikin, policeman, postman
mand	command, demand, mandate, mandatory
mania	maniac, pyromania, Kleptomania
manu	manual, manuscript, manufacture
mar	mariner, submarine, marina, maritime
mark	marker, demarcation
mascul	masculine, masculinity
mater	maternity, matrix, matrimony
mechan	mechanical, mechanize, mechanic

ROOT	EXAMPLES
med	medical, medication, meditate
med	median, medieval, mediocre
membr	member, membrane, membership
memor	memory, memoir, memo, memento
mend	mendacious, mend, mendacity
mens	mensal, immense, immensurable
ment	mental, mentality, mention
mer	merchant, merchandise, mercenary
merg, mers	immerge, immerse, submerge
meter, metr	meter, perimeter, metrical
migra	migration, emigrant, migrant
milit	militant, military, militia
mim	mimic, mimicry, mime, pantomime
mit, miss	dismiss, remit, admission
moni	admonish, monitor, monition
mort	mortal, remorse, mortify, mortician
mov, mot, mob	mobile, movable, remove
mut	mutual, mutuality
nam	name, rename, nameless
nect	connect, connection
nerv	nervous, nerve, nervy
noc, nox	nocturnal, noxious, obnoxious
nom, nomin	nominal, nominate, nominee
norm	normal, norm, normalize
nov	novel, novice, novelty

ROOT	EXAMPLES
numer	numeral, numerator, numerical
nunc, nounce	announce, enunciation, pronounce
nutri	nutrition, nutritive, nutritious
ocul	oculist, binoculars, ocular
od	odyssey, odometer
onym, onoma	homonym, synonym, antonym
op	optical, optometrist, optic
oper	opera, operation, operator, cooperate
opt	adopt, option, optional
optim	optimist, optimistic, optimism
orb	orbit, orb
ordin	ordinance, ordinary
organ	organism, organic, organize
orn	ornament, ornate, ornamental
own	owner, disown
pact	pact, compact, impact
par, part	apparent, apparition, apparently, preparation preparatory, prepare
part	partial, particle, particular, partition
pat, pass	passive, passion, passionate
pater	paternal, patriotic, patron
path	empathy, sympathy, pathetic
ped	pedal, pedestal, pediatrician, pedestrian
pel, puls	compel, expel, repulse, impulsive
pend, pens	pendulum, depend, appendix

ROOT	EXAMPLES
per	expert, experience
physic	physical, physicist, physician
pict	pictorial, depict, picture
plac	placate, placable
plain	complain, plaintiff, plaintive
plaud	applaud, plaudit, plausive
plex, plic	replicate, explicate, replica, replication
plor	implore, deplore, explore
plus, plur	plural, plus, plurisyllabic
pod, pus	podiatrist, podium, podiatry
popul	population, populate, popular
port	portable, import, report, transport
pot, poss	possible, impossible, potent, potential
prehend	comprehend, apprehend, reprehend
press, print	pressure, impress, compress
prim, prin	primary, primate, primitive, principal
put	computation, compute, computer
qual	quality, qualify, qualification
quant	quantity, quantitative, quantum
quest, quir, quis	inquisitive, question, inquire
rad	radiation, radiate, radiator
rap	rapture, rapid, rape
ras, rad	rash, abrasive, abrasion
rat	rational, irrational
rect, reg	correct, regiment, regimen

ROOT	EXAMPLES
rode, ros	erode, corrode, erosion
roll, rol	roller, rolling pin
run	rerun, runway, runner
rupt	rupture, erupt, disrupt
san	sane, sanitary, sanity, insane
sat	satisfy, saturate, insatiable
scend, scent	descend, ascent, descent
scope	telescope, microscope
scrib, script	scribble, transcript, script
sect, sec	dissect, section
sed, sid, sess	reside, sedentary, sediment
see	foresee
sell	seller, resell
sens, sent	sentiment, sense, sensitive
sequ, sec	sequence, sequel, sequential
ser	serial, series
serv	service, server, servitude
shape	shapely, reshape
side	sideline, sideways, sidestroke, sidewalk
sign	signature, design, insignia
simil	similar, simile, similarity
sist	resist, insist, persist
sit, set	situate, settlement, settle, settler, situation
soci	sociable, social, association
sol	solitary, solitude, solar

ROOT	EXAMPLES
solv, solu	resolve, solution, soluble
son	resonance, sonnet, sonic, sonata
sort	resort, consort
spec, spic	spectacular, speculate, spectacle
spell	spelling, misspell
spir	inspire, aspire, respiratory
spound, spons	respond, sponsor, correspond
sta, stit	statue, constitution, stationary, institute
stall	stall, install
stasis, stat	stasis, statute, statutory
stead	homestead, bedstead
stig, sting, stinct	distinct, distinguish, stigma
stil	distill, distilled, still
string, strict	constrict, stringent, strict
struct	structure, construct, instruct, obstruct
suad, suas	persuade, persuasion, dissuade
sum, sumpt	consumption, consume, resume
tail	curtail, retail, entail
tang, tact	tangible, contact, tactile
tard	retard, tardy
tax, tact	tactful, tactile, tactics
teg, tect	protect, detect
tell, tal	teller, tally
temper	temperament, temperate, temperamental
tempo, tempor	tempo, temporary, extemporaneous

ROOT	EXAMPLES
tempt	tempting, temptation, tempt
ten, tin, tain	tenant, tenacity, maintain, retain
tend, tens, tent	tension, intend, attention, intense
tenu	tenuity, tenuous
termin, term	terminate, exterminate, terminal
terr	terrify, inter, terrific
test	testify, contest, protest
text	texture, context, pretext
the, theo	theology, atheist, theologian
thes, thet	thesis, hypothesis, hypothetical
tim	timid, intimate, timocracy
ting, tinct	tinge, extinct
tol	extol, tolerate, toleration
tom	atom, atomic
tor	torment, torture, extortion
tot	total, totality
tourn	tourniquet, tournament, tourney
tox	toxin, intoxicate, toxemia
tract	tractor, detract, contract
trib	contribute, attribute, tribute
trud, trus	intrude, protrude, intrusion
turb	perturb, disturb
typ	type, typical, typify, typist
ultim	ultimate, ultimatum, ultimately
urb	urban, suburban, urbanize
us, ut	utility, useless, useful, utilize
vac	vacuum, evacuate, vacant

ROOT	EXAMPLES
vad, vas	invade, evasive, evade
vag	vagabond, vagrant, vague
val	valor, valiant, value
var	variation, variable, variegate
veh, vect	vehicle, vehement, convection
ven	event, adventure, convene
vend	vendor, vendible, vending
verb	verbatim, verbal, verbose
verg	verge, converge, diverge
vert, vers	invert, reverse, versatile
vest	vest, investment, invest
vid, vis	vision, video, provide, television, visualize
vinc, vict	victory, convince, evict
vir	virile, virtue, virility, virus, virulent
vita	vital, vitamin
viv	vivacious, revive, vivid
voc, voke	vocal, revoke, vocation
volv, volu	revolution, evolve, revolve, involve
vot	vote, votive, voter
vuls	revulsion, revulsive
wak	awaken, wake, wakeful
ward	ward, warden, warder
warn	warning, warn, forewarn
wit, wis	wisdom, witness, wise, witty
worth	worthy, worthless, worthwhile
zeal	zealot, zealous, zeal

Suffix	Meaning	Examples
-able -ible -ile	able to be	portable curable sensible reversible mobile fertile docile sterile
-acy	quality, act	infancy accuracy literacy
-age	act of, related	courage package dosage percentage
-al	related	pedal maternal familial moral
-an -ean -ian	one who	magician optician artisan Mexican
-ance -ence -ancy -ency	doing	resistance significance dependence residence urgency constancy emergency
-ant	quality	irritant colorant militant emigrant
-ar -ary	one who / like, related	beggar liar / dictionary temporary circular
-ate	quality of	saturate dictate populate imitate
-dom	state of	kingdom freedom wisdom serfdom
-en	to make / quality of	harden weaken loosen strengthen / rotten swollen wooden brazen
-ent	related to / one who	consequent competent intelligent president regent
-er -eur -eer	one who, like	worker singer amateur volunteer
-et -ette -let	little	leaflet cabinet dinette statuette bracelet booklet pirouette
-ful	full of	truthful cheerful hopeful eventful
-fy -ify	to make	satisfy terrify intensify magnify
-hood	state of	knighthood brotherhood livelihood
-ic -iac	like, made of	terrific dramatic rustic heroic zodiac maniac
-cle -cule	little	molecule corpuscle particle article
-ier -ist	one who	carrier cashier dentist artist
-id	state of	fluid vivid placid lucid
-ism	being	materialism ritualism organism
-ise -ize	to make	fertilize realize oxidize socialize
-ive	having power	curative narrative talkative
-ity -ty	state of	nobility hostility capacity fidgety
-less	without	fearless careless friendless
-ly	quality	miserly motherly wickedly manly
-ment	state, quality / that which	excitement abasement nourishment sediment impediment department

Suffix	Meaning	Examples
-ness	state of	happiness kindness faithfulness
-or	one who	actor director doctor donor
-ory -orium	quality place	regulatory monitory circulatory factory lavatory auditorium
-ous -ious -eous	full of	amorous cautious amphibious igneous dangerous bounteous marvelous
-some	full of	lonesome tiresome worrisome
-tion -ion	action	vacation tension graduation division
-tude	state,quality	magnitude habitude fortitude
-ty	state of times ten	beauty property liberty safety fifty twenty seventy
-ward	toward	forward upward windward westward

SYLLABICATION

vc/cv

accept	circus	gallop	lettuce	pillow
admire	coffee	garbage	market	pretty
almost	collar	garden	marry	pretzel
angel	contest	ginger	member	puppy
army	cotton	grammar	mermaid	rabbit
arrow	cuckoo	hammer	mirror	ribbon
attack	curtain	happen	mitten	sandal
balloon	daddy	harbor	monkey	shelter
basket	danger	harness	muffin	signal
better	dinner	hello	napkin	sister
blanket	doctor	helmet	number	sudden
bonnet	drafty	holly	offer	supper
bunny	early	hunger	office	target
butter	elbow	index	often	tennis
campus	enjoy	indoors	organ	under
candy	enter	insect	pancake	until
canvas	escape	into	pattern	wedding
carpet	expect	kitten	pencil	window
carrot	fellow	ladder	penny	wonder
center	folder	lesson	perfume	yellow
cinder	furnace	letter	picnic	zipper

v̄/cv

acorn	crater	human	obey	repeat
baby	crisis	humor	odor	reward
bacon	decide	idea	open	robot
basin	defend	ivy	over	rotate
basis	define	label	paper	ruler
became	delay	labor	pecan	secret
become	delight	later	photo	shady
before	demand	lazy	pilot	siren
began	depend	legal	pirate	soda
begin	design	lilac	polar	sofa
behave	diver	local	police	solo
behind	elect	locate	pony	station
belong	erase	lower	prefer	stupid
below	even	lunar	prepare	tiger
beware	evil	major	prevent	total
brazen	famous	meter	private	unit
brocade	favor	miner	protest	unite
cedar	female	minor	pupil	voter
china	fever	minus	razor	waken
cider	fiber	moment	recess	wary
climate	final	motor	record	widen
climax	hazy	nation	relax	
clover	hotel	notice	remain	

SYLLABICATION

v̆c/v

banish	dragon	logic	panic	second
blemish	ever	magic	patent	seven
body	exact	manage	pedal	shadow
boxer	exit	medal	petal	shiver
cabin	finish	melon	pity	shovel
camel	fragile	menace	planet	spinach
chisel	govern	metal	prison	suburb
civil	granite	mimic	profit	talent
closet	gravel	model	proper	taxi
color	habit	modern	punish	timid
comet	honey	modest	radish	topic
comic	image	money	rapid	tragic
cover	legend	never	rebel	travel
credit	lemon	novel	relish	upon
damage	level	olive	rigid	visit
denim	limit	opera	river	wagon
desert	linen	oven	robin	
devil	liver	palace	salad	
dozen	lizard	panel	satin	

/_le

able	cuddle	mumble	shingle	whistle
amble	dabble	muscle	shuffle	whittle
angle	dazzle	nibble	simple	wiggle
apple	dimple	nipple	sniffle	wobble
baffle	dribble	noble	snuggle	wrinkle
bangle	drizzle	noodle	sparkle	
battle	fable	nozzle	speckle	
beagle	fiddle	nuzzle	staple	
bottle	freckle	paddle	startle	
bramble	fumble	people	steeple	
bridle	gamble	pickle	struggle	
bubble	gargle	poodle	table	
bugle	gentle	puddle	tackle	
bundle	gobble	purple	tattle	
bristle	grumble	puzzle	thistle	
candle	handle	raffle	tickle	
castle	hurdle	rattle	tinkle	
cattle	hustle	riddle	title	
circle	jingle	rifle	toddle	
couple	juggle	ripple	trouble	
crackle	kettle	ruffle	tremble	
cradle	knuckle	saddle	tumble	
crinkle	little	sample	twinkle	
cripple	maple	scribble	uncle	
crumble	middle	settle	waffle	

ADJECTIVE FORMS

Positive	Comparative	Superlative
big	bigger	biggest
brave	braver	bravest
clean	cleaner	cleanest
clear	clearer	clearest
cold	colder	coldest
dark	darker	darkest
easy	easier	easiest
fat	fatter	fattest
fine	finer	finest
happy	happier	happiest
hard	harder	hardest
heavy	heavier	heaviest
lazy	lazier	laziest
light	lighter	lightest
long	longer	longest
loud	louder	loudest
new	newer	newest
poor	poorer	poorest
sad	sadder	saddest
safe	safer	safest
short	shorter	shortest
slow	slower	slowest
soft	softer	softest
sunny	sunnier	sunniest
tall	taller	tallest
white	whiter	whitest

IRREGULARS

Positive	Comparative	Superlative
bad	worse	worst
good	better	best
little	less	least
many-much	more	most

HOMONYMS

ant	aunt	knot	not
ate	eight	know	no
bare	bear	lie	lye
bass	base	loan	lone
beat	beet	made	maid
bee	be	mail	male
blew	blue	meddle	medal
board	bored	moan	mown
cell	sell	morn	mourn
chord	cord	new	knew
close	clothes	none	nun
creak	creek	oh	owe
dear	deer	one	won
die	dye	pail	pale
doe	dough	pain	pane
eye	I	pair	pear
fair	fare	paws	pause
find	fined	peace	piece
fir	fur	plain	plane
flea	flee	rain	rein
flour	flower	read	reed
for	four	read	red
foul	fowl	right	write
gait	gate	sail	sale
grate	great	sea	see
groan	grown	sew	so
guessed	guest	sole	soul
hair	hare	some	sum
hall	haul	son	sun
hay	hey	steal	steel
him	hymn	tail	tale
ho	hoe	their	there
hoarse	horse	toe	tow
hole	whole	wail	whale
hour	our	wait	weight
idol	idle	weak	week
inn	in	wear	ware
knead	need	which	witch
knight	night	wood	would

bye	by	buy
cent	sent	scent
dew	do	due
I'll	isle	aisle
marry	merry	Mary
praise	prays	preys
to	too	two
vain	vein	vane

238

absent	away	always	never
act	behave	bad	good
afraid	fearful	before	after
aid	help	begin	end
always	forever	boy	girl
ask	question	city	farm
bad	evil	dark	light
base	bottom	day	night
begin	start	dirty	clean
big	large	dry	wet
chief	leader	easy	hard
close	near	empty	full
cool	cold	father	mother
desire	wish	forget	remember
earth	world	found	lost
enjoy	like	front	back
fact	truth	gave	took
firm	solid	go	stop
gift	present	happy	sad
guide	lead	hard	soft
hard	firm	here	there
house	shelter	him	her
huge	great	in	out
idea	thought	last	first
ill	sick	laugh	cry
keep	hold	lead	follow
land	ground	left	right
little	small	little	big
loud	noisy	lost	found
make	build	morning	night
name	title	near	far
odd	strange	now	then
odor	smell	off	on
open	start	old	young
plan	plot	open	close
price	cost	push	pull
problem	puzzle	queen	king
quiz	test	rich	poor
real	true	right	wrong
rear	back	run	walk
reply	answer	sell	buy
rich	wealthy	sick	well
shape	form	sit	stand
shout	yell	start	stop
steal	rob	stay	go
stop	end	take	give
street	road	under	over
sum	total	up	down
tale	story	white	black
thief	robber	whole	part
town	city	work	play
train	teach	yes	no
warrior	soldier	young	old

239

HETERONYMS

Key:

N	-	Noun
V	-	Verb
Adj	-	Adjective
Adv	-	Adverb

accent   N   (ăk´sĕnt) He has a Southern accent.
              V   (ăk-sĕnt´) Accent the second syllable.

bow   N   (bō) He carried a bow and arrow.
              V   (bou) They will bow their heads to pray.

close   N   (klōz) Let us bring this day to a close.
              V   (klōz) He will close the door.
             Adj (klōs) They worked in close quarters.
             Adv (klōs) Stay close to me.

combat   N   (kŏm´bat) The soldiers engaged in combat.
              V   (kŏm-bat´) Our army will combat the enemy.

compact N   (kŏm´păkt) The lady found her compact.
              V   (kŏm-păkt´) A machine is used to compact the
                                garbage.
             Adj (kŏm-păkt´) Jim's car is a compact model.

complex N   (kŏm´plĕks) The children's teasing gave John
                                an inferiority complex.
             Adj (kŏm-plĕks´) This is a complex situation.

compound N   (kŏm´pound) H$_2$O is a chemical compound.
              V   (kŏm-pound´) The interest will compound daily.
             Adj (kŏm´pound) Doghouse is a compound word.

compress N   (kŏm´prĕs) He put a cold compress on the bruise.
              V   (kŏm-prĕs´) The garbageman will compress the trash.

content N   (kŏn´tĕnt) The newspaper content is excellent.
             Adj (kŏn-tĕnt´) The cat is happy and content.

contest N   (kŏn´tĕst) He won the contest.
              V   (kŏn-tĕst´) She will contest the lawsuit.

contract N   (kŏn´trăkt) We signed the contract.
              V   (kŏn-trăkt´) He did not contract the disease.

contrast N   (kŏn´trăst) There is a great contrast between
                                night and day.
             V   (kŏn-trăst´) A white rose will contrast with
                                her black dress.

converse   N   (kŏn′vŭrs) The converse of "hot" is cold.
                V   (kŏn-vŭrs′) We converse with her neighbor.

convert   N   (kŏn′vûrt) He is a convert to Christianity.
                V   (kŏn-vûrt′) Why not convert the old house
                                         into a restaurant?

convict   N   (kŏn′vĭkt) The convict is in prison.
                V   (kŏn-vĭkt′) A jury will convict the criminal.

costume   N   (kŏs′tūm) Mary wore a Halloween costume.
                V   (kŏs-tūm′) She will costume the actors for
                                         the play.

defect   N   (dē′fĕkt) One car had a defect and would not run.
               V   (dē-fĕkt′)The spy will defect to the U.S.A.

duplicate   N   (dū′-plĭ-kāt) This copy is a duplicate of the
                                           original.
              V   (dū′plĭ-kāt) Duplicate these important papers.
          Adj (dū′plĭ-kāt) Our typist made a duplicate copy.

frequent   V   (frē-kwĕnt′) We will frequent the theater.
          Adj (frē′kwĕnt) There are frequent delays in the
                                         schedule.

intern   N   (ĭn′tûrn) The intern is in the hospital.
               V   (ĭn-tûrn′) They intern all enemy ships.

intimate   N   (ĭn′tĭ-mĭt) He is an intimate of the president.
              V   (ĭn′tĭ-māte) She did intimate disapproval of
                                         the plan.
          Adj (ĭn′tĭ-mĭt) She told her intimate friends.

lead   N   (lĕd) The weight is made of lead.
              V   (lēd) The general will lead his troops.

         Adj (lĕd) He wrote with a lead pencil.

live   V   (lĭv) The Andersons did live in Chicago.
          Adj (līv) The performance was live.

minute   N   (mĭn′ĭt) Wait a minute.
          Adj (mī-nūt′) Describe the minute details of the plan.

permit   N   (pûr′mĭt) She has a permit to enter.
              V   (pĕr-mĭt′) Mr. Stevens won't permit students
                                         to chew gum in class.

premise   N   (prĕm′ĭs) The premis is: man must work to live.
              V   (prē-mīz′) Let's premise the speech with a short
                                         history of the topic.

present   N   (prĕz′ĕnt) On birthdays we give a present.
            V   (prė-zĕnt′) Present an award to him.
         Adj   (prĕz′ĕnt) He used the present tense.

produce   N   (prŏd′us) Farmers take their produce to market.
            V   (pro-dūs′) Orange trees produce a lot of fruit.

progress   N   (prŏg′rĕs) Some patients make rapid progress to
                          recovery.
            V   (prō-grĕs′) Work on the building did progress
                          rapidly.

project   N   (prŏj′ĕkt) Work has begun on the science project.
            V   (prō-jĕkt′) They project the movie on the screen.

protest   N   (prō′tĕst) Who made a protest against the new
                          mayor's proposal?
            V   (prō-tĕst′) He will protest that he wasn't
                          treated fairly.

read   V   (rēd, rĕd) He will read the book
       Adj   (rĕd) She is a well-read woman.

rebel   N   (rĕb′ĕl) The rebel opposed the existing government.
        V   (re-bĕl′) He began to rebel against his dictator.
     Adj   (rĕb′ĕl) The rebel forces lost the war.

rebound   N   (rē′bound′) The basketball player caught the
                          rebound.
           V   (rė-bound′) A ball will rebound from the wall.

recess   N   (rē′sĕs) The children went out for recess.
         V   (rē-sĕs′) Congress will recess for the holidays.

record   N   (rĕk′ĕrd) They listened to a record.
         V   (rė-kord′) He will record the music.
      Adj   (rĕk′ĕrd) He ran the race in record time.

refund   N   (rē′fŭnd) You will receive a refund for the things
                          returned.
        V   (rė-fŭnd′) I will refund your money.

refuse   N   (rĕf′ūs) All that was left after the fire was a
                          pile of refuse.
        V   (rė-fūz′) The boys refuse to go.

regress   N   (rē′grĕs) One dangerous mission offered no regress.
        V   (re-grĕs′) The old woman did regress to a child-
                          like state.

reject   N   (rē′jĕkt) The sale item was a factory reject.
        V   (rē-jĕkt′) The company did not reject his idea.

| relay | N | (rē'lā) The eighth graders ran the three-mile relay. |
| | V | (rē-la') Relay the message to your mother. |

| repeat | N | (re'pēt) They are broadcasting a repeat of the one I saw yesterday. |
| | V | (rė-pēt') Can you repeat the question? |

| row | N | (rō, rou) They were involved in a terrible row. |
| | V | (rō, rou) Please row the boat. |

| sow | N | (sou) The farmer fed the hungry sow. |
| | V | (sō) The farmer will sow the seeds in May. |

subject	N	(sŭb'jĕkt) Jean Winters studies five subjects in school.
	V	(sŭb-jĕkt') Firemen are subject to the intense heat of flames.
	Adj	(sŭb'jĕkt) Name a subject nation.

| suffix | N | (suf'ĭks) What is the suffix in the word helpless? |
| | V | (sŭ-fiks') Suffix this ending to the word. |

| survey | N | (sûr'vā) The U.S. took a survey of unemployment. |
| | V | (sẽr-vā') Several men will survey the land. |

| suspect | N | (sus'pĕkt) He is not a suspect in the robery. |
| | V | (sŭs-pĕkt') The police suspect several people. |

| tear | N | (tĭr) A tear rolled down her cheek. |
| | V | (târ) Do not tear the paper. |

| wind | N | (wĭnd) The wind blew through the trees. |
| | V | (wīnd) Wind the rope around this post. |

| wound | N | (woond) The wound would not heal. |
| | V | (wound) He wound the clock. |

ACCENT

1 In two-syllable words, accent the first syllable

2 In two-syllable words where the second syllable contains two vowels (but only one vowel sound) accent the second syllable

3 The root word is accented in affixed forms

4 Accent the syllable preceding -ious, -ic, -ity, -ion, -ical, ian, ial, -tion, or -sion

1	2	3	4
ba′con	a·live′	art′ist	cap·tiv′i·ty
bus′y	be·come′	a·wake′	char′i·ty
but′ter	be·ware′	bak′er	co·me′di·an
daugh′ter	con·sume′	bi·lin′gual	com′i·cal
gra′vy	de·spite′	dis·suade′	cre·a′tion
kitch′en	ex·cite′	frac′tion	dra·mat′ic
la′dy	for·give′	il·le′gal	fran′tic
lead′er	im·merse′	im·press′	na′tion
meas′ure	im·pure′	in·flate′	on′ion
mon′key	mis·take′	min′ing	per·mis′sion
nick′el	ob·serve′	re·turn′ed	phy·si′cian
o′pen	por·tray′	re·wind′	por′tion
pa′per	pre·pare′	rob′ber	ra′cial
per′son	re·move′	sail′or	re·la′tion
pock′et	re·play′	say′ing	sec′tion
pu′pil	sa·lute′	tact′less	se·lec′tion
rea′son	un·safe′	tire′some	sen·sa′tion
se′cond		un·kind′	ses′sion
shal′low		un·well′	
ta′ble			

⑤ Accent the third-to-last syllable in a three or more syllable word ending in silent "e."

con′fi·dence
con′tem·plate
cor′re·late
du′pli·cate
ex′er·cise
grad′u·ate
par·tic′i·pate
pen′e·trate
rec′og·nize
sub′ju·gate
tem′per·ate
ter′mi·nate
un·for′tu·nate
u′ni·verse
var′i·ance
veg′i·tate

⑥ Polysyllabic words usually have a major and minor accent (alternating syllables)

ca′pa·bil′i·ty
dis′ap·point′ment
dis′pen·sa′tion
ex·traor′di·nar′y
flu′o·res′cent
gen′er·os′i·ty
hab′i·ta′tion
hor′ti·cul′ture
in′cli·na′tion
leg′is·la′ture
mat′ri·mo′ny
ob′ser·va′tion
pen′i·cil′lin
per′spi·ra′tion
rep′e·ti′tion
sat′is·fac′tion
tam′bou·rine′
var′i·a′tion

CONSONANT SOUND LIST

Consonants - b c d f g h j k l m n p r s t v w y z

Consonant Blends - bl cl fl gl pl sl
br cr dr fr gr pr tr
sc sk sl sm sn sp st sw
dw tw sw

scr spr squ str spl shr thr

Consonant Digraphs - ch sh th wh qu ph gh ng ck

Variant Consonant Sounds - c = "k" c = "s"
g = "g" g = "j"
s = "s" s = "z"

Silent Consonant Letters - k̸n g̸n w̸r mb̸ t̸ch c̸k ig̸h̸

VOWEL SOUND LIST

Short Vowels - ă ĕ ĭ ŏ ŭ

Long Vowels - ā ē ī ō ū

"R" Controlled Vowels - ar er ir or ur

Vowel Diphthongs - oy oi   ou ow

Vowel Digraphs - ēc̸ ōc̸ ēa̸ ēy̸ ēi̸ īc̸ āi̸ āy̸ ei c̸ā ōa̸ ōw̸

Miscellaneous Vowel Sounds - o͞o o͝o ĕa̸ ēa̸ c̸ā al ȳ y̆ aw au ew ue

LIST OF COMMON RHYMING ENDINGS

Pattern	A		E		I		O		U	
˘VC	ab ad ag al am an	ap at as	eb ed eg eck ell em	en ep ess et	ib id iff ig ick ix ill	im in ip is iss it izz	ob od ock on ox om	op ot	ub ud uff ug uck ull um	up us uss ut uzz
˘VCC	asp ack ass ant atch aft act	amp and ang ank ant ash	end eft eld elf elm elp elt	ence ent ept esh est	itch ift ilt imp inch ing ink	int ish isk ist	otch ond		uch udge ulk ulse ump und ung	unk unt ush usk ust
CV̄	a		e		i		o		u	
V̄V̸	ay aid aik ail aim ain	aint ait	ee ead eed eef eek eel eam	ean een eep eap east eat eet	ie ied		oe oach oad oam oat ow̸ oast		ue	
V̄CE̸	ade age ake ale ame ane ange	ape ace ase aste ate ave aze	eme ese ete		ibe ide ife ike ile ime ine	ire ice ite ive ise ize	obe ode oke ome one ope ote	ove ose oze	ube ude uke ule ute use	
"R" Controlled	ar arch ard arge arl arm arp	art arve ark	er erd erb erk erm ert erve		ir irch ird irk irl irm irt	irth irst	or ore orch orn ort orch orm	orn orse ort orth ord	ur url urn urse urt urb	

Vowel Dipthongs: oi - oy / oy oid oil oin oint oice oist oise

ou - oe / ow ouch owd oud owl own ound ounce
ount our out outh ouse

Others: o̅o̅ - ŏŏ / ood ook ool oom oose oon ooth

al - au - aw / aw awk all alk awl alt awn aunt aught ause aul

air are ĕad y̅ i̅g̸h i̅nd i̅g̸ht i̅ve o̅ugh o̅ll o̅ld o̅lt o̅w̸n o̅st o̅w̸s

off og odge ove ome ong oss ew

COMMON VARIANT SPELLINGS FOR CONSONANT AND VOWEL SOUNDS

Consonants

b

c　k　ck

d

f　ph　gh

g

h　wh

j　g　dge　d

k　c　ck　ch　qu

l

m　m͟b　m͟n

n　k͟n　g͟n　p͟n

p

qu

r　w͟r　(er/ir/ur vowels)

s　c　p͟s

t　p͟t

v

w

x　ks　gz

y

z　s

sc　sk

ch　t͟ch

sh　s　t　c

th

wh　hw　h

ph　f　gh

Vowels

Short:

ă

ĕ　ĕa　iĕ

ĭ　y　ee　eĭ

ŏ

ŭ　ȧ　ė　o̊

Long:

ā　āi　āy　eā　ei　ey　eigh　ā_e̸

ē　ēa　ēe　ēi　ēo　ēy　y̆　iē　ē_e̸

ī　eī　īe　īg͟h　uy　ȳ　ī_e̸　ȳ_e̸

ō　ōa　ōe　ōh　ōu　ōw　ō_e̸

ū　ew　ūe　ūi　eū　ū_e̸

"R" Controlled:

är

or

er　ir　ur　(ȯr)

Other Vowels:

o͞o　ū　ū_e̸　ew

o͝o　ṳ

oi　oy

ow　ou　ough

aw　au　a̤(ll)

CONSONANTS

DIGRAPHS

CONSONANT BLENDS

SHORT VOWELS

LONG VOWELS

R-CONTROLLED VOWELS

OTHER VOWELS

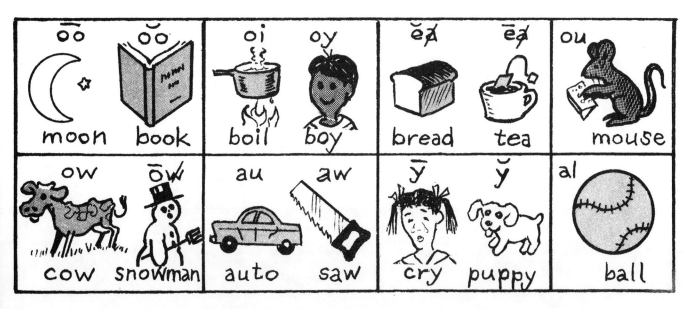